# THE BRITISH PRESS SINCE THE WAR

# THE BRITISH PRESS SINCE THE WAR

*Edited by*

Anthony Smith
*St Antony's College, Oxford*

ROWMAN AND LITTLEFIELD
TOTOWA, NEW JERSEY

First published in the United States, 1974 by
ROWMAN AND LITTLEFIELD, Totowa, N.J.

© Anthony Smith 1974

All rights reserved. No part of this publication
may be reproduced, stored in a retrieval system
or transmitted in any form or by any means,
electronic, mechanical, photocopying, recording
or otherwise, without the prior permission of
the publisher

**Library of Congress Cataloging in Publication Data**

Smith, Anthony, 1938–    comp.
   The British press since the war.

   Bibliography: p.
   1. English newspapers.    I.    Title.
PN5118.S5        072        74–7178
ISBN 0-87471-550-4

PN
5118
.S5

Printed in Great Britain
by Latimer Trend & Company Ltd Plymouth

This book is dedicated to
Willie and Marina

# Contents

|  |  | PAGE |
|---|---|---|
|  | INTRODUCTION | 15 |
|  | PART ONE: FLEET STREET—FINANCE, OWNERSHIP AND STRUCTURE | 24 |
| 1 | Wickham Steed. *The ideal newspaper* | 26 |
| 2 | Printing and Kindred Trades Federation. *Survey of the industry* | 30 |
| 3A | Royal Commission on the Press, 1947-9. *The standard by which the Press should be judged* | 32 |
| 3B | Royal Commission on the Press, 1947-9. *Conclusions and recommendations* | 35 |
| 4 | Denis Thomas. *The character of the* News Chronicle | 41 |
| 5 | Editor of the *Sunday Telegraph. An addition to the quality Press* | 45 |
| 6 | *Sunday Express* and *Sunday Dispatch. Increasing polarisation* | 48 |
| 7A | Royal Commission on the Press, 1961-2. *The television interests of newspaper companies* | 49 |

| | | |
|---|---|---|
| 7B | Royal Commission on the Press, 1961–2. *Plan for an amalgamations court* | 51 |
| 7C | Royal Commission on the Press, 1961–2. *Nicholas Kaldor and Robert Neild's scheme for a 'Levy'* | 55 |
| 8 | *Daily Leader. An attempt to start a new paper* | 60 |
| 9 | *Sun. The birth of a new daily paper* | 63 |
| 10A | The Economist Intelligence Unit. *The National Newspaper Industry Survey* | 65 |
| 10B | The Economist Intelligence Unit. *Estimated savings through greater efficiency* | 69 |
| 11 | *The Times. A change of format* | 69 |
| 12 | Monopolies Commission. *The merger of* The Times *and the* Sunday Times | 74 |
| 13 | *Sunday Citizen. A farewell* | 82 |
| 14 | Monopolies Commission. *Thomson Newspapers Ltd and the independence of its editors* | 85 |
| 15 | National Board for Prices and Incomes. *The earnings of journalists* | 90 |
| 16A | PIB. *The changing technology of newspapers* | 93 |
| 16B | PIB. *Average daily circulation—a chart* | 97 |
| 16C | PIB. *The ownership of newspapers—a chart* | 98 |
| 16D | PIB. *The chain of distribution—a chart* | 100 |
| 17 | International Publishing Corporation Staff. *An attempt to prevent the merger with Reed* | 100 |
| 18 | James Curran. *The impact of television on the audience for national newspapers* | 105 |

## PART TWO: THE PRESS AND THE LAW— THE EROSION OF NEWSPAPER FREEDOM 108

### A Contempt of Court

19 'Justice' Report. *The legal profession pleads for reform* 112

20 Sir Elwyn Jones, QC, Attorney General. *The Aberfan Tribunal extends the concept of contempt* 115

21 Press Council. *Fleet Street expresses its indignation* 119

22 Royal Commission on Tribunals of Inquiry, 1966. *Tribunals and the Press* 121

23 Committee on Contempt in Tribunals. *Lord Justice Salmon proposes reform* 126

24 White Paper of 1973. *The Government's views on the two Salmon committees* 127

25 *The Times* Law Report. *The* Sunday Times *and the thalidomide affair* 131

26 Law Lords. *Final judgment on the thalidomide affair— the banning of the* Sunday Times *article* 142

27 *Sunday Times. Reply to the Law Lords* 153

28 Harold Wilson. *The Law Lords' judgement and the Parliamentary process* 159

### B Official Secrets

29 Official Secrets Act, 1911. *Section two* 164

30 Radcliffe Committee, 1962. *The D-Notice system* 166

31 Radcliffe Committee, 1967. *Chapman Pincher and the cable-vetting affair* 170

32A Labour Government's White Paper. *The Radcliffe Report 'rejected'* 173

| | | |
|---|---|---|
| 32B | Lord Radcliffe. *Government and a free press* | 175 |
| 33 | Chapman Pincher. *Press freedom and national security* | 177 |
| 34 | Biafran Secrets Trial. *Mr Justice Caulfield's summing up* | 179 |
| 35 | Jonathan Aitken. *An attack on a 'law in disrepute'* | 180 |
| 36A | Franks Committee. *Memorandum of the Institute of Journalists* | 183 |
| 36B | Franks Committee. *The case for criminal sanctions* | 187 |
| 36C | Franks Committee. *Proposals* | 189 |
| 37 | Editorial Liaison Committee. *Opposition to the Franks Report from the Press* | 190 |
| 38 | Granada Television and the D-Notice Committee. *The secrecy of secrecy* | 192 |

### C Privacy

| | | |
|---|---|---|
| 39 | 'Justice' Report. *What is privacy?* | 199 |
| 40 | Right of Privacy Bill, 1967. *An attempt to legislate* | 200 |
| 41A | Younger Report on Privacy. *The problem of a general right* | 201 |
| 41B | Younger Report on Privacy. *Proposals* | 203 |
| 42 | Harold Evans, Editor of the *Sunday Times*. *Privacy and the Lambton/Jellicoe affair* | 205 |

### D Libel

| | | |
|---|---|---|
| 43 | Cecil King. *News and abuse* | 215 |
| 44 | Porter Committee. *The extension of qualified privilege* | 217 |
| 45 | 'Justice' Working Party. *The defence of qualified privilege, and the admissibility of evidence of bad character* | 222 |

CONTENTS 13

46 Lord Thomson of Fleet. *On reform of the libel laws* 225

E PARLIAMENTARY PRIVILEGE
47 Committee of Privileges. *The Garry Allighan case* 229

48A Select Committee on Parliamentary Privilege, 1967. *Historical origins of privilege* 234

48B Select Committee on Parliamentary Privilege, 1967. *The jurisdiction of the House* 236

F OBSCENITY
49 Select Committee on the Obscenity Bill of 1958. *Sir Alan Herbert's evidence on the definition of obscenity* 239

50 Select Committee on Obscene Publications, 1958. *Recommendations* 242

PART THREE: THE PRINCIPLES AND PRACTICE OF THE PRESS 244

51 Cecil King. *The behaviour of the Press* 245

52 National Union of Journalists. *Code of Professional Conduct* 249

53 Vassall Tribunal. *Protection of the confidentiality of sources* 252

54 Scotsman. *How much privilege for the Press?* 258

55 John Whale. *The Parliamentary lobby and its system* 260

56 *The rules of the lobby* 262

57 Anthony Lewis. *An American criticism of the Parliamentary lobby system* 267

58 Royal Commission on the Press, 1947–9. *Lord Kemsley's fears about the effects of a Press Council* 269

| | | |
|---|---|---|
| 59 | Press Council. *Constitution* | 271 |
| 60 | Press Council. *A statement on four-letter words* | 275 |
| 61 | Press Council. *Unsavoury memoirs deplored* | 277 |
| 62 | Press Council. *Cheque-book journalism* | 279 |
| 63 | Press Council. *Statistics on adjudications* | 282 |
| | PART FOUR: NEWSPAPERS AND WORKERS' PARTICIPATION | 283 |
| 64 | Jeremy Tunstall. *The career of the journalist* | 284 |
| 65 | Free Communications Group. *Newsroom democracy* | 290 |
| 66 | Jak. *Cartoon on the electrical workers—homo-electrical-sapiens Britannicus* | 294 |
| 67 | Scottish Daily Express. *The IRA and Father O'Brezhnev* | 296 |
| 68 | Press Council. *The Council's warning on Press censorship from within* | 298 |
| 69 | Editor of the *Observer*'s Memorandum. *The problem of the 'unqualified' journalist* | 299 |
| 70 | *Guardian* House Agreement. *Journalists on the board* | 302 |
| | SUGGESTIONS FOR FURTHER READING | 309 |
| | ACKNOWLEDGEMENTS | 315 |
| | INDEX | 317 |

# Introduction

'In this country,' wrote Lord Palmerston to Queen Victoria, in an effort to condone certain transgressions of *The Times*, 'all thriving newspapers are commercial undertakings, and are conducted on commercial principles, and none others are able long to maintain an existence. Attempts have often been made to establish newspapers to be directed by political men, and to be guided by the same considerations by which these men would govern their own conduct, but such papers have seldom succeeded.'* The newspaper of opinion is a mirage long pursued by English journalism but only briefly achieved. Economics has always been the prime anxiety of newspaper owners—even those whose chief aim has been to influence opinion—and it is arguable that British journalism has reached its highest peaks in those periods when Fleet Street as a whole, or at least a relevant section of it, has been passing through a period of high profit. It has never been possible to separate the great issues of Press freedom from the equally great ones of Press ownership and circulation. Newspapers have been firmly and irretrievably locked into the economy of Britain, even before the 'taxes on knowledge' disappeared and the delivery of a daily newspaper was no longer a luxury which only the middle and upper classes could afford.

In looking at the newspapers which remain in circulation in the 1970s, people from outside Britain are often puzzled to

* *Letters of Queen Victoria*, Vol 3 (1907), 463

perceive the lack of a 'working class' paper on the news-stands, apart from the unsuccessful Communist *Morning Star*. In fact there are one or two radical sheets of the very far left, but there is no mainstream paper attached to working class politics, and there has been none since the *Daily Herald* ceased to have any links with the trade union movement. (It later became the *Sun*.) The last real working class Press began to disappear over 100 years ago, when the stamp tax on newspapers was removed; until that time a healthy mass circulation radical Press was distributed illegally but was unable to compete with the normal newspapers when, untaxed and cheaper, these were able to start extending their circulation downwards through the social strata. If one attempted to express the internal structural problem of the British Press in very simple terms, one might say that no national daily paper can survive unless it belongs firmly to one or more sections of the middle class in editorial content and advertising appeal, or unless it circulates among an extremely high proportion of the working class; a working-class minority paper cannot collect the revenue to survive, and even a working-class majority paper has to struggle fiercely within a tiny group of competitors.

The modern newspaper in Britain is derived historically from *The Times* and the other thriving middle-class papers of the mid-nineteenth century. The mass Press which began at the end of the last century was a cheap (halfpenny) version of the great middle-class papers; its populist style was borrowed from the mass circulation papers of the United States, its politics from its millionaire owners, its wealth from its advertisers. The twentieth century has seen a rapid concentration of ownership and a series of circulation struggles which have forced the readerships of any paper which manages to survive into a series of demographic moulds. The contents are heavily influenced by sophisticated surveys of what different types of reader require. Only in the three 'quality' dailies—*The Times*, the *Guardian* and the *Daily Telegraph*—does anything survive of the daily battle for the minds of men which a reading of the newspapers of the last century shows was once a prime function of the daily newspaper. Newspapers, through their advertising columns, have always clustered around the interests, customs and priorities of their readers, but today the whole struggle for survival in Fleet Street revolves around the unequal and apparently irrational distribution of advertising revenue in the conditions of modern economics. The whole contemporary debate about the nature of Press freedom and newspaper independence revolves around the strange economics of Fleet Street. This situation is producing tensions within the various professions involved in making newspapers that once again throw absolutely fundamental questions into prominence: *whose* freedom is the freedom of the Press, that of editor, owner or reporter? How can the proper relationship between journalism and the advertiser be maintained when advertising is responsible for so high a proportion of total revenue?

The vastness of the enterprises which own the national Press of Britain throws up another equally traditional theme—the relationship between journalism and government. When the interests of large corporations are so intimately involved with major governmental policies, how are those corporate interests restrained from influencing the policy of newspapers which they control? And how are journalists to behave towards government and bureaucracy when they are increasingly dependent editorially on contact with and information from ministers and civil servants? The main purpose of this book is to illustrate these themes, in their contemporary forms, from the literature of the Press since the end of World War II.

Less than one-fifth of the 132 countries represented at the United Nations enjoy a Press free of overt governmental interference. The vast majority of the world's citizens, even within the economically developed part of the globe, have no opportunity to receive information on current events untainted by the hand of censorship. To the outside observer, Britain appears to have newspapers that are plentiful, lively and argumentative; their editors are free to select for themselves the issues which they regard as important at any moment; no government for a century and more has attempted to impose its will on the Press, by means of bribery or strongarm methods. At the same time, Britain, in comparison with many countries, has an abundant and prosperous Press; the British public buys a larger number of daily papers per head than almost any other nation, and in addition to local and provincial papers supports no fewer than nine national dailies and a small host of national weeklies, of differing political persuasions, ranging from the radical left to the orthodox right and including satirical and 'underground' publications.

From inside Britain, however, the picture is very different. Several of the national dailies have undergone periods of extreme financial emergency despite their very high per capita circulation. The British Press suffers from a structural disease which has brought about a wave of amalgamations and which is caused by an over-dependence on advertising revenue. Newspapers selling more than a million copies have died in the last quarter century, not for lack of readers but because the distribution of that readership through the income levels of the population has been inadequate to ensure survival. Every old-age pensioner buying a newspaper causes its publisher a net loss; every high wage-earner brings him a profit. To survive, a newspaper has to reach a high proportion of relatively wealthy readers.

The British journalistic situation is by foreign comparisons startlingly irrational. Its national dailies are large in number and most of them have recorded profits for most of the last 20 years. Yet the country, unique among the developed nations, can support no news magazine and depends for the most part on foreign imports for illustrated magazines. All efforts to create illustrated magazines in recent years have collapsed in financial disaster. Three national papers (two of them Sundays) have started colour 'supplements' in this period, but in periods of national economic stagnation these lucrative magazines have been accused of milking advertising from their parent-papers to the extent of endangering their lives; there has even been an appeal for a supplement 'truce' by which all three would be simultaneously abandoned, leaving the available revenue to prop the shaking structures of the newspapers they were intended to 'supplement'. A weekly colour magazine started by the *Daily Mirror* was obliged to close after some painful months. Part One of this book examines the development of this central financial anguish of the British Press and presents documents which help to explain the rationale of its frightening economics.

There is an older generation of journalists still at work which tends to see the development of the Press in Britain as a story of ever-enlarging editorial freedoms—'the swelling tide of freedom' as the late Lord Francis-Williams called it.* In the British Press of the late nineteenth century the editorial column set the character of a newspaper; before the arrival of the mass popular daily, traditions had established in the journalist, communicating with relatively small middle-class readerships, the sense of being an opinion-leader in society. The self-confidence has died only very slowly; the language of leader columns still frequently employs the idiom of the 1880s and 1890s, when editors weighed their words as if each could help to sway an influential section of public opinion. The newspaperman of today has shed that sense of burgeoning independence; he works along lines of demography, trying to help his newspaper fit the contours of a carefully worked out readership survey. Newspapers have become remoter from their owners, who have created modern rationalised structures of internal management. Multiple ownership has spread, joining Sunday papers to dailies, and placing dailies with diverse political views inside single managements. Journalists work in a precarious industry. They try less hard to lead opinion. Their work reveals fewer political certainties.

At the same time the major newspapers of Fleet Street are less closely tied by informal links to government and the

* In *The Right to Know* (1969), 30

'Establishment'. Less can be achieved by a telephone call from Westminster to Fleet Street than was the case in the 1930s. The formal restraints of government on the Press have, however, been growing steadily. Until 1911 it was not a statutory offence in Britain to publish government secrets even in time of war. Gradually the area of information covered by the Official Secrets Act has grown to encompass almost every document passing out of Whitehall. At the same time the area of society with which Whitehall is concerned has grown enormously. The result is that Britain has acquired in this century an increasingly secret form of government about which the Press is able to do very little without infringing the provisions of the Official Secrets Act. A committee set up under the chairmanship of Lord Franks ostensibly to liberalise the law or at least render it more workable has made the controversial recommendation that a new system should be created whereby documents can be declared 'secret' at the discretion of the relevant minister. It is hardly surprising that the question of the official secret has become a major vexation in British journalism.

There are many other areas in which the formal constraints on the Press have grown stronger: the laws of libel and, to a lesser extent, of obscenity, and the rules governing contempt of court and parliamentary privilege have all, in varying degrees, acquired authoritative reinterpretations which are tending to make the work of the journalist more difficult. At the same time there is considerable political and public pressure to legislate on the protection of personal privacy in a way which would further inhibit the collecting of certain kinds of data. Journalism is increasingly being forced to operate inside an area of legal restraint which has replaced the less formal social restraints of the past. Part Two of this collection attempts to indicate the way in which the laws affecting journalism have developed and the directions in which reform is being currently discussed.

The Press (together with broadcasting) has arguably acquired a new and important role within the political process of modern society—that of discerning or deciding the priorities among contemporary public issues, that of 'setting the agenda'. It is difficult to see whether this role is a new *power* or merely a new and half-accidental *function*; none the less it means that the journalist processing the vast quantities of information which today pour from government and elsewhere stands as a kind of unofficial broker providing his readers with a rough moral chart of contemporary affairs. The relative smallness of the journalistic profession and the concentration of editorial outlets puts the journalist in a new relationship with his readers. The public demands to see the *credentials* of the journalist for fulfilling this position in society and for exploiting his *de facto* privileges. The journalist has access to powerful people; he is responsible for rationalising, selecting and transmitting the waves of new information. He has become in the eyes of many readers a kind of substitute government and, inevitably, his whole way of working has increasingly been subject to public investigation and debate.

There has been since the war the steady development of a new view of the role of the Press—what Theodore Peterson\* calls the 'social-responsibility' theory of the Press—which provides the newspaperman with a range of social duties to match his privileges. The two Royal Commissions on the Press in Britain held since the war have helped to increase the public interest in the role of the Press; the Press Council was formed as a result of the first Commission and strengthened as a result of the second. Its existence means that journalism is no longer the private affair of newspaper entrepreneurs; newspapers are necessary to the political as well as the financial processes of society, and they therefore exist within the public domain as much as the private. This strand of thinking represents a major change in the social position of the Press, and Part Three of this volume presents some basic documents in the history of the Press Council and some of its characteristic statements.

\* In *Four Theories of the Press* (1956)

One of the by-products of the strange economics of the newspaper in Britain in this period is the increased remoteness of ownership from the process of journalism. Newspapers have been the cherished property of wealthy men rather than mere investments forced to sustain a steady return. The central tension within British journalism in its golden age, the latter part of the last century, was between owners and editors; in the age of the mass popular daily (which dates from the acquisition in 1896 of the *Daily Mail* by Alfred Harmsworth) there has been a shifting balance of power between the principal shareholders in newspapers and their more dynamic editors. As ownership has become more concentrated, however, newspapers of different political persuasions have found themselves housed beneath the same corporate roof, often surviving by reason of a virtual subsidy from the publisher; sometimes the diversification of newspaper publishing into the more lucrative business of commercial television has helped to sustain a paper through the more difficult periods. But an owner who does not share the political views of his own papers inevitably comes to be seen as a journalistic oligarch, an entrepreneur without deep emotional links to his newspaper property. Alternatively his retention of the paper and its staff may become a kind of social service.

In either case the situation inevitably provokes the discussion of the whole question of editorial control; if an owner has not created a newspaper or nurtured it creatively during the period of his ownership, then the journalists who spend their lives working on the paper inevitably begin to ask fundamental questions about the choice of the editor, the choice of the editorial line.

In France many of the very prosperous provincial papers and some of the nationals are owned by men who acquired them in the period of chaos which immediately followed the ending of the Nazi occupation. The title deeds of ownership are in a sense morally insecure; the journalists ask who should rightly be in editorial control of a paper especially on the death or retirement of the original owner (who may have acquired his position through his role in the Resistance). This has encouraged the vigorous development of a movement for 'newsroom democracy' in France (most prominently in *Le Monde*), a movement which has spread to Fleet Street and has begun to exercise a considerable influence on the journalistic identity of a new generation of Fleet Street reporters containing a high proportion of graduates. Of all the new relationships within the world of newspapers in Britain this growing interest in internal newsroom autonomy could be the most far-reaching in its influence on the content of newspapers in the future. If the position of editor becomes a quasi-elective office (as is now the case with the *New Statesman*, and several journals on the continent of Europe), then inevitably the system by which a paper's news values and policies are generated will change. As yet, however, this movement has produced only a small literature, which Part Four of this book attempts to illustrate.

PART ONE

# Fleet Street—Finance, Ownership and Structure

*Even in an age in which their indigence is widely proclaimed, newspapers do not adhere to a strict application of the laws of economics. The newspaper industry is an emotional one in which owners and shareholders seem at times prepared to sustain losses of an extraordinarily high order without flinching. An ordinary commercial product would have been swept away at a far earlier stage in its struggle for survival than many of the newspapers which have expired in recent years or than many which still fight to exist. In 1968* The Times *lost £3,000,000, and in 1971 announced, almost with pride, that it had in that year lost 'only £1,200,000'. The* Evening Standard *was kept going for ten years without declaring a single profit, until it finally climbed back into the black.*

At the same time Fleet Street can provide even now the opportunity for a company or a dynamic individual to seize hold of a failing product and make it into a commercial success. The Sun *newspaper was acquired for a minute sum in 1969 by Rupert Murdoch, owner of the* News of the World *and within three years had achieved a circulation of nearly 3,000,000 daily without appearing to flag. Any major advance by one of the popular papers in Fleet Street, however, nearly always involves a retreat by its rivals, and the appearance of the revivified* Sun *has caused the* Daily Mirror, *for instance, to alter its selection and presentation of news towards the brasher 'cheekier' style of the former. The circulation* war of the early 1970s has in some ways resembled the fierce competition of the 1930s, when the Daily Herald won the battle to be first to reach a daily circulation of two million; at that time newspapers almost destroyed themselves financially in an effort to stay at the head of the promotional race. Fleet Street now spends severeral million pounds a year on television advertising in its modernised promotional race, at a time when the total number of purchasers of daily national newspapers has been on the whole drifting downwards. In 1972 the Sun alone spent £1.16 million on television commercials, plus a large sum on a house-to-house promotion campaign in which colour-printed samples were thrust down 13¼ million letterboxes.

The success of the Sun has helped to emphasise the growing polarisation between the 'quality' Press and the 'popular'; the Daily Mirror, which in the mid-1960s achieved a circulation of 5¼ million while acquiring for itself an increasingly serious character, has moved 'down-market' in the early 1970s, while shedding at least a million copies a day. The Times, the Guardian and the Daily Telegraph have remained fairly steady in circulation and improved their financial security, while the wealthy specialist Financial Times has steadily increased its circulation to something approaching 200,000. The struggle for survival is at its fiercest among the popular papers. Since the war Fleet Street has watched the demise or amalgamation of the Daily Graphic, the News Chronicle, the Herald, and the Sketch among the dailies, plus a number of Sunday papers. It was these losses which brought about the two major Royal Commissions, extracts from whose reports are contained in this section, as well as various other enquiries into newspaper finance conducted by the Prices and Incomes Board and the Monopolies Commission.

The fear which hung over the newspaper industry in the aftermath of war was that ownership of the major part of the Press would devolve upon a tiny group of men, several of them highly politically motivated. There was also anxiety that the political affiliations of the remaining newspapers would be overwhelmingly right-wing and that the Labour Party would lack, especially between elections, a vigorous and loyal ally in Fleet Street. With the death of the New Chronicle the Liberal Party lost a paper which had consistently, from the moment of its birth, been tied to the policies of that party; in the Manchester Guardian (later the Guardian) the Liberal Party enjoyed only partial and general support until more recent years when that paper has tended at election times to support the Labour Party.

Part One of this book attempts to show how rising costs, changing reading habits and the shifting class affiliations among the public have altered the structure of Fleet Street, and also to identify the corporate pressures which are still at work altering the pattern of ownership and the editorial character of daily and Sunday newspapers.

Since the 1950s many newspapers have been given the chance by government to acquire holdings in commercial television and radio companies which have in most (though not all) years been extremely profitable. Diversification into these and other fields has kept the newspaper chains far from the poverty line, even though the newspapers themselves have often drained company resources. The social and political questions involved in the problems of newspaper concentration, therefore, are inseparable from the issue of commercial broadcasting and the method by which franchises are distributed.

At the root of the whole problem of newspaper finance lies the question of what newspapers should be and do. There is a permanent temptation to 'degrade' the product in order to reach an audience wide enough to sustain advertising revenue; there is a simultaneous public and professional pressure beyond the mere market for newspapers to provide the public with attractively presented information and discussion of the urgent issues of the day. That is why this section begins with a quotation from a journalist of great fame, written on the eve of the war against Nazism, in which he argues that the downward pressures can be overcome by an owner or editor determined to maintain a traditional journalistic ethic of public service.

## 1 Wickham Steed
## THE IDEAL NEWSPAPER

*Wickham Steed's name is one of the most famous in British journalism of this century; he edited* The Times *for several years when it was owned by Lord Northcliffe (formerly Alfred Harmsworth), but when the latter died in 1922, the paper was taken over by Lord Astor and John Walter, who saw Steed as a 'disturbing influence' and removed him. Steed continued writing throughout the 1930s, attacking those in Fleet Street who supported the policy of appeasement of Germany. At the time of Munich he wrote a book summing up the ideals of journalism as he saw them, of which this is an extract.*

Like most journalists who dream dreams I wonder sometimes what kind of paper I should try to turn out if I had, say, a million pounds or more to play with, and could either start a paper of my own or take over and transform an existing journal. Would it be possible, under the present conditions of the 'newspaper industry,' for a paper to rise superior to those conditions or to turn them to account in such fashion as to restore and to safeguard the freedom of the Press? It ought to be possible, though I am ready to admit that the man who should do it might need far higher ability than I could command. The need of the hour may call forth the man—or it may not. During the Great War there was urgent need for a military commander of outstanding ability or genius among the Allied armies. If he did not appear was it or was it not because conditions were too complicated for any man to master? . . . Here is a chance for a newspaper-maker of vision with an ideal and a purpose of his own, both of which he might perhaps hide in his heart lest they be mocked by fools before he could vindicate them. The newspaper I dream of would reflect the distractions of modern life no less faithfully than existing papers reflect them, but it would treat them as distractions, not as the things that matter. It would search out the truths behind these appearances and proclaim them, sparing no shams, respecting no conventions solely because they happened to be conventions, giving honour where honour might be due, but calling cant and humbug by their names.

It would be quite fearless. It would not 'hedge' in its treatment of thorny subjects; and if, as would be inevitable, it made mistakes, it would avow them. It would accept only such advertisements as it thought honest, so that its acceptance of them would be a moral guarantee to advertisers and to readers alike. Net sales certificates it would steadfastly refuse to publish, and it would scorn to canvass for subscribers or to offer them free insurance or other benefits. If advertisers or their agents should seek to bring it to heel, it would publish their names; and it would ruthlessly expose all underhand 'business' practices that came to its knowledge. A good part of its capital would be spent in winning the confidence of young and eager minds who would soon learn to trust its judgment and to heed its counsel. From its first 'editorial' column to the last it would be a militant journal, tied to no 'interests,' careless of hostility, sure that none would be able to ignore it.

My newspaper would, of course, make every effort to get the news, and would put its main news on the front page—where it ought to be. It would not fear to print several consecutive columns of one good 'story.' It would treat with contempt the time-wasting device of sending readers from one page to another so as to put the beginning of a different 'story' at the top of every column. Nor would it cheat its readers by superabundant headlines or by vain repetitions. Good and careful typography can help readers to see what is in a paper without defrauding them of reading matter.

My ideal newspaper would give 'all the news that's fit to print' as vividly as possible, whether the news suited its 'policy' or not. For its policy would fit the facts; it would not suppress or gloss over facts to suit 'policy.' In cases of doubt whether discretion might not be the better part of publicity it would give publicity the benefit of the doubt. To no Government, statesmen or person would it lend support for other than public reasons, publicly stated. It would be the servant of the public, to whose welfare alone it would acknowledge allegience, albeit without the misguided sycophancy that flatters an imaginary public and assumes that readers 'would not stand' plain speaking. A faithful servant tells his master the truth.

My paper would be national, not nationalist. It would be

liberal, not Liberal. It would strive for Peace, without pacifism. It would make clear the vital things for which nations and men may fitly fight and fitly die, if there be no other way of upholding them. Never would it fall into the grievous error of thinking the avoidance of conflict the same thing as peace. Against the brutal stupidity of the war-method of dealing with disputes between nations it would strive with all its might; yet always remembering that the hearts of men will never be weaned from war, with its spirit of life-risking adventure, unless peace enlist the spirit of self-devotion and self-sacrifice in ways worthier than those of war. My newspaper would seek to link the nations not only against war but in defence of individual freedom and of human right, so as to open the way for constructive international helpfulness; just as, in matters national and social, it would work to harness all classes of citizens to the task of constructive improvements in the edifice of society.

Could such a paper as this—technically well-made, trustworthy, news-giving, hard-hitting, full of vim and drive—hope to gain a circulation sufficient to command, not to solicit, enough advertisement revenue to balance its budget? I think it could, provided it were rich enough to 'stand the racket' until it had won its public.

One day, perchance, some newspaper-making genius with a soul of his own will do something like this. Then our advertisement-courting, dividend-seeking, circulation-mongers will rub their eyes and wonder how it has been done. Till then my ideal newspaper may remain in the realm of the ideal, and the British Press—if, indeed, it escape totalitarian servitude—will plod along its pedestrian way far below the breezy heights whereunto the heart of every true journalist aspires.

SOURCE: Wickham Steed. *The Press* (1938), 244–8

## 2 Printing and Kindred Trades Federation
## SURVEY OF THE INDUSTRY

*As the general discussion on the prospects for Fleet Street mounted in the 1970s, several of the unions involved in the newspaper industry produced their own policies and surveys of the problems. One of these contained a valuable 'Diary of Events' listing every major alteration in newspaper ownership for the preceding decade (in which fears about amalgamations within the industry became most apparent). The 'Diary' shows how a number of examples of rationalisation in the organisation of the printing of newspapers meant that the newspaper chains were even more dependent on one another than the mere structure of ownership suggests.*

### DIARY OF EVENTS

1959 Acquisition of Kemsley Newspapers Ltd., and with that the 'Sunday Times', by Thomson Organisation Ltd.
Odhams Press Ltd. acquired George Newnes Ltd.
Daily Mirror Newspapers Ltd. acquired Amalgamated Press Ltd. 'Manchester Guardian' became the 'Guardian' and started printing in London and Manchester.

1960 The 'News Chronicle' and the 'Star' ceased publication in October. Taken over by Associated Newspapers Ltd.
'Empire News' owned by Thomson Organisation Ltd. ceased publication in October, and was incorporated into the 'News of the World'.
'Sunday Graphic' owned by Thomson Organisation ceased publication in December.
In December, 1960 the 'Sunday Times' ceased being printed on the 'Daily Telegraph' machines, and transferred to Thomson House.
The TUC gave up political control of the 'Daily Herald'.

1961 'Sunday Dispatch' of Associated Newspapers Ltd. closed in June after being merged with the 'Sunday Express'.
In March Daily Mirror Newspapers Ltd. acquired Odhams Press Ltd.

A Royal Commission on the Press was set up in March.
'Sunday Telegraph' commenced publication in February.
'Sunday Times' commenced its colour magazine.
1962 'Reynolds News' changed its name to 'Sunday Citizen'.
Royal Commission on Press reported in September.
1963 International Publishing Corporation Ltd. was formed in January—March to implement merger of Daily Mirror Newspapers Ltd. and Sunday Pictorial Newspapers Ltd. The 'Sunday Pictorial' changed its name to the 'Sunday Mirror'.
1964 In September the 'Sun' was published as a successor to the 'Daily Herald'. The 'Sun' has no connection with the TUC.
Colour supplements were started by the 'Observer' and 'Daily Telegraph'.
1966 Thomson Organisation Ltd. acquired 85 per cent of 'The Times', and set up Times Newspapers Ltd., to publish 'The Times' and 'Sunday Times'.
1967 In December the 3 Lord Cowdray companies, Financial Times Ltd., Financial News Ltd., and Westminster Press Provincial Newspapers Ltd., were merged to form S. Pearson Publishers Ltd., now called Pearson Longman Ltd.
1968 In October the battle for News of the World Organisation Ltd. commenced, with Rupert Murdoch's Australian company News Ltd., acquiring the company in January 1969.
1969 The 'Sun' was taken over by the News of the World Organisation Ltd. in November.
'Daily Mirror' commenced publishing a colour supplement in September.
The Manchester Guardian & Evening News Ltd. and Associated Newspapers Ltd. started work on a joint printing venture in Manchester.
1970 In March the Reed International Ltd./International Publishing Corporation Ltd. merger was agreed.

In May the 'Daily Mirror' colour supplement ceased publication.

In August Lord Thomson's family company undertook responsibility for any losses sustained by 'The Times'.

The northern edition of the 'People' started being printed on the press in Manchester jointly owned by Manchester Guardian & Evening News Ltd. and Associated Newspapers Ltd.

1971 The 'Sketch' closed in May and the 'Daily Mail' became a tabloid.

SOURCE: Printing and Kindred Trades Federation. *National Newspaper Industry—a survey conducted for the Federation by the Labour Research Department* (December 1972), 75–6

### 3A Royal Commission on the Press, 1947–9
### THE STANDARD BY WHICH THE PRESS SHOULD BE JUDGED

*On 29 October 1946 the House of Commons held a major debate on the performance of the Press, in which a number of members, led by Maurice Webb of the National Union of Journalists, pressed successfully for the establishment of a Royal Commission, on the grounds that existing forms of control, management and ownership were prejudicial to the free expression of opinion and the accurate presentation of news. The NUJ, through Webb, had argued that the concentration of ownership had in fact led to the suppression of opinion and the distortion of news. The increase in the size of newspaper chains meant that journalists were being subjected to the views of a tiny group of owners and 'to the commercial considerations governing the employment of great accumulations of capital'. The opponents of the motion (which was passed by 270 votes to 157) argued that the motion was itself politically motivated from the left, that nothing approaching monopoly existed in Press ownership and that a Royal Commission could open the way to government interference.*

*The Commission's conclusions were not nearly as pessimistic as the promoters of the Commission had hoped. It evidently felt that its terms of reference, which included the relation of free expression of opinion to the prevailing pattern of newspaper ownership, were hampering. Above all, the Commission realised that the abnormal conditions of the immediate postwar period would render any observation they might make unusual, temporary or anomalous. Before the war, for instance, British newspapers consumed 1,250,000 tons of newsprint a year; in 1948 they were allowed to use only 350,000 tons. However, in a period of obligatorily thin papers (down to three four-page and three six-page issues per week), circulations were abnormally high: in 1937 total circulations had been 17,800,000; ten years later they stood at 28,503,000. Newsprint at £45 per ton was four times the price of prewar years. The* Daily Mail *before the war had carried 1,308 column inches of advertising; now it carried only 326in. Advertisers clamoured for the space available; unable to find it in the national Press, the advertising would spread out to the provincial. Much 'suppression' of news was ascribed to the sheer shortage of space in which to print it. Although no new titles appeared on Fleet Street, the Press was enjoying a period of high profits.*

*The Commission performed a valuable task of describing in detail the ownership, structure, shareholdings and methods of operation of the Press. In endeavouring to rationalise its own terms of reference the Commission set out several valuable statements of the position of newspapers in postwar societies.*

361. The Press may be judged, first, as the chief agency for instructing the public on the main issues of the day. The importance of this function needs no emphasis.

362. The democratic form of society demands of its members an active and intelligent participation in the affairs of their community, whether local or national. It assumes that they are sufficiently well informed about the issues of the day to be able to form the broad judgments required by an election, and to maintain between elections the vigilance necessary in those whose governors are their servants and not their masters. More and more it demands also an alert and informed participation not only in purely political processes but also in the efforts of the community to adjust its social and economic life to increas-

ingly complex circumstances. Democratic society, therefore, needs a clear and truthful account of events, of their background and their causes; a forum for discussion and informed criticism; and a means whereby individuals and groups can express a point of view or advocate a cause.

363. The responsibility for fulfilling these needs unavoidably rests in large measure upon the Press, that is on the newspapers and the periodicals, which are the main source from which information, discussion, and advocacy reach the public. In recent years this function has been shared with the radio; but the impermanence of broadcasting, together with the limitations on the quantity and character of controversial material which can be diffused over the air, still leaves the Press in a central position. A useful service is being rendered on a small scale by the factual publications of specialist societies and learned bodies, such as the Royal Institute of International Affairs and the British Society for International Understanding; and a number of newsletters of differing value supply information and comment to subscribers; but any shortcomings of the Press in this field are unlikely to be adequately made good by any other agency...

383. There are, however, two essential requirements which in our view newspapers individually and the Press collectively ought to fulfil, and we propose to take these as our own standard of judgment. . . .

384. The first of these requirements is that if a newspaper purports to record and discuss public affairs, it should at least record them truthfully. It may express what opinions it pleases —and nothing we may say hereafter is intended to criticise the opinions of any newspaper, or to question its right to express them—but opinions should be advocated without suppressing or distorting the relevant facts. If a paper adheres to a political party it should be plain to the reader that it does so, but from the columns of opinion, not from the colouring given to the news. A paper's politics and those of its readers will inevitably and legitimately affect its judgment of the relative interest of

certain items of news, but the news it reports it should report truthfully and without excessive bias. The second requirement is that the number and variety of newspapers should be such that the Press as a whole gives an opportunity for all important points of view to be effectively presented in terms of the varying standards of taste, political opinion, and education among the principal groups of the population.

385. These two requirements are not stated as alternatives: they are complementary. We recognise that even if they are satisfied, the pre-occupation of the Press with the exceptional, and the limited range of interests of the readers of any paper, must continue to throw the picture of events presented by the Press out of focus; but if the Press gives its readers the means of forming judgments on the problems of most immediate interest to them, that is perhaps as much as need be asked of it at present.

SOURCE: Royal Commission on the Press, 1947–9. *Report* (Cmnd. 7700, Chapter XI, paras 361–3, 383–5)

## 3B Royal Commission on the Press, 1947–9
## CONCLUSIONS AND RECOMMENDATIONS

*In summarising its own thinking on the state of the Press in postwar Britain, the Commission employed a series of questions which it had set itself at the beginning of its work, in an effort to rationalise the terms of reference Parliament had given it. Clearly the promoters of the Commission did not receive the kind of justification of their fears which they hoped the Commission would provide. The only major change proposed was the creation of a Press Council (which is the main subject of Part Three). Simultaneously, on the other side of the Atlantic, the Hutchins Commission into the Freedom of the Press (see p 314) reached similar conclusions. In Britain the Press Council was eventually set up; in America the discussion has continued until the present day.*

*What degree of concentration of ownership of newspapers, periodicals, and news agencies exists?*

664. There is nothing approaching monopoly in the Press as a whole or with the single exception of the London financial daily, in any class of newspaper: nor is there in those classes of periodical which we have examined.

665. The largest single aggregation of newspapers in one ownership, that controlled by Kemsley Newspapers Ltd., accounts for 17.18 per cent. of the total number of general daily and Sunday newspapers in the country. Concentration of ownership has gone farthest among provincial morning newspapers, 24 per cent. of which are members of the Kemsley chain.

666. In 58 towns out of 66 in Great Britain in which daily newspapers are published there is a local monopoly, in the sense that there is only one daily newspaper or all the dailies are in one ownership. Twelve of these towns neither import provincial dailies published elsewhere nor publish separately owned weeklies. More extensive monopolies in the publication of daily newspapers exist in the extreme North of England, in Devon and Cornwall, and in South Wales. But the importance of any local monopoly is qualified by the fact that national newspapers circulate throughout the country.

667. Concentration of ownership of local weekly newspapers is negligible.

668. Among political periodicals (the only ones of this class which we have studied in any detail) there is no appreciable concentration of ownership and no marked combination of the ownership of newspapers with that of periodicals.

669. Two news agencies supply a comprehensive service of home news to the British Press and four supply a comprehensive service of foreign news.

*Is there a tendency towards further concentration of ownership?*

670. Between 1921 and 1948 there was a marked tendency away from concentration of ownership in the national Press. We see no reason to expect a reversal of this tendency. In the provincial Press the trend was strongly towards concentration

between 1921 and 1929: thereafter the trend was much less pronounced and in terms of the largest single newspaper chain was reversed. There is no reason to expect that the aggressive expansion of chain undertakings which characterised the earlier period will be resumed.

671. Neither in the local weekly nor in the periodical Press nor in the news agencies do we expect a significant trend towards further concentration of ownership.

*Is such concentration as exists on balance disadvantageous to the free expression of opinion or the accurate presentation of news?*

672. The present degree of concentration of ownership in the newspaper Press as a whole or in any important class of it is not so great as to prejudice the free expression of opinion or the accurate presentation of news or to be contrary to the best interests of the public. Newspaper chains are undesirable not in themselves, but only if they are so large and so few that they unduly limit the number and variety of the voices speaking to the public through the Press. We should not be alarmed by an increase in the number of relatively small chains; but we should deplore any tendency on the part of the larger chains to expand.

673. Local monopoly is in some areas inevitable but it has certain inherent dangers and where it is not inevitable it is clearly to be deprecated.

674. The decrease in the number of newspapers, which is an aspect of concentration of ownership, has not been so great as to prejudice the public interest; but any further decrease in the number of national newspapers would be a matter for anxiety, and a decrease in the provincial morning newspapers would be a serious loss.

675. The existing concentration in the ownership of news agencies is not harmful.

*Do any other factors in the control, management, or ownership of the Press or of the news agencies, or any external influences operating upon those concerned in control, management, or ownership, militate against the free expression of opinion and the accurate presentation of news?*

676. In considering this question we have taken as our standard two requirements, first that, while the selection of news may be affected by a newspaper's political and other opinions the news it reports should be reported truthfully and without excessive bias, and second that the number and variety of newspapers should be such that the Press as a whole gives an opportunity for all important points of view to be effectively presented in terms of the varying standards of taste, political opinion, and education among the principal groups of the population.

677. The first requirement is satisfied in very different measure by different papers. A number of quality papers do fully or almost fully meet its demands. But all the popular papers and certain of the quality fall short of the standard achieved by the best, either through excessive partisanship or through distortion for the sake of news value. The provincial newspapers generally fall short to a lesser extent than the popular national newspapers.

678. As to the second requirement, the Press provides for a sufficient variety of political opinion but not for a sufficient variety of intellectual levels. The gap between the best of the quality papers and the general run of the popular Press is too wide, and the number of papers of an intermediate type is too small.

679. The causes of these shortcomings do not lie in any external influences upon the Press (other than those exerted by public demand). The policy of the Press is dictated neither by the advertisers, nor by the Government, nor by any outside financial interests. It is the policy of those who own and conduct the Press. Nor do the causes of the shortcomings lie in any particular form of ownership.

680. The Press is part of our political machinery, which is essentially partisan, and it is a highly competitive industry, the principle of whose being is to maintain high circulations. The

increasing complexity of public affairs and the growth of the reading public have created a need for public instruction on an entirely new scale, without producing as yet either the corresponding demand or the corresponding supply. The failure of the Press to keep pace with the requirements of society is attributable largely to the plain fact that an industry that lives by the sale of its products must give the public what the public will buy. A newspaper cannot, therefore, raise its standard far above that of its public and may anticipate profit from lowering its standard in order to gain an advantage over a competitor. This tendency is not always resisted as firmly as the public interest requires. The Press does not do all it might to encourage its public to accept or demand material of higher quality.

681. Nevertheless the Press has considerable achievements to its credit. It provides cheaply and efficiently a mass of information and entertainment for which there is a wide public demand. It acknowledges high standards of public responsibility and service. It is jealous of its own independence and reputation and many of those employed in it have a sense of vocation.

*How this freedom and accuracy may best be promoted*

682. We do not see a solution to the problems we have indicated in major changes in the ownership and control of the industry. Free enterprise is a prerequisite of a free Press, and free enterprise in the case of newspapers of any considerable circulation will generally mean commercially profitable enterprise.

683. Nor do we see the solution in any form of state control of the Press. We prefer to seek the means of maintaining the free expression of opinion and the greatest practicable accuracy in the presentation of news, and, generally, a proper relationship between the Press and society, primarily in the Press itself.

684. Accordingly *we recommend:*—

1. That the Press should establish a General Council of the Press consisting of at least 25 members representing proprietors, editors, and other journalists, and having lay

members amounting to about 20 per cent. of the total, including the chairman. The lay members should be nominated jointly by the Lord Chief Justice and the Lord President of the Court of Session, who in choosing the other lay members should consult the chairman. The chairman, on whom a heavy burden of work will fall, should be paid.

The objects of the General Council should be to safeguard the freedom of the Press; to encourage the growth of the sense of public responsibility and public service amongst all engaged in the profession of journalism—that is, in the editorial production of newspapers—whether as directors, editors, or other journalists; and to further the efficiency of the profession and the well-being of those who practise it.

In furtherance of its objects the General Council should take such action as it thinks fit:

(1) to keep under review any developments likely to restrict the supply of information of public interest and importance;

(2) to improve the methods of recruitment, education, and training for the profession;

(3) to promote a proper functional relation among all sections of the profession;

(4) by censuring undesirable types of journalistic conduct, and by all other possible means, to build up a code in accordance with the highest professional standards. In this connection it should have the right to consider any complaints which it may receive about the conduct of the Press or of any persons towards the Press, to deal with these complaints in whatever manner may seem to it practicable and appropriate, and to include in its annual report any action under this heading;

(5) to examine the practicability of a comprehensive pension scheme;

(6) to promote the establishment of such common services as may from time to time appear desirable;

(7) to promote technical and other research;

(8) to study developments in the Press which may tend towards greater concentration or monopoly;

(9) to represent the Press on appropriate occasions in its relations with the Government, with the organs of the United Nations, and with similar Press organisations abroad;

(10) to publish periodical reports recording its own work and reviewing from time to time the various developments in the Press and the factors affecting them.

2. That powers of inquiry similar to those of the Board of Trade under sections 172 and 173 of the Companies Act, 1948, should be conferred on the Registrar of Friendly Societies in respect of any societies registered under the Industrial and Provident Societies Acts which publish newspapers or periodicals or engage in the business of a news agency.

3. That chain newspapers should be required by law to carry on the front page a formula clearly indicating their common ownership.

4. That if local monopolies in a considerable area whether rural or urban should be found not to be within the purview of the Monopolies Commission, the Monopolies and Restrictive Practices (Inquiry and Control) Act, 1948, should be amended to bring newspaper monopolies in areas of this size within its scope.

5. That the present agreement in the industry to refrain from non-journalistic forms of competition should be prolonged indefinitely.

SOURCE: as Document 3A, paras 664–84

## 4 Denis Thomas
## THE CHARACTER OF THE NEWS CHRONICLE

*It was the sudden demise, and some said callous execution, of the* News Chronicle *that triggered off the debate about the British Press of the*

*1960s which has lasted until the present day. The* News Chronicle *was a radical paper, of quality, with a majority of working-class readers; it had a very large circulation throughout its last decade, even though it was slowly falling. It was not the actual number of its readers, however, which caused its downfall, but the fact that not enough of them were in upper income brackets to sustain the interest of the advertisers. So long as the* News Chronicle *remained in existence there was a kind of optimism that high principles and popular presentation could exist side by side with first-rate and successful journalism. An interesting description of the paper was given in a pamphlet published by the Truth Publishing Company in 1957.*

At the foot of a column on the back page of the *News Chronicle* is to be found the longest imprint on Fleet Street. It begins: 'News Chronicle, incorporating the Daily News, the Daily Chronicle, the Daily Dispatch, Westminster Gazette and Morning Leader. Printed by the Daily News Limited and published by News Chronicle Limited.' From the title on the front page, and the heading to the leader column, it appears that the paper should properly be called *News Chronicle and Daily Dispatch*. And any Londoner who might buy a copy in the Manchester area would find that there the second half of the title is printed only a little less prominently than the first.

These are significant details, because today's *Chronicle* is the chief exponent, in a popular sense, of British Liberal journalism. Its reputation, and most of its readership, have survived the eclipse of the Party it traditionally stands for. It is of course true that it has broadened the base of its appeal in recent years, though without achieving a readership solid enough to attract much advertising support. At a time when even the giants of Fleet Street are looking around for new golden geese it is almost painfully vulnerable.

There must, however, be something essentially durable about a newspaper which, while supporting a Party which is at the nadir of its fortunes, nevertheless manages to outsell such a powerful Conservative paper as, for instance, the *Daily Tele-*

*graph*, and which runs Labour's *Daily Herald* to within two hundred thousand readers. Its most distinctive feature is probably its editorial consistency; and that in turn stems from the fact that it is the only national daily paper to be owned not by a joint stock company but by a trust. With its stable-companion, the evening *Star*, it is owned by a company—the Daily News Limited—in which the majority shareholding belongs to the Daily News Trust. Of the trustees, two-thirds are members of the Cadbury family, whose other trust, Bournville Village, is named in the original articles of association as beneficiary if the Daily News Trust should not be renewed.

The income, meanwhile, is paid proportionately to charity, to the company and to the staff. Philanthropy and strong family conscience, therefore, have their place in the *News Chronicle* set-up. (So, less altruistically, do legitimate means of avoiding heavy death duties.) Instead of a proprietor or a board of directors, the editor is in this case answerable to trustees, who may be expected to set a higher value on principles and standards than on commercial expediency alone. To that extent, successive editors have been spared the more demoralising aspects of the Fleet Street rat-race (an expression which journalists themselves invented). But they have not been spared much else. . . .

### ACCENT ON INDUSTRY

Michael Curtis, the editor, believes that industry, as a collective audience, is on the whole disregarded by the national Press. He himself misses no opportunity of reaching into it for news and features likely to interest an increasingly science-conscious readership: 'I think of our newer readers as being largely young, skilled men with minds of their own.' Industrial areas are producing such new readers faster than the others, and the *News Chronicle*—with a special edition, for instance, for Wales—now addresses them more directly than ever.

Another direction in which Mr Curtis is leading his paper is towards fuller coverage of foreign affairs. This derives in part from the influence of television on reading habits: it tends, says Mr Curtis, to stimulate new interests in events abroad. The paper has not only stepped up its foreign news service but has also begun presenting such stories in the form of illustrated features. Thus its page two, in particular, usually carries an expanded background story in the form of news-with-comment: 'The Eclipse of Mr France', 'The Great Wall of China Closes Around Mr K.'. James Cameron, latest in a long line of brilliant columnists, keeps up a staccato—and sometimes discordant—crossfire from his strongpoint on the leader page.

All this, even if it is not pulling in new readers fast enough to save the paper, is in the *News Chronicle*'s tradition of clear thinking and free speaking. Its editorial tone these days is more strident than it has been in recent years, and in raising its voice to command attention it loses something of its traditional register. But tradition is something of which Michael Curtis takes a realistic view. 'Every editor inherits it, and the danger is that he might think of it as sacrosanct in every part. I don't think so. That's the way to reaction, and no great newspaper can hope to go forward on that basis.'

### JOURNALISTS' SOFT SPOT

Towards the end of 1955 it acquired the Manchester *Daily Dispatch*, whose 400,000 readers were presumed to be mostly supporters of the Government, and claims to have lost 'an insignificant 8,282' of those of them who came over. 'It would have been astonishing', said a front-page announcement some weeks ago, 'if every one of the old *Dispatch* readers had stayed with the *News Chronicle*. . . . The lasting success of this merger is an outstanding achievement.' In fact, the circulation is now just about back to what it was in 1945. But it is falling steadily.

Significantly, the *News Chronicle* is a newspaper greatly respected by journalists themselves—a race of men who, for all their supposed ignobility of character, nevertheless find it necessary to believe in the particular journals they serve. They watch the declining fortunes of most rivals with a dry eye; but if the *News Chronicle* is forced to surrender to the pressure of sheer economics, they would feel that something worthwhile had dropped out of the profession of journalism itself. Journalists' soft spot for this one newspaper possibly derives from their occupational sense of frustrated idealism, for certainly the paper itself is not without blemish from a purely professional point of view—it has never, for instance, successfully modernised its make-up.

Still, Mr Curtis and his team *are* modernists. And there are no laughs, these days, for trade jokes about chocolate and cocoa.

SOURCE: Denis Thomas. *Challenge in Fleet Street—a candid commentary on today's national newspapers* (1957), 35–8

## 5 Editor of the Sunday Telegraph
### AN ADDITION TO THE QUALITY PRESS

*One of the major developments of the 1960s in journalism was the polarisation of papers towards the popular and the 'quality'. While the* News Chronicle *went under, and the* Daily Herald *lingered only a little longer, the 'middle-class' press enjoyed a period of relative prosperity. The* Daily Telegraph *launched a Sunday paper designed to compete with the* Observer *and the* Sunday Times, *which were enjoying the benefits of a new wave of lush consumer advertising. The* Sunday Telegraph *has, for most of its life, been supported by the profits of its prosperous daily parent. In its first edition, its editor described the purpose and style of the new Sunday.*

There have been many helpful, useful and friendly letters in recent weeks from potential readers of the *Sunday Telegraph*, anxious to express their goodwill and curious to know what we are about.

What, for example, is the 'gap' that the *Sunday Telegraph* claims to fill? Not Sir Charles Snow's notorious division between the scientists and the rest of us, but something no less challenging: the gap that exists between the Sunday papers which set out to be popular and those which lay claim to quality.

To us, with the example of the *Daily Telegraph* to point to, so sharp a distinction seems out of date: like insisting that there are only rich and poor, highbrow and low-brow, U and non-U, Left and Right. Nowadays more and more people aspire to the middle position; they are moving into 'the gap' where quality and popularity meet and co-exist.

*In response to their needs we offer not a rival to the week-end magazines, but a newspaper designed for Sunday.*

### THEIR AIMS

It has been planned and produced by daily newspaper men, applying the lessons of many years' experience with the steadily growing and flourishing *Daily Telegraph*. They aim first at the clear, simple, accurate presentation of news—news that has been looked for, worked at and thought about.

They believe, too, in the inquisitive, topical, forward-looking approach to everything that interests readers in current affairs, in the arts, in games and hobbies, in investment and personal finance, in sport, in the world of women and the family, in property and the home. The idea of service to readers is expressed in the guides to reading, shopping, painting, films and music that will be found in these pages.

Readers of the *Daily Telegraph* will find on the front and middle pages a presentation that is familiar, but in fact redesigned down to the smallest detail. Expert typographical advice has been used to make all parts of the paper easily legible. A larger body size has been used for the text type throughout, and for the news headlines we have introduced Caledonia, a type face never before used for this purpose in Britain.

### OUR CRITICS

One way in which a newspaper of 28 pages can bridge the gap is by its balance of news and features. What is new about the features in the *Sunday Telegraph*?

First, the emphasis on Sunday as the day when the tasks and

pleasures of the week are planned. Our critics write with this need in mind. On books, on the theatre, on music, television and radio, on art and on films it is useful and stimulating to be fortified before the event. Regular reviewers will include Dame Rebecca West, J. J. M. Stewart, Nigel Dennis and L. P. Hartley.

Then there is the emphasis on news in the feature pages— on things happening and about to happen. That will specially mark the column called Talking of Politics on page 14, which is supplemented by a full service of news from our Political Correspondent. Those British connoisseurs who say there is no political reporting outside Washington will have to think again.

News is also a feature of the two pages for women edited by Winefride Jackson—news and practical advice on cooking, clothes, entertainment, education, and all the problems of home life that men also share.

Reporting in depth is applied to the churches on page 9. How they and their members express their faith and principles in the tasks of everyday life is full of human interest. By its candid and impartial scrutiny this column invites controversy.

### AMATEURS TOO

In the City pages news and service are provided for the men and women who invest and who find their financial problems getting more complex and more interesting as their affairs prosper. The City Editor caters for amateurs as well as experts.

On pages 4 and 5 each week will be found what we hope will be an outstanding feature of the paper. To-day's main item is one of two extracts from a major book and these will be used frequently. But there will also be much specially written material. Here we shall revive the art of reportage, either by bringing the imaginative writer to the news situation or by giving the news reporter the time and space for his imagination to spark.

If our readers find that they have not been given all the news, views, facts and forecasts that they need to understand and enjoy the world they live in they will, no doubt, say so. In making their suggestions, however, they are asked to remember one thing: this is meant to be a paper that you can read through—and finish in one day.

THE EDITOR

SOURCE: *Sunday Telegraph* (5 February 1961)

## 6 Sunday Express and Sunday Dispatch
### INCREASING POLARISATION

*One by one the papers, dailies and Sundays, which filled the gap between quality and popular disappeared. In June 1961 a Sunday paper, the* Dispatch, *with a small circulation was amalgamated with the* Sunday Express, *which published the following message to its new readers.*

Today the *Sunday Express* welcomes into its existing vast readership the readers of the *Sunday Dispatch*.

For the *Sunday Express* there is both pride and sorrow in the events which have led to the transfer of the title and goodwill of the *Sunday Dispatch* to this newspaper.

Sorrow that a vigorous rival has been forced, by the harsh economics of newspaper production, to cease separate publication. Sorrow that an independent voice has been silenced.

But the *Sunday Express* takes immense pride in the fact that the proprietors of the *Dispatch*, in considering the future of the paper's millions of readers, turned to the *Sunday Express*.

The *Sunday Express* believes that the *Dispatch*'s readers will agree that this was a wise choice. Indeed the only one.

Consider the strange position now existing in the field of Sunday journalism.

At one extreme are the ponderous, pompous, small-circulation 'heavy' papers.

At the other are those papers which have built up large sales by sensarionrlism and salaciousness. IN THE IMMENSE CHASM BETWEEN STANDS THE SUNDAY EXPRESS—AND ONLY THE SUNDAY EXPRESS.

We hope that the *Sunday Dispatch* readers who join us today will like their new paper. They will find in its pages some of the features which delighted them in the *Sunday Dispatch*.

But there is one thing which remains completely unaltered in the *Sunday Express*. Its character.

THE SUNDAY EXPRESS STAYS NOW AND ALWAYS A PAPER FIT FOR ALL THE FAMILY TO READ.

SOURCE: *Sunday Express* (18 June 1961)

### 7A Royal Commission on the Press, 1961-2
### THE TELEVISION INTERESTS
### OF NEWSPAPER COMPANIES

*The death of the* News Chronicle *sent a shock wave throughout the Press industry. The newspaper had been owned by the Cadbury family which, by reason of its ownership, had been awarded a substantial shareholding in one of the regional commercial television companies. Despite the ending of its control of the paper, the family was able to retain this interest. The second aspect of the* Chronicle's *death which shocked many in Fleet Street was that it had been sold to Associated Press and amalgamated with the* Daily Mail, *a paper which had always been diametrically opposed politically to the* Chronicle. *Many of the best journalists were kept on the new paper but a very large number left, some going out of Fleet Street altogether. A few years earlier it might have been possible for the* Chronicle *to have been sold to a company, such as Thomson's, which might have kept it in existence; alternatively it might have amalgamated with the* Daily Herald, *which was also a paper of the left, thereby creating a financially sound radical newspaper. The suddenness of the final announcement, the ideologically alien nature of the amalgamation, and the small compensation paid to the staff caused a wave of indignation. With the* Chronicle *disappeared the* Star, *a prosperous London evening paper, which had committed no sin other than to be printed by the same machinery as the* Chronicle.

*The* Daily Herald *had been successful in the early 1930s in being the first of the populars to reach a daily circulation of two million, but* had been slowly in decline since the war. Its owners, Odhams Press, also owned the People, a Sunday paper, and soon after the death of the Chronicle decided to sell out to Daily Mirror Newspapers Ltd. This meant that the latter company controlled two rival daily papers aimed at similar readerships and two rival Sundays also competing in similar markets. The acquisition clearly spelt danger for the Herald.

Such were the origins of the second postwar Royal Commission on the Press. Since the 1947-9 Royal Commission had reported ('that the decrease in the number of newspapers . . . has not been so great as to prejudice the public interest'), seventeen daily and Sunday papers had ceased publication in London and the provinces; it was therefore decided that a new Commission, under Lord Shawcross, should be asked to inquire 'not into the rights or wrongs of these events, but into the economic factors affecting the Press generally'. One of the matters investigated was the position of newspapers in commercial television companies.

## Interests in Television

244. The combination of television and newspaper interests has been a source of controversy, but we have concerned ourselves only with its economic consequences and not its social implications, which are not within our terms of reference. Had they been we should have expressed some misgivings about it. The representatives of The Scotsman Publications Ltd. told us of some of the advantages which flow from the interest of the Thomson group in Scottish Television Ltd.:

'We have some mutual and convenient arrangements. We give them their news service, and charge them for it, of course. Otherwise it would be enormously costly for them to set up a news service in the area. We get certain publicity from them, which is nominally paid for, which is unfortunately now subject to this ten per cent. advertising tax. Recently we made certain premises avilable to them to set up a television bureau during the Edinburgh Festival, but there is no enormous homogeneity of interest and convenience between us . . . At the moment with Scottish Television being part of the Thomson newspaper group, and having a minority interest to consider, we do pay for our publicity, because that would be taking money out of the minority's pocket, as it were, but we have come to an agreement with them that we only use available free time—filler, as they call it—and we do get a reduced rate for that in actual fact ... It ought to be said, because this is an economic hard fact, if we had no association whatever with Scottish Television there would be a decision to be made as to whether we wanted this particular form of advertising'.

Newspapers published in competition with those owned by an undertaking with a controlling interest in a television contracting company do not enjoy similar advantages; in view of the statutory monopoly enjoyed by television contracting companies we consider it to be contrary to the public interest for such companies to be controlled by newspaper undertakings. We recommend that such arrangements be terminated at the earliest possible date.

245. Newspaper proprietors with minority interests in television may not enjoy such advantages as are described in the preceding paragraph. Their sole benefit usually lies in the earnings of the investment, which are often very great. Any tendency for the large profits of television companies to diminish would obviously affect the revenue of newspaper undertakings. It might make some undertakings less able to enlarge their Press interests through the purchase of other newspapers or periodicals.

SOURCE: Royal Commission on the Press, 1961–2. *Report* (Cmnd. 1811, 1962, paras 244–5)

### 7B Royal Commission on the Press, 1961-2
### PLAN FOR AN AMALGAMATIONS COURT

*The Shawcross Commission was very severe with the Press Council. 'Full advantage has certainly not been taken of the existence of a body representing the Press as a whole to enlarge public knowledge of the problems which the Press have to face.' The Press Council, in the economic field, had restricted itself to providing a bald factual account* of certain financial aspects of the work of the Press. The Commission demanded reform of the Press Council in a number of respects, not only to provide the 20 per cent lay representation which the previous Royal Commission had recommended, but also to widen the Council's terms of reference through the creation of a special Press Amalgamations Court.

326. As well as expressing the hope that a reformed Council would be able to devote itself more effectively to its present stated objects we recommend that it should undertake the following additional functions:—

(a) To scrutinise changes in the ownership, control and growth of Press undertakings (including periodical undertakings so far as they are relevant to the public interest), and to give wide publicity to authoritative information on these matters in annual reports or by special report if the need arose.

(b) To keep up to date and publish statistical information relevant to concentration in the Press on the lines of that given in the appendices to this report.

(c) To secure enforcement of the requirements recommended in paragraph 318 that newspapers should bear the name of the company or individual in ultimate control of their affairs.

The proper discharge of these functions should assist in enlarging the public knowledge of developments which must be of concern to the citizens of a free country. In view of the disquiet about the possible dangers to the free expression of opinion arising from the potential conflict of interest between editors and advertisers, we suggest a further function:—

(d) That the Council should have authority to hear complaints from journalists of undue influence by advertisers or advertising agents, and give full publicity to their findings.

It might be possible to extend this function to hearing complaints by editors or other journalists that they have been improperly obliged by their employers or superiors to suppress opinion, distort the truth or otherwise engage in unprofessional conduct. An editor or journalist who had made such a complaint might well be unable or unwilling to remain in the same employment, but the existence of a forum for such complaints might act as a deterrent to undue pressures.

336. We do not suggest that there should be a wholesale prohibition of all future amalgamations or expansions. There can be no public interest in preventing such transactions as the merger of the *News Chronicle* with the *Daily Mail* or the *Sunday Dispatch* with the *Sunday Express* when in each case the former newspaper would have gone out of existence in any event. There are, however, other possible circumstances in which amalgamations may take place, some of which may be obviously contrary to the public interest, some of no consequence in this regard, some beneficial and some requiring scrutiny. A case in point was of course the recent acquisition of Odhams Press Ltd. by the Daily Mirror group. Odhams Press could have survived economically on its own. There were some, including its own board, who thought that if it were to be taken over at all it would have been more in the public interest for it to be amalgamated with the group controlled by Mr. Roy Thomson. Others asserted the opposite view. We express no opinion at all on which of these three possibilities might at that time have been the most consistent with the public interest in the context of our terms of reference. What in fact happened was decided wholly by the financial interests of shareholders who were not, as such, concerned with the public interest. This seems to be an example of the sort of transaction which in future might justify scrutiny from the point of view of the public interest.

*A Press Amalgamations Court*

337. We therefore recommend that a tribunal should be established to scrutinise transactions involving the purchase of newspaper titles or of controlling interests in companies which, either directly or indirectly through subsidiaries, own newspapers. Not all such transactions need be subjected to scrutiny; those involving a mere merger of title when one newspaper is

going to cease publication in any event (as occurred in the case of the *News Chronicle*) would be excluded. We should also limit the scheme to daily and Sunday newspapers, and require a transaction to be scrutinised only if the purchaser controlled aggregate weekly sales of daily or Sunday newspapers of more than 3,000,000 copies either before or as a result of it. The tribunal (which we think should be a specially constituted court, akin to the Restrictive Trade Practices Court, rather than an advisory or administrative tribunal) would grant consent to a transaction only if it were shown to be in the public interest in the accurate presentation of news and the free expression of opinion. Criteria for determining whether transactions were in the public interest would be specified by the statute; we suggest in paragraph 348 certain principles to be followed. Transactions to which the statute applied would be presumed to be contrary to the public interest unless the applicants could show that freedom and variety of opinion were not likely to be reduced by the transaction, or that any reduction in such freedom and variety was likely to be less, by the avoidance of a diminution in the number of newspapers published or otherwise, if consent were granted than if it were withheld. . . .

339. The first objection that might be raised to legislation of this kind is that it involves an interference with the freedom of the Press. This we think is not so. Here perhaps the words of Mr. Justice Douglas in the United States case of *Associated Press* v. *The United States* may be quoted:—

> 'Finally, the argument is made that to apply the Sherman Act to this association of publishers constitutes an abridgement of the freedom of the press guaranteed by the First Amendment.... It would be strange indeed however if the grave concern for freedom of the press which prompted adoption of the First Amendment should be read as a command that the government was without power to protect that freedom. The First Amendment, far from providing an argument against applica-

tion of the Sherman Act, here provides powerful reasons to the contrary. That Amendment rests on the assumption that the widest possible dissemination of information from diverse and antagonistic sources is essential to the welfare of the public, that a free press is a condition of a free society. Surely a command that the government itself shall not impede the free flow of ideas does not afford non-governmental combinations a refuge if they impose restraints upon that constitutionally guaranteed freedom. Freedom to publish means freedom for all and not for some. Freedom to publish is guaranteed by the Constitution but freedom to combine to keep others from publishing is not. Freedom of the press from governmental interference under the First Amendment does not sanction repression of that freedom by private interests. The First Amendment affords not the slightest support for the contention that a combination to restrain trade in news and views has any constitutional immunity.'

340. Then it may be said—and said truly—that the proposal involves treating the newspaper industry differently from industry in general. The answer is that the public interest in relation to the newspaper industry is different. The discrimination is based on the proposition that freedom and variety in the expression of opinion and presentation of news is an element which does not enter into the conduct of other competitive industries and that it is a paramount public interest. Similar reasoning would apply to the objection that legislation of this kind would interfere with the property rights of shareholders.

SOURCE: as Document 7A, paras 326, 336-7, 339-40

## 7C Royal Commission on the Press, 1961-2
## NICHOLAS KALDOR AND ROBERT NEILD'S SCHEME FOR A 'LEVY'

*There have been various schemes put forward ever since the problem of Press concentration became a national issue for creating systematic financial disincentives to rising circulation. The general plan behind these has been to render it no longer desirable or profitable for a newspaper to increase its circulation by promotional devices, beyond a certain point.*

*Several plans of this kind were presented to the Shawcross Commission, of which the plan of Kaldor and Neild was the most prominent. It survives in discussion until the present day, although it was rejected by the Commission.*

*The scheme is based upon a desire to counteract the tendencies towards standardisation of what is set before the public, which is the universal result of the economies of scale which are achieved in modern mass production. The two economists argued that whereas in food, clothing and transport we are prepared to accept the reduction of choice in exchange for the higher living standards offered by mass production, we should not be prepared as a society to accept this in the sphere of 'intellectual goods'. The tendencies towards concentration operate more powerfully in the newspaper industry than in others because the producer who has an initial lead can outbid his rivals by devoting his extra profits to increasing his fixed as opposed to his variable costs (ie increase staff, expensive equipment, special features). Advertising, they argued, has come to dominate newspaper costs to the extent that it actually subsidises the basic costs of production, revenue from sales being less than the total cost of production. The paper that succeeds in the circulation battle also enjoys, therefore, the benefit of having the extra advertising cover a larger part of his production costs. Marginal success and failure produce exaggerated advantages and disadvantages. The Kaldor-Neild scheme is designed to counteract this aspect of the market by means of a special levy.*

*Remedies*

10. Any effective remedy must make large circulations less profitable relative to smaller ones, and reduce the size that a paper must achieve if it is to stay in business (i.e. reduce the 'break-even point'). The most convenient instrument for this purpose is a levy graduated so as to increase the effective cost to the publisher when circulation increases beyond a certain figure, combined with an equalisation payment which has the effect of raising the proportion of revenue that is directly geared to sales. We therefore propose that a levy should be imposed on the newspaper industry, the proceeds of which are returned to the industry in such a way that the net result is to change the

relative profitability of small and large circulations. Since advertising revenue is a kind of bounty to newspapers, which arises from performing a service which is incidental to their functions as newspapers and bears little relation to the cost of providing that service, the most reasonable method of achieving this end is to impose a levy on revenue from advertising; the rate of the levy as a percentage of (gross) advertising revenue should be graduated according to circulation, and there should be total exemption for newspapers whose circulation is below a minimum level. The following schedule is constructed as illustration; we do not have the information necessary to calculate what in practice would be the appropriate schedule.

NATIONAL DAILY MORNING NEWSPAPERS

| Circulation | Rate of levy on Gross Revenue from advertising Per cent. |
|---|---|
| The first 500,000 | Nil |
| 500,000–1 million | 7·5 |
| 1 million–2 million | 20 |
| 2 million–3 million | 40 |
| Above 3 million | 50 |

11. In order to avoid large jumps in the liability when certain circulation levels are reached, we suggest that the actual schedule should be broken down into a larger number of small steps. In the above example, the actual schedule might be stated in terms of an increase of 1 per cent. for every 50,000 of circulation, or an increase of 2 per cent. for every 100,000 of circulation, above the level of 500,000. In order to prevent people from evading the levy by producing the same newspaper under a variety of titles, and also to prevent excessive concentration of ownership, the circulations of all daily morning newspapers belonging to one proprietor should be added together for the purpose of assessing the levy. Sunday papers should be dealt with in the same way. We propose that the proceeds of the levy should be returned to the papers embraced in the

scheme in the form of a flat rate equalisation payment of so much per copy sold, subject to a limit of, say, 2 million copies per day. Thus, supposing that the levy were to yield £10 million per annum, and the total circulation of newspapers (excluding that part of the circulations which is in excess of 2 million per day) is 10 million copies per day, the equalisation payment would be £1 a year per copy, or approximately 0·8d. per copy per day subject to maximum payment of £6,667 per day, or £2 million a year, for any one paper.

12. The main feature of a scheme of this kind (of which many variants can be devised) is that it causes the 'cost curve' of newspaper production to turn upwards beyond a certain level of circulation; that is, it causes profits per copy to diminish (and ultimately total profits to diminish) when certain circulation figures are exceeded. In our example 'the optimum circulation' beyond which profits per copy (though not necessarily *total* profits) begin to diminish is around 2 million. This is not an unreasonable figure, having regard to the total number of newspaper readers in the United Kingdom; before the Second World War, the most popular daily newspaper scarcely exceeded this figure. Had a scheme on the above lines been put into operation then, it would not have actually weakened the financial position of any particular newspaper, but it would have effectively discouraged the process of concentration that has occurred since that time. But if a scheme of this sort is to be introduced at the present time, the issue will have to be faced whether the scheme should merely serve to prevent further concentration from taking place (that is, prevent a further reduction in the number of papers with its attendant increase in the circulation of the leading papers above the present figure of around 4,000,000) or whether it should effectively penalise the papers which at present have the largest circulations (i.e. the 'Daily Express' and the 'Daily Mirror') and induce them to contract, thereby helping to preserve the existing number of papers and to make room for more. Even if it were felt that the 'acquired rights' or 'acquired circulations' of the existing Press

should not be penalised, it would be possible to work out a scheme which safeguarded the position of the papers which have attained peak circulations well in excess of 2,000,000 in the years prior to the introduction of the scheme. This object would be served if, for example, papers could subtract from their present circulations a number equal to 10 times the amount by which their present circulation is below their peak monthly circulation during the last three years, provided that does not reduce its imputed circulation to below 2 million. Thus supposing the peak circulation of a paper in the past three years was $4\frac{1}{2}$ million, when the scheme came into operation (say in 1962) it could reduce the tax payable on its advertising revenue to that pertaining to a paper of 2 millions by keeping its circulation about $\frac{1}{4}$ million or more below the peak, i.e. at about $4\frac{1}{4}$ million or less. But after three years, say in 1965, it would have to reduce its circulation to around 4 million in order to continue to be taxed in the 2 million circulation bracket. There are of course numerous other ways in which a scheme could be introduced that would discourage further concentration (and over a longer period promote deconcentration) without actually imposing heavy financial burdens on the newspapers which initially had the largest circulations.

13. No doubt a proposal of this kind would be heavily criticized by interested parties as an interference with 'freedom' and as a scheme which 'penalises the strong in order to support the weak'. We should like to emphasize again that in this field, more than in any other, commercial success is no criterion of public advantage. It is well established that it is the duty of the State in a free society to take whatever steps are necessary and appropriate to keep the market free, and to check the aggregation of monopoly power which itself constitutes a menace to freedom. In the newspaper industry such aggregation of monopoly power has far worse consequences than in other fields, implying as it does a dictatorship over the sources of knowledge, accompanied by irresponsible power to condition the mind and to sway opinion. The Royal Commission on the

Press of 1947–48 stated in its Conclusions (para. 674) that 'any further decrease in the number of national newspapers would be a matter for anxiety'. Since that time the number of national newspapers has decreased further. Indeed, it was the public anxiety created by the disappearance of an important newspaper last year which led to the appointment of the present Royal Commission. The time for action has arrived.

SOURCE: Royal Commission on the Press, Documentary Evidence, Vol VI (Cmnd. 1812–19, 55–6)

## 8 Daily Leader
## AN ATTEMPT TO START A NEW DAILY PAPER

*Several efforts were made by groups on the right and on the left, to start new daily papers in the 1960s. By means of voluntary sellers the Trotskyite Socialist Labour League managed by gradual steps to create in the* Workers' Press *an organ which appears daily. A similar venture on the far right died after two years of struggle. A group of religiously oriented people had tried in 1963 to start a new daily paper committed to 'good news', to counteract the allegedly pessimistic values of the bulk of daily journalism. This is the advertisement they placed in* The Times *to announce the formation of the project, which never came to fruition.*

### ANNOUNCING A NEW FORCE IN DAILY JOURNALISM
#### GOOD NEWS—EVERY DAY

Do you want a daily newspaper that puts the emphasis upon the good instead of the evil; the pure instead of the corrupt; the heroic instead of the mean; the generous instead of the selfish; upon high ideals instead of depravity; upon the stars in the sky instead of the mud in the gutter?

Are you ready to welcome a daily newspaper that strives to respond to the challenge:

*Whatsoever things are true, whatsoever things are honourable,*
*Whatsoever things are just, whatsoever things are pure,*

*Whatsoever things are lovely, whatsoever things are of good report:
If there be any virtue, and if there be any praise, think on these things.*
—(Philippians iv 8).

Any group of fallible human creatures that announced its intention fully to live up to such standards would fairly be charged with arrogance. But the promoters and controllers of a new newspaper—*Daily Leader*—do profess, in deep humility, that as God gives them grace they will strive towards these principles.

A basic duty of any newspaper is to inform its readers of matters of importance that come into the news, whether or not they make pleasant reading. The *Daily Leader* accepts that duty and will endeavour to fulfil it. That is to say, there will be no censorship, and no attempt to cover up harsh truth. But always there is good news to be presented—good news quite literally, for splendid things are happening in the world every day. In defiance of charges of self-righteousness and censoriousness that we know are inevitable, we say that the Press in Britain has slipped into the way of emphasising the dark side of life and human behaviour, and the *Daily Leader* will seek to do precisely the opposite.

That many families will welcome this statement is certain. The vital question is: Do enough people care enough about the matter to make possible the creation and maintenance of the *Daily Leader*?

Do you care enough about it?

How much—as well as how little—must be achieved to gain the objective is stated frankly and briefly: The *Daily Leader* cannot be sold for less than 6d. a day; and it needs the promise of support of 80,000 people. Under those minimum conditions the *Daily Leader* will be self-supporting, even without advertising revenue. The support of one-eighth of one per cent of the people of Britain, or of four out of every thousand households, is therefore what we seek.

The *Daily Leader* will not be priggish or precious or pharisaical or parsonic; but it may not always avoid cheap sneers that it is puritanical, as against the prurience that is tending to become a journalistic norm.

The *Daily Leader* will give proper—even generous—coverage to church news that matters, news of affairs and news of persons. It will not, however, be cluttered up with ecclesiastical items or pietistic features.

The *Daily Leader* will be governed by a Trust Deed that guarantees its independence and editorial integrity for all time. It will declare its position in every issue thus: A Newspaper pledged to promote the good and resist evil.

We believe the *Daily Leader* can become an immense force for good in the land. Now, if ever, the evil forces which threaten to debase our standards of national behaviour must be resisted. The *Daily Leader* can do exactly what its title implies—give the nation a firm lead every morning.

If you agree that this is work worth doing, and worth supporting, this is how we ask for your co-operation:

*We ask you to undertake to order the* Daily Leader *to be delivered from your newsagent regularly every morning from the first issue, and to continue to take it for a period of not less than three years. This will give us time in which to get the paper properly known and established.*

*Only if 80,000 people are ready to give us that undertaking is it possible for us to go ahead with publication. No purpose would be served by publishing a paper that was losing money and could only continue for a short while.*

*Donations towards the considerable costs of establishment will also be very welcome but, let us stress, are not nearly so important as enrolment as a regular reader. Any donations received will not be banked but will be retained until the decision to publish or not to publish is taken. If it is decided not to go ahead because of inadequate support, all donations will be returned intact to the donors.*

SOURCE: *The Times* (25 July 1963)

## 9 Sun
## THE BIRTH OF A NEW DAILY PAPER

*When Daily Mirror Newspapers took over the Daily Herald in the course of buying Odhams Press, they promised to keep it alive for seven years. It had started originally as a strike sheet in the early years of the century, for many years under the editorship of George Lansbury. Later it became the property of the Trades Union Congress, which sold part of the interest in it in the 1930s in an effort to raise the capital to make it more attractive. The TUC retained a certain interest in the paper even after the Odhams-Mirror merger, and the new owners had promised to do their best to keep it going. The Herald was the victim of its image and of demographic change; its readers were gradually dying off and were not being replaced by the new consumption-oriented generation of workers. The new owners decided to relaunch the paper under a new title and with a great deal of publicity. The experiment worked very briefly until it became clear that apart from the title very little had changed between the old Daily Herald and the new Sun. This was the lead story in the Sun's first edition.*

### GOOD MORNING! YES, IT'S TIME FOR A NEW NEWSPAPER

*The British public believe it is time for a new newspaper, born of the age we live in. That is why the SUN rises brightly today.*

Here it is—Number One issue of the first new popular daily in this country for 34 years.

What does this newspaper stand for? What is its sense of purpose? What is it all about?

The Sun is politically free. It will not automatically support or censure any party or any Government.

It is an independent paper designed to serve and inform all those whose lives are changing, improving, expanding in these hurrying years.

We welcome the age of automation, electronics, computers. We will campaign for the rapid modernisation of Britain—

regardless of the vested interests of managements or workers. But we will crusade against any Government which drives the evolution forward without farsighted schemes for retraining, and generous compensation where unemployment arises.

The Sun is a newspaper with a social conscience. A radical paper, ready to praise or criticise without preconceived bias. Championing progressive ideas. Fighting injustice. Exposing cruelty and exploitation.

Above all, the Sun is a gay—as well as informative—paper for those with a zest for living.

THE NEW THINKING

Look how life has changed.

Our children are better educated. The mental horizon of their parents has widened through travel, higher living standards and TV.

Five million Britons now holiday abroad every year. Half our population is under 35 years of age.

Steaks, cars, houses, refrigerators, washing-machines are no longer the prerogative of the 'upper crust,' but the right of all. People believe, and the Sun believes with them, that the division of Britain into social classes is happily out of date.

Public taste has been uplifted. People are interested in new homes, new inventions, new foods, modern ideas, the latest car, the newest everything.

For all these millions of people with lively minds and fresh ambitions the Sun will stimulate the New Thinking, hoping to produce among its readers the leaders of tomorrow, knowing that they are more likely to emerge from a College of Advanced Technology than from Eton or Harrow.

THE NEW WOMEN

The present role of British women is the most significant and fruitful change in our social life.

Women are no longer trapped between four walls. They are released from household drudgery by labour-saving devices, gadgets and intelligent home-planning.

In 1938 only one married woman in ten went to work: the figure is now ONE in THREE and will soon increase.

The emancipation of their minds has been accelerated at a fascinating pace by wider human contacts outside the home.

Women are the pacesetters now and there is no country with a higher sense of fashion, coiffeur and chic. The Sun will cater for their needs in every issue. Indeed, the Pacesetters on Page 14 is for all homebuilders and all men and women determined to keep in the van of social progress.

THE HIGHEST STANDARDS

A word about the Sun as a newspaper. It does not merely LOOK different: it IS different.

It will set itself the highest journalistic standards. If inadvertently, though in good faith, we ever fall below the objectives of truth and accuracy we have set ourselves the facts will be corrected with frankness and without delay. We want to hear our readers saying, 'You can believe it because it is in the Sun.'

We believe, with the public, that it is time for a new newspaper born of the age we live in. We hope with your daily support that the Sun will achieve your ideals and its own ideals.

SOURCE: the *Sun* (15 June 1964)

## 10A The Economist Intelligence Unit
## THE NATIONAL NEWSPAPER INDUSTRY SURVEY

*In 1966 the Joint Board for the Newspaper Industry commissioned an inquiry by the Economist Intelligence Unit into the costs of producing newspapers in Britain. The unit's report described its own findings as formidable. Like the Shawcross Commission, the EIU pointed out that Fleet Street had been grossly inefficient for many years; newspapers are protected by their nature against foreign competition and, during a period of rising demand immediately after the war, had found it convenient to accept the imposition of a series of restrictive practices within the industry rather than fight them. The Shawcross Commission had said of the death of the* News Chronicle: '*Different and more consistent managerial policy might have saved this newspaper.*' Now the EIU made a similar judgment of the management of Fleet Street as a whole.

In these conclusions and comments we itemise the main problems which we believe are facing the industry. As we stated in the Introduction to this Part of our report we do not attempt to suggest solutions to these problems, as to do so would be to go far beyond our brief. We would, however, be pleased to submit suggestions for the consideration of the Joint Board if we are invited to do so.

## MANAGEMENT

(i) There is an urgent need for more detailed budgetary and cost control schemes in most organisations. The use of inter-firm comparisons would help the industry, therefore there would be advantages in installing similar cost control systems throughout the industry.

(ii) There are some 700 Circulation Representatives, yet few organisations make any attempt to measure the effectiveness of their Representatives.

(iii) The natural respect for Editorial freedom has, in some areas, been allowed to overshadow business principles. Although the Editorial policies of the various newspapers must necessitate variations in the size and structure of the Editorial staff, the differences disclosed by our management survey are wider than we would have expected. Some facets of Editorial organisation and competition appear to warrant further investigation.

(iv) Publicity expenditure for the industry as a whole is running at a rate of about £5 million a year. Our analysis of publicity expenditure and circulation trends indicates that sharp changes in publicity expenditure have little or no effect on the circulation trend.

(v) There must be some doubt if the present level of competition in some sectors is really necessary. Greater co-operation on various items of research might be of benefit to the industry without harming any individual organisation.

(vi) It seems likely that under the present conditions costs will rise faster than revenue over the next five years.

(vii) Increases in the price of newspapers brings a declining percentage increase in total revenue. Already a penny increase in the price of some newspapers increases total revenue by only 4 or 5 per cent. This indicates that the present revenue pattern is likely to make the industry place a continually greater reliance on advertisement revenue.

(viii) Approximately half of the industry is operating at a loss, and our projection to 1970 indicates that the closure of some newspapers is likely.

## PRODUCTION

(i) Little use is made of normal production engineering, planning and control techniques in the industry, and few organisations are large enough to recruit specialists of high calibre.

(ii) Although new equipment is at times installed, the evaluation of new equipment and techniques often appears to be carried out in a haphazard manner. Where new equipment is installed it is not always used to its full effectiveness due to difficulties in agreeing manning standards.

(iii) Manning standards are usually set by horse trading, and often bear little relationship to the needs of the job. This leads to anomalies in work load and rewards between departments and sections.

(iv) The present wages structure is a jungle, and the basic wage bears no relationship to the take home pay. This leads to continual demands for extras of all kinds, and is a basic cause of friction and unrest.

(v) Many departments are heavily overmanned, and there will clearly be major problems in reducing this overmanning without serious hardship.

(vi) Many department supervisors have little or no authority over the staff in their departments.

## THE TRADE UNIONS

(i) The number of unions represented on the production floor naturally leads to some friction between unions attempting to protect their own members.

(ii) There is a gap between Branch and Chapel level, and Branch Officials have little influence in the operation of the Chapels.

(iii) Some F.O.C.s and Chapel Officials are unsuitable as representatives of their union, and most union Executives have insufficient control over the selection of Officials at all levels.

(iv) The salaries and security of many union Officials is not commensurate with their responsibilities.

## TRAINING

(i) There is little training of either management or trade unionists. This is perhaps the greatest weakness of the industry.

(ii) Many organisations are too small to provide their own training facilities.

(iii) The present system of apprentice training is, in our opinion, unsuitable for the future needs of the industry.

(iv) There are very few facilities for retraining men to take full advantage of the techniques which must surely come.

## SOCIAL SECURITY

(i) Although no redundancy agreements are in existence there is a feeling of insecurity in the industry. This is to be expected with the present level of overmanning and the technological changes which are inevitable.

(ii) New pensions schemes have been introduced by a number of organisations. In general these are good, but often they relate only to basic rates and not to take home pay, and are less attractive to the older employee with comparatively short future service. Little provision has been made for the transferability of pension rights within the industry.

(iii) Although the use of casual labour has been reduced

over the last few years there are between 3,000 and 4,000 men who have permanent employment only on Saturday nights.

(iv) The possible reduction in staff is unlikely to take place in an acceptable time by normal attrition methods.

(v) Large-scale reductions in staff other than by normal attrition will cost a vast amount of money if hardship is to be reduced to a minimum. Some organisations would probably be unable to finance this out of their own resources.

## SAVINGS

If large scale savings are shared on the present basis of 50 per cent to the department where the saving was made and 50 per cent to the company, very serious anomalies are likely to occur. We suggest that an equitable basis for the sharing of savings should be agreed before the savings are achieved.

SOURCE: EIU. *The National Newspaper Industry—a survey*, Part IV, Summary and Conclusions (1966), 59–62

### 10B The Economist Intelligence Unit
### ESTIMATED SAVINGS THROUGH GREATER EFFICIENCY

*The Economist Intelligence Unit attempted to add up the total potential savings in production costs which could be made in Fleet Street in a single year if the Press adopted the recommendations contained in the report. The total in the EIU's estimation was £4,850,000, which was calculated in the table on p 70.*

### 11 The Times
### A CHANGE OF FORMAT

*In the nineteenth century most newspapers placed advertisements on their front pages. The news began on page 2. In the case of* The Times *this layout, which dated back to 1785, when it was a good way of extracting maximum revenue from advertisers, was continued until the last decade. In the course of a long programme of modernisation,* The Times

## SAVINGS IN PRODUCTION COSTS

| Newspaper | Composing and Readers per cent men | Composing and Readers £'000s pa | Process per cent men | Process £'000s pa | Foundry per cent men | Foundry £'000s pa | Machine Room per cent men | Machine Room £'000s pa | Publishing per cent men | Publishing £'000s pa | Total £'000s pa |
|---|---|---|---|---|---|---|---|---|---|---|---|
| The Daily Telegraph | 0 | 14.45 | 50 | 36.10 | 18.5 | 20.00 | 46.0 | 356.00 | 10 | 66.00 | 492.55 |
| The Daily Express | 0 | 20.10 | 50 | 51.45 | 20.6 | 26.00 | 51.6 | 529.00 | 10 | 45.00 | 671.55 |
| The Sun | 15 | 41.70 | 50 | 62.00 | 14.4 | 7.40 | 56.5 | 150.00 | 10 | 25.50 | 286.60 |
| The Daily Mail | 0 | 11.90 | 50 | 76.00 | 13.0 | 13.30 | 50.0 | 277.80 | 10 | 39.25 | 418.25 |
| The Daily Mirror | 0 | 8.50 | 50 | 51.85 | 12.0 | 12.60 | 47.5 | 621.00 | 10 | 52.50 | 746.45 |
| The Evening Standard | 0 | 10.70 | 50 | 32.37 | 7.0 | 4.80 | 39.0 | 165.40 | 10 | 51.20 | 264.47 |
| The Guardian (London) | 0 | 4.60 | See Sunday Times | | 12.5 | 3.40 | 37.7 | 34.00 | 10 | 6.75 | 48.75 |
| The Times | 0 | 19.50 | 50 | 21.85 | 14.0 | 8.75 | 40.5 | 64.00 | 10 | 19.50 | 140.60 |
| The Daily Sketch | 0 | 6.85 | 50 | 25.90 | 14.7 | 11.00 | 55.0 | 156.00 | 10 | 13.00 | 212.75 |
| The Sunday Express | 20 | 13.75 | See Daily Express | | See Daily Express | | 47.0 | 160.50 | 10 | 36.00 | 210.25 |
| The Sunday Mirror | 15 | 9.25 | See Daily Mirror | | See Daily Mirror | | 53.0 | 235.00 | 10 | 33.00 | 277.25 |
| The Sunday Times | 10 | 12.90 | 50 | 24.75 | 20.3 | 11.55 | 58.0 | 331.50 | 10 | 27.20 | 407.90 |
| The News of the World | 15 | 13.00 | 50 | 9.62 | 13.5 | 7.10 | 41.2 | 140.60 | 10 | 42.00 | 212.32 |
| The Observer | 0 | 4.50 | See The Times | | 25.0 | 9.15 | 57.2 | 103.40 | 10 | 21.00 | 138.05 |
| The People | 0 | 3.25 | See The Sun | | 20.3 | 6.60 | 29.2 | 100.00 | 10 | 26.40 | 136.25 |
| The Sunday Telegraph | 0 | 5.00 | See The Daily Telegraph | | 12.0 | 3.60 | 47.8 | 81.00 | 10 | 15.60 | 105.20 |
| The Financial Times | 0 | 10.00 | 50 | 9.60 | 17.3 | 14.00 | 51.4 | 63.00 | 10 | 9.30 | 105.90 |
| Totals | | 209.95 | | 408.49 | | 159.25 | | 3,568.20 | | 529.20 | 4,857.09 |

SOURCE: as Document 10A, Table 1

*decided to abandon this tradition and to put news on the front page in the same way as all other newspapers, and it explained its new policy in a leader.*

## MODERN TIMES

'Change', said RICHARD HOOKER, 'is not made without inconvenience, even from worse to better'. We hope that any inconvenience the unfamiliar look of today's issue of *The Times* may cause old readers will be short-lived, and that once they have become accustomed to finding their way about the redesigned paper—which we believe they will do quickly—they will agree the changes are for the better.

The question has been asked why there should be change at all. Change is the law of life. If things do not evolve they die. *The Times* of yesterday was not *The Times* of 1916 or of 1856. Every newspaper is evolving all the time. Newspapers serve society; if they are to do so successfully they cannot divorce themselves from its habits. Placing news on the front page of *The Times* is one more step along a road this paper has been treading for 181 years. Uniqueness is not a virtue if it becomes mere eccentricity. There is no future for any newspaper as a museum piece.

The world-wide interest in the change is a measure of the deliberateness with which the step has been approached. News first began to appear regularly on the front page of an English newspaper in the 1900s. Between the wars there was a general switch-over. When *The Manchester Guardian* put news on its front page in 1952 only *The Times* was left among English newspapers. Now *The Times* also puts first things first. The prime purpose of a newspaper is to give the news. It should do so in the quickest and most convenient manner.

The consequent rearrangement of the other pages has been kept as simple as possible. The home and overseas news pages remain grouped together. Their order has been reversed so as to make what journalists call 'the left-hand middle spread' of the paper—that is the page which has hitherto been the main news page—the principal home news page. The leader page stays in its usual position; but the weather forecast has been removed in order to expand this information and bring it all together. From now on, weather information will appear with the television and radio programmes on page 3.

Today's Arrangements have been removed from the leader page to the court page. They too have been extended and made national (as distinct from London) and international. The page opposite the court page has been assigned to matters principally concerning women and the home. A Diary has been introduced on the leader page. Some readers have been alarmed by reports that it is to be a gossip column. There were far more vehement fears when *The Times* started a crossword puzzle. (That angry and vituperative correspondence from the eminent and the unknown was one of the social curiosities of the age.) We hope *The Times* diary will come to be as eagerly awaited and as highly regarded as *The Times* crossword now is.

In the ideal newspaper every feature would appear in the same place on the same page every day. Years ago, when all costs were less and paper was only £8 a ton, that was possible. In recent years, when paper has been £60 a ton and inflation has forced the cost of everything to do with newspaper production far beyond comparison with the modest increase in the selling price of newspapers, this has not been possible. But gradually, in the course of recent years, *The Times* has managed to anchor more and more of its contents. The progress towards a completely consistent and coherent make-up will go on.

In order to ensure this, what must now be thought of as the old front page of *The Times* has been moved to page 2. Birth, marriage, and death announcements will always lead that page, followed in sequence by the Personal and other long-established columns of advertisements. Theatre, cinema, and other entertainment advertisements will always lead page 4. The Personal columns are now set in a larger type to improve legibility.

The determination to make *The Times* as a whole easier to

read has led to a major typographical change. Paradoxically this is the one reversion to the past. A few years after the last war, when the flood of news was rising, and newspaper sizes were still restricted by the Government, *The Times* compressed its main body type in order to get it on a slightly slimmer body, and therefore have more lines in each column. MR. STANLEY MORISON's Times New Roman is so fine a type that it stood up well to this operation. The time has now come to restore it to its original purity, and to place it on its proper body. The result is more open and more legible columns. The new headings on the news pages are all chosen from MR. MORISON's original designs.

We have dealt at this length with the appearance of *The Times* because it is what immediately strikes the reader. But news on the front page, even of *The Times*, will be a few days' wonder. Readers will rapidly become as accustomed to the new look as they were to the old. It is what a newspaper is that matters.

There is no intention of altering the essential character of *The Times*. The same people have produced today's issue as did yesterday's. They will produce tomorrow's. They will continue to have the same sense of responsibility and the same standards. They will at the same time use all their professional skill to make *The Times* more comprehensive, more interesting, more explicit, more lucid. *The Times* aims at being a paper for intelligent readers of all ages and all classes. The more it can have of them the better. Some people have expressed the dark suspicion that one of the reasons *The Times* is modernizing itself is to get more readers. Of course it is. And we shall go on trying to get more readers for as long as we believe in our purpose.

SOURCE: *The Times* leader (3 May 1966)

## 12 Monopolies Commission
## THE MERGER OF THE TIMES AND THE SUNDAY TIMES

The Times' *circulation had been static for four years from 1961 and its share of the readership for quality papers had been falling. Seventy per cent of its circulation was concentrated in London and South East England which meant that the cost of advertising in* The Times *was higher in pence per copy than in the* Guardian *or the* Telegraph. *Trading profits had been falling since 1960 (apart from 1964) and although a vigorous advertising campaign had increased circulation in 1966 (after the changes in layout) by 17 per cent, it would take some time before the increase in advertising revenue actually materialised; nothing could prevent the paper losing anything up to £300,000 in 1966. It needed a net sale of 400–450,000 copies before its advertising rate could go up to the £15 an inch (from £12) which would be needed to break even. It needed an injection of £2–3 million in capital in the coming years.*

The Times *under Sir William Haley had held discussions with the* Manchester Guardian and Evening News, *the* Observer *and the* Financial Times *to consider whether a basis could be found for some kind of joint working or merging of interests. No satisfactory outcome could be reached, but several tentative approaches had been made by Lord Thomson in 1964 and 1965. In August 1966 Thomson approached* The Times' *financial advisers (Hill, Samuel & Co) through an intermediary and the result was a proposal to merge* The Times *with the* Sunday Times. *The Monopolies Commission was charged with the task of investigating whether this merger would be in the public interest. They concluded that it would not operate against that interest, though 'It would no longer be the same voice or the same* Times *as in the past, and it is important that it should be recognised, both at home and abroad, that it would have no claim to any special role or status; but we do not regard that as contrary to the public interest.'*

*In its report the Commission attempted to assess the impact on the content and role of* The Times *of the merger.*

*How the proposed transfer might affect the public interest*

156. In assessing the implications of the proposed change in the ownership of the Times, we consider first the particular position which it occupies. Some witnesses argued that the Times is a national institution of unique importance and prestige which should not be permitted to come under the control of a company actuated by considerations of commercial profit. Others took the view that its position is not essentially different from that of competing quality newspapers. Indeed, some of these considered that its pretension to be in a quite different class from that of other newspapers had done positive harm.

157. We recognise that there was a time, in the 19th century, when the Times stood virtually alone, and even when other newspapers overtook it in popularity it still retained great influence. It no longer enjoys the same position of dominance nor the same influence on public affairs as it has done at some periods in the past, but some of the prestige arising from its historical position still clings to it and, in the minds of some people, differentiates it from other newspapers. Moreover, on occasion in the past, the editor of the Times allowed himself and the newspaper to be used by the Government of the day as an instrument for moulding public opinion. This may in part account for the fact that, particularly abroad, the Times is still sometimes believed to have an authority which it does not now possess.

158. We do not accept that the role of the Times is in any way special. Its prestige and the authority with which it speaks should depend entirely on the quality of the newspaper itself. By this criterion it deserves a high reputation. Although we do not consider that the Times has any right to be accorded a special status or unique role, we recognise that it occupies a position of importance and that its loss would be a serious matter, as indeed would be the loss of any of the quality newspapers with which it competes.

159. It is valued for two qualities. The first is the nature and range of its news reporting. The Times Publishing Company told us that it would like to widen and improve its news

coverage, but it is generally accepted that in the news that it prints it sets a high standard of accuracy and freedom from bias. Moreover the Times still, as a matter of course, provides a record of some matters which may not appear in any other newspaper, e.g. Parliamentary reports, public and university appointments, the law reports, the obituaries and the Court Circular. The other quality that the Times has is freedom to express opinions on great issues of the day without regard to popularity or to political or other pressures. The Times is not unique in this, but there are few newspapers whose editors are completely free to express forthright views uncoloured by special or sectional interests.

160. It is against this background that we must consider whether the public interest might suffer as a result of the proposed transfer. The questions are:
   (i) whether the transfer would cause an excessive concentration of newspaper power;
   (ii) whether there would be a threat to the survival of other newspapers;
   (iii) whether changes in the nature of the Times are likely to result which would rob it of the qualities which make its preservation a matter of public interest.

*Concentration of ownership*

161. As regards the first question, the transfer of the Times would, in form, be to a company which would publish only one daily and one Sunday newspaper. Although this does not in itself suggest a serious concentration, 85 per cent of the shares of this company would be owned by The Thomson Organisation, which would also have the right to buy the remaining 15 per cent if the Astor interests should wish to sell them. We cannot therefore regard the device of the creation of a separate company as effectively separating control of the Times and the Sunday Times from the rest of the Thomson interests. Thus the result of the transfer would be to add the Times to a group which in the United Kingdom, apart from the Sunday Times,

also owns the Scotsman and about 100 magazines and provincial newspapers and has various interests outside the newspaper industry, including Scottish television, book publishing, 'package holiday' tours and an airline. The addition of an important vehicle of opinion such as the Times represents a material increase in power to this group. It would be a continuation of the movement towards concentration in the ownership of the press, which must ultimately tend to stifle the expression of variety of opinion.

162. If the danger to be anticipated from such concentration is that one man or company might have an undue degree of influence on public opinion, there are factors which suggest that the present proposal need not be regarded as a matter for serious concern. The first is that The Thomson Organisation does not at present own an English national daily newspaper, and even with the Times its share of the circulation of all national and provincial daily newspapers would be only about 7 per cent*. Another factor is that, apart from the Sunday Times and the Scotsman, the other interests of The Thomson Organisation do not give it much influence over public opinion; it is not permitted to control opinion expressed on Scottish television, and its provincial newspapers, although numerous, can scarcely be regarded as influential by comparison with national newspapers. Furthermore the avowed approach of The Thomson Organisation to newspaper businesses is to select good editors and editorial staff and to leave the editors free to decide editorial policy. The Organisation claims that it is concerned only with efficient and profitable management and does not interfere in matters of opinion, even if its various newspapers contradict one another. Ultimately of course the needs of commercial profitability may lead a management which adopts such an approach to remove an editor who expresses such

---

\* It would have a larger share of the circulation of the quality newspapers considered separately, namely:
    13 per cent of the circulation of national quality dailies;
    44 per cent of the circulation of quality Sundays (unchanged);
    33 per cent of the circulation of national quality dailies and Sundays combined.

unpopular opinions that the paper is commercially prejudiced, but our witnesses generally confirmed that The Thomson Organisation has in practice given its editors a great deal of freedom. Although there can be no guarantee that The Thomson Organisation or its successors will always abide by this policy, nevertheless the transfer of the Times to a company with such a policy involves little risk. It certainly involves less risk of stifling variety or of the misuse of power to influence opinion than would the transfer of the Times to a proprietor who regarded newspapers as vehicles for his own views. Accordingly, we do not consider that the proposed transfer would lead to an undue concentration of newspaper power.

163. Although most of our witnesses readily accepted that The Thomson Organisation would be unlikely to interfere with the expression of opinion in the Times as long as the company was controlled by Lord Thomson, some concern was voiced about the position after Lord Thomson's death and also about the fact that, following the transfer, the ultimate ownership of the Times would be outside Britain, i.e. with the Thomson family trust in Canada. Most of us see no objection in principle to a British newspaper being controlled from Canada. In fact, however, control over The Thomson Organisation is exercised by Lord Thomson through his shareholding in Thomson Television Ltd. and the question does not therefore arise during his life as long as he retains his control. Upon his death the controlling interest would pass to his son, who, we have been told, intends to live in Britain. We have no reason to expect that the change in control of the Organisation upon Lord Thomson's death will lead to any change in its approach to newspaper management, but there can of course be no assurance that future owners will not adopt different policies.

*Competition*

164. The concentration of newspaper and other interests may not only afford power to control the expression of opinion but may also bring commercial and financial power. This leads

to the second question posed in paragraph 160, whether the proposed transfer of the Times threatens the survival of other newspapers. If the Times were preserved only at the cost of losing one or more other newspapers the public interest could suffer as much as by the loss of the Times. The question falls into two parts: the first concerns the special position of the Guardian and the Observer, both of which would be printed by the new company, and the second concerns the effect on these and other newspapers generally of increased competition from the Times.

165. The Observer and the Guardian have discussed their position with The Thomson Organisation and have informed us of the outcome. Both were nervous of the difficulties that could arise through being printed by the same company, if not in the same building, as their principal competitors. The Observer has sought to protect its position by negotiating terms on which its printing contract could, if necessary, be terminated. The Guardian's negotiations are not yet completed. We hope that a satisfactory agreement will be reached covering the two points on which Lord Thomson has already offered to meet the Guardian's wishes and also mutually acceptable provisions for the extension of the printing contract for a further period after 1976. We recognise that both newspapers would be in a vulnerable position and could yet be put to considerable difficulty. But we consider that this is a matter which must be left to negotiation between the parties and we do not think it would be appropriate to suggest any special safeguards in the public interest.

166. As regards competition more generally, there is no doubt that if the Times is to be made commercially successful it will have to compete for readers and moreover that, supported by the marketing skill and strength of the Thomson Organisation, it would compete very strongly for advertisers. If it were successful, the circulation or advertising revenue, or both, of other newspapers would be bound to be affected adversely, although we were told that in some respects newspapers in the

quality group could benefit from the competition, if for instance it enhanced the value of quality newspapers generally in the eyes of advertisers. There is a risk that, in the foreseeable future, one or more national newspapers will cease publication, and their heavy dependence on advertising revenue makes the quality newspapers especially vulnerable. Such a situation would be unlikely to be attributable solely to greater competition from the Times. Some newspapers are already financially weak and their difficulties are currently being aggravated by advertisers' caution in the present economic climate. The Guardian indeed has recently issued public warning of its present difficulties. Competition from the Times could add to the difficulties of these newspapers, but the evidence of witnesses leads us to the conclusion that the consequences of the transfer would not of themselves suffice to kill any newspaper which would otherwise have survived.

167. We have been struck by the situation which results from the dependence of newspapers, especially the quality newspapers, upon advertising revenue. This places such a high premium on circulation that a newspaper which is losing circulation or is not gaining circulation as rapidly as its competitors may have to cease publication. Under these conditions an important effect of competition may be that large numbers of readers are deprived of the paper of their choice. It was put to us that this difficulty bore especially on papers which gave vigorous expression to minority views and on left-of-centre papers, because the readers that they appealed to were believed by advertisers to command less purchasing power than those of less provocative quality papers. But this view was not supported by those of our witnesses who were directly concerned. The problem appears primarily to be one of relative circulation figures; a newspaper may have a substantial readership but, if other papers competing in the same section of the market can point to much higher circulation figures, it may fail for lack of advertising revenue. Some of our witnesses took the view that if this difficulty led to a severe reduction in the num-

ber of national newspapers further consideration would have to be given to the ideas for removing or offsetting inequalities in advertising revenue which were examined and rejected by the Royal Commission on the Press (Cmnd. 1811, paragraphs 285–313). Another suggested solution was a body on the lines of the National Film Finance Corporation. However, this general problem, serious as it may be, lies outside the terms of our reference.

168. Nevertheless it is against the background of the situation outlined in the previous paragraph that we have had to consider the effect of greater competition from the Times. Such competition might prove to be the last straw for some other newspaper, but any alternative plan to strengthen the Times might carry the same threat. We do not think therefore that the prospect of increased competition is a reason for objecting to the transfer of the Times or for placing any restraint on its ability to compete. Furthermore action on either line could be open to the objection that it might endanger the survival of the Times itself.

## Changes in the Times

169. We turn now to the question whether changes in the nature of the Times would be likely under the new management which would be detrimental to the public interest. As mentioned in paragraph 159, the value of the Times to the public lies both in the extent of its news reporting and in the freedom of its editor in matters of opinion. As to the former, The Thomson Organisation assured us that it was not intended to make any change in the nature of the Times as a newspaper of record. It would still be aimed basically at the same section of the public as it is now, and those features which make it valuable to that public would be retained. Future policy would be primarily a matter for the new editor, when appointed, but it was not expected that any of the present news features would be dropped; there would no doubt be changes in the news pages, but these were likely to be in the direction of making the reporting of

both home and foreign news more comprehensive, in order further to improve the value of the Times as a newspaper.

170. Certain witnesses drew attention to the danger that the extensive commercial interests of The Thomson Organisation at home and abroad might influence the reporting of matters which affected these interests. They did not necessarily mean that the Organisation would require the editor to refrain from expressing opinions or publishing material which might have an adverse commercial effect on these interests, but it was suggested that the editorial staff might themselves feel inhibited in this respect. Mr. Hamilton assured us that he would make it clear to the editor and the staff of the Times that they would have his complete protection in honestly reporting in the Times whatever they regarded as right even if it affected other Thomson interests. In the light of this assurance we accept that the danger of biased reporting of matters affecting Thomson interests in the Times would be negligible, although the possibility would remain and there could be no guarantee that future managements of the company would follow the same policy. In any case, other journals might be expected to draw attention to biased reports or acts of omission.

171. We conclude therefore that there is little danger that the public interest would suffer from changes in the Times as a purveyor of news.

SOURCE: Monopolies Commission. *The Times Newspaper and the Sunday Times Newspaper* (20 December 1966), paras 156–71)

### 13 Sunday Citizen
### A FAREWELL

*By the late 1960s the survival of the* Sunday Citizen *(originally* Reynolds News), *which was the property of the Co-operative Movement, seemed to be something of an anachronism. It belonged to the category of ideological newspapers which the conditions of the modern market had made obsolete. It was a minority paper of the working class, and stood no chance of existing for long in the normal system of distribution. Founded by the Chartists, it retained until its last issue (18 June 1967) a powerful element of the Victorian radical fighting spirit.*

## OUR FINAL MESSAGE:
## SPEAK OUT! FIGHT ON!

When the Sunday Citizen began publication as Reynolds's Weekly Newspaper on May 5, 1850, Britain was a land full of good will to all men but evil performance towards most men.

Victorian sentimentalists wept over Oliver Twist in Fagin's den. And then went to their factories to fight in the name of the iron law of wages against any concession that would add sixpence a week to the income of an underfed family.

Or they petitioned their MPs against legislation that would soften the savagery of industries in which steam power devoured human life as surely as it increased the output of goods.

George William McArthur Reynolds was one of the great number of men and women of his day who rebelled against a system that multiplied wealth but destroyed people.

He founded his newspaper to support the People's Charter, which included the demand for manhood suffrage, secret ballot and payment of MPs—rights so elementary that we take them for granted nowadays.

But all the powers of the State, Parliament, Church, Throne, and Law, Army and Navy, middle class special constables, spies and agents-provocateur, the gallows and transportation, *were mobilised to savage the Chartists who read the first issue of this newspaper.*

The long and mainly unsuccessful—*at the time*—struggle of the Chartists was not a fight for more pay, shorter hours, longer holidays (no working man could then *imagine* a holiday except unemployment!), safety legislation, trade union rights.

More than anyone now living in Britain, the Chartists had every reason to fight for reforms in working conditions and wage rates that were foul beyond anything we know today. But those were not their primary objectives.

*They fought for the vote. They fought for peaceful access to political power.*

It was a fight that could have taken for its slogan the words of an even earlier advocate for the common people: Colonel Rainborough, one of the captains of the Commonwealth Army that routed Charles I. When the leaders of the victorious army met at Putney to debate the future of England, he argued for manhood rather than property sufrage on the grounds that 'The poorest he that is in England hath a life to live as the greatest he.'

*Rainborough knew what he was about.*

*The Chartists knew what they were about.*

They knew that in the last resort political power is one source of power that dominates all others, *the final power that must be won and held by those who want to introduce great changes and great reforms.*

That was the philosophy George William McArthur Reynolds stamped on this newspaper.

For 117 years, under four proprietors and not many more editors, the Sunday Citizen has insisted that the goal for the people and their Movements must be political power.

UNIONS AND CO-OPS

*Trade unions* are bastions of the worker's rights on the job. They are more essential than ever today, as industry and commerce become more complex, employers more powerful and remote.

*Co-operative societies* are the main safeguard of the consumer. So long as they exist, there is a check on monopoly and an alternative to private profit in the distribution of food, household and personal goods.

But it is *political power* that controls and conditions the effectiveness of these two Movements of the people. It is *political power* that all through history has been the key to reform—or to reaction when it falls into the wrong hands.

That is the last message we leave to the broad Labour

Movement—to Socialists, Co-operators, Trade Unionists, to radicals and to all who are instinctively on the Left but not connected with the established Movements of the Left.

SOURCE: *Sunday Citizen* (18 June 1967)

## 14 Monopolies Commission
### THOMSON NEWSPAPERS LTD AND THE INDEPENDENCE OF ITS EDITORS

*In late 1967 the Monopolies Commission was asked to investigate a proposal by Lord Thomson to take over a small group of local newspapers owned by Crusha & Son Ltd. The Commission allowed the merger and in doing so presented its observations on the question of interference with editorial rights by owners of large newspaper chains. It concluded that editors within the Thomson group are better protected against local pressures than many editors who enjoy financial independence.*

*Thomson ownership in relation to news presentation and free expression of opinion*

101. We were told that The Thomson Organisation, as such, had no editorial view; it had 'no axe to grind' and the editors of its papers were free to present the news and their views in the manner they thought fit. The Organisation maintained, indeed, that 'because of their almost parochial nature, editorial independence in the case of weekly newspapers is, in our view and experience, not only the virtue it is in the case of local daily newspapers but also an absolute commercial necessity'. In its view, the primarily commercial attitude of the management to its newspapers and its success in pursuing its commercial aims gave the editorial staff both a background of financial stability and confidence and better facilities for developing their service to the public; the fair presentation of news and views was to a large extent a matter of the professional standards of journalists, and while these could on the whole be relied upon they involved the ability and determination to resist outside

pressures, whether from advertisers or elsewhere, to modify, colour or suppress news or comment upon news. In local weekly newspapers the Organisation doubted whether editorial opinion, in any event, could have much influence upon public opinion, but fair and accurate presentation of the news was important. Editors who have the backing of The Thomson Organisation are, in its view, better able to resist pressures—particularly at the local level— than those whose proprietors were more vulnerable or might themselves have an axe to grind in local affairs. They could also give the public a better service. The Organisation put plant and specialist skills at their command such as were not available to small independent newspapers. So far as the development of the advertising side was concerned this, the Organisation told us, generally meant larger papers with a higher proportion of advertising space but with some increase in editorial space.

102. Most of the witnesses who commented upon this aspect agreed that The Thomson Organisation allowed its editorial staff substantial freedom in presenting and commenting upon news, and we accept that this is Lord Thomson's policy. But we cannot regard this as the end of the matter, first because no proprietor can guarantee that a policy is immutable and secondly because some indirect influence on editorial policy by the proprietors is inescapable, if only because it is the proprietors who must be responsible for the kind of editors and editorial staff they select and support. The main questions that seem to us to arise in this connection are (*a*) whether there can be any serious danger of a change in policy on editorial freedom, (*b*) whether the grouping of a number of local newspapers under Thomson control is liable to lead to some loss of contact by editors and their staffs with the local community to the detriment of the service provided, and (*c*) what effect an attitude on the part of the proprietor of neutrality in editorial matters, subject only to commercial success, is likely to have upon the character of the newspaper concerned.

103. As to the possibility of a change of policy, it is, of course,

a fact that Lord Thomson cannot undertake that his successors will pursue the same policy as himself. Although he argues that the policy is a commercial necessity for local weekly newspapers, another newspaper proprietor could think otherwise or be more concerned with influencing opinion than with maximising profits. It remains debatable whether any proprietor has ever succeeded in influencing public opinion by pursuing a determined personal line of editorial opinion. It is all the more questionable whether such a policy could succeed in present conditions where news and views are disseminated daily by radio and television as well as through the newspaper. It is perhaps most questionable of all in the case of local weekly newspapers, which offer little scope for the discussion of national issues and whose readers can generally gauge the facts about local issues and are open to other local influences in forming their opinions about them. No newspaper proprietor can be wholly immune from the temptation to procure the publication of news slanted to suit his own convictions or commercial interests. The professional standards of editorial staff provide some safeguard against pressure of this kind, but the risk that such pressure will be applied and that editorial staff will succumb to it seems to us no greater when the newspaper is owned by The Thomson Organisation than when there is a local proprietor with local interests.

104. Many newspaper witnesses emphasised to us their view that the editors and staff of local newspapers should have 'local roots' and belong to the community they serve. Some of them thought that The Thomson Organisation paid little regard to this need, that it moved its staff around from newspaper to newspaper, and that where it owned a number of neighbouring papers these tended to take on a common aspect with a great deal of common content, with the result that none of the individual communities concerned continued to receive a full local news service. The Organisation itself agrees that there is considerable movement of staff; it believes that varied experience and the prospects of promotion produce better staff. It

appreciates, however, that the editor of a local paper and some of his staff must be men who have spent a good many years in the local community, and it says that there is less movement of senior editorial staff than of junior reporters and of managerial and advertising staff. The Organisation says that if the proposed merger takes place 'the same staff will produce the papers in the same manner as heretofore, under the same editors'.

105. In the view of the Shawcross Commission the main danger of chain ownership in the provincial press was that the local press might be deprived of its local character, but it was also of the opinion that concentration of ownership among local weekly newspapers, though it had increased slightly, was still negligible. As we have shown in chapter 1 concentration has continued to increase in this field in the past five years though it is still by no means intense. There is possibly some danger in the future of the formation of regional monopolies, which could have the effect not only of depriving the papers within the monopolies of their truly local, or parochial, character but also of eliminating variety. It is possible that managements and even editors might become more detached from the towns and districts whose names their papers bear and that these papers would become uniform purveyors of regional rather than parochial news. This can be a serious risk, however, only where a block of neighbouring papers is in the hands of one proprietor. The local newspapers of the Thomson group are, in fact, considerably more scattered geographically than those of some smaller existing groups, and so far as the Crusha newspapers are concerned there could be no question at present of their falling into a regional pattern.

106. This point apart, all large organisations are open to the risk of losing—or at any rate of being accused of losing—intimate contact with the local markets they serve. Local knowledge and local roots are important advantages of independent local papers. Possibly no large group can achieve quite the same intimate relationship with a local community. But The Thomson Organisation is of course conscious that if

its local papers are to be successful they must provide the kind of news service that the local communities demand. It is worth mentioning in this context that, to a greater extent than any other class of newspapers, local weekly papers are bought by the public for the sake of some of the advertisements appearing in them, that is for the classified advertisements. These may be regarded as virtually an essential part of the news service of such papers and we have no doubt that The Thomson Organisation is particularly expert in providing this part of the service.

107. As to the last of the three questions mentioned in paragraph 102, one of the accusations frequently levelled against much of the press is that, in order to sell its products, it emphasises those superficial, personal or sensational aspects of the news that it expects will attract immediate attention and is afraid of boring or irritating its less reliable customers by offering them an objective analysis of public issues. Insofar as The Thomson Organisation itself takes a neutral attitude on editorial policy it may be presumed that it is the editors who decide how the news shall be treated; but it may also be presumed that the Organisation tends to appoint editors who, in its view, are likely to present the news in such a way as to attract readers and contribute to the commercial success of their papers. Whatever may be the case in other sections of the press, however, we doubt whether the local weekly press offers much scope for variety in treatment of the news. These weekly papers by their very nature deal with news which from a national point of view might be called trivial. Much of this news is personal, in the sense that it deals with the activities of small groups or individuals in the local community. Its accuracy can more easily be checked from the personal knowledge of many readers than that of much of the 'national' news. In these circumstances the likelihood of sensationalism is reduced. There are occasions, of course, when an issue which is a subject of national interest arises in a particularly acute form in a local area; any local paper might then be tempted either to over-emphasise its more dramatic local and personal aspects or, if there is deep con-

troversy on the issue, to avoid expressing an opinion or to suppress minority opinion. We see no reason, however, why Thomson-owned papers should be more subject to these risks than any others. In general, it appears to us that the suggestion that a commercial attitude on the part of the proprietor might affect the character of the paper to the detriment of the public interest is less relevant to local weekly papers than to other sections of the press.

108. Thus to sum up our view under this heading we have found no reason for thinking that the transfer to Thomson ownership of the three Crusha weekly newspapers is likely to have any adverse effect on the presentation of news or the free expression of opinion in those papers.

SOURCE: Monopolies Commission. *Thomson Newspapers Ltd and Crusha & Son Ltd—a report on the proposed transfer* (17 January 1968), paras 101–8

## 15 National Board for Prices and Incomes
## THE EARNINGS OF JOURNALISTS

*While Fleet Street at corporate level was undergoing a period of major structural change, there were other changes affecting the life of the newspaper industry which were likely to prove equally important in the long run. Changes in the career pattern of journalists was brought about by the existence of the new electronic media and new training methods. The old system by which a journalist was apprenticed in the provinces and gradually worked his way up to London and Fleet Street was being modified by a new career pattern in which a large number of university graduates strove to work in Fleet Street earlier in their careers, regarding it only as part of the 'summit' of journalism, the other parts being television and radio news and current affairs. The National Board for Prices and Incomes, in investigating a planned pay increase for journalists, published the following information.*

32. There would appear to be three main issues to be resolved: first, whether the increases in the minima are justified in the

light of the extent of wage drift prevailing in the industry; secondly, the relationship in pay between journalists and production workers employed by newspapers; thirdly, the relationship in pay between different groups of journalists. When the N.P.A. and the N.U.J. nearly 50 years ago first made an agreement to determine the minimum rate which should be paid to Fleet Street journalists, Fleet Street journalism was generally regarded both in money and status terms as the apex of a journalist's career. Apart from some provincial and Scottish papers, a journalist looked to Fleet Street for his career prospects. Editors recognised performance at their discretion by 'merit' payments, and the national negotiations were limited to the establishment of minimum rates. These arrangements governing pay have lasted until the present settlement.

33. In the last twenty years there has been an expansion in other communications media—in radio and television, and in a whole range of public relations functions which a journalist is specially qualified to perform. Fleet Street journalism still retains a large part of its appeal for the journalist, but there are now also other goals for him to aim at. For some journalists experience in Fleet Street is a stage in their career, not necessarily the end of it. As we saw in Chapter 3 the negotiated minimum rates for Fleet Street journalists have fallen out of step with negotiated minimum rates for journalists in other parts of the communications industry.

34. This development comes at a time when journalists in Fleet Street are expressing growing dissatisfaction with the system of 'merit' pay. They feel that this system, while providing scope for individual recognition by editors, has not worked fairly in that some journalists, in particular the older and less mobile, have been overlooked. The assessment of 'merit' can also differ from editor to editor. Indeed the process of annual review is commonly known in some parts of Fleet Street as the 'November Handicap'.

TABLE 1
*Proportion of journalists in each occupation: January 1964 and January 1969*

| Occupation | 1964 Number | 1964 Percentage | 1969 Number | 1969 Percentage | Percentage increase in journalists 1964–1969 |
|---|---|---|---|---|---|
| Editorial executives | 419 | 15·6 | 556 | 17·5 | 32·7 |
| Feature and specialist writers | 534 | 19·9 | 607 | 19·1 | 13·7 |
| Photographers | 202 | 7·5 | 209 | 6·6 | 3·5 |
| Reporters | 632 | 23·6 | 716 | 22·5 | 13·3 |
| Sub-editors | 582 | 21·7 | 678 | 21·3 | 16·5 |
| Other journalists | 313 | 11·7 | 415 | 13·0 | 32·6 |
| All journalists[1] | 2,682 | 100·0 | 3,181 | 100·0 | 18·6 |

[1] All full-time journalists covered by the survey excluding those on *The Guardian* who were unable to supply information prior to 1969.

TABLE 3
*Average, median and quartile weekly earnings by location: January 1969*

| Location | Number of journalists | Average £ s | Median £ s | Lower quartile £ s | Upper quartile £ s |
|---|---|---|---|---|---|
| London | 2,662 | 51 10 | 45 0 | 38 9 | 56 12 |
| Manchester | 683 | 39 10 | 36 19 | 34 8 | 41 12 |
| Fleet Street | 3,345 | 49 1 | 43 1 | 36 16 | 53 15 |

SOURCE: PIB Report No 115. *Journalists' Pay* (June 1969, Cmnd. 4077, paras 32–4 and Tables 1 and 3)

## 16A PIB
## THE CHANGING TECHNOLOGY OF NEWSPAPERS

*After the Shawcross and EIU reports, the newspaper industry made the effort to operate more realistic levels of manning in the production departments of most papers. Large reductions were made in casual workers and in 'ghost' workers (notional workers whose wages are shared among the crew actually working). The PIB investigated the use of manpower in a number of production areas and concluded that manning levels had been reduced on average by 5 per cent. Productivity at the same time had risen by 9 per cent and wage costs by between 7 per cent and 21 per cent. The Board pointed out that the economic problems of the national newspaper industry do not arise solely or even principally from labour costs or the resistance of trade unions to technical change; nonetheless, substantial reduction of labour costs could mean the difference between life and death for an individual paper. The Board also criticised managements which gave low priority to industrial relations because of the urgency of producing a product which depended upon marginal economies of time if it was to be fully competitive. The success of the Sun, however, had shown that difficulties with the unions and between unions could be resolved despite the phenomenal complexity of the problems involved. 'Negotiating situations are created by management, and while it is important that the trade unions settle their differences, the continuation and effectiveness of productivity bargaining mainly depends upon the strength and determination of management.' The Board then outlined the technological situation which confronted the Press, its managers and unions, in the next period of time and listed a number of developments which could have a major impact on the production methods of the national Press.*

*Technology*

57. So far our comments have in the main been made within the context of the industry's existing technology, which has changed little over many years. In the following sections we attempt to assess the possibilities for technological change,

which could have far-reaching effects on efficiency and which are to some extent conditioned by the climate of industrial relations.

58. At present all national newspapers in the UK are printed by rotary letterpress machines fed by webs of newsprint drawn from large reels. The matter to be printed is first cast, line by line, in type metal, using manual methods. The production process is labour intensive, due partly to the type of equipment used but also to management policies and labour practices which have produced severe overmanning. Nevertheless, the existing methods possess certain advantages of flexibility and speed which satisfy editorial requirements and offer the possibility of low production cost.

59. It is, however, indisputable that actual costs are higher than those technically possible with existing methods owing to the extent of overmanning. It has been suggested that to attempt to reduce costs by introducing new methods, involving considerable capital investment, would be inadvisable until more efficient working practices have first been established, as the transfer of existing manning restrictions to the new situation might nullify the benefits of technological advance, making the return on the investment uneconomically low.

60. Restrictive labour practices do undoubtedly constitute an important constraint on the introduction of new and improved techniques, though in our view they are not the only important constraint. In most cases profit levels are such that there are considerable difficulties in generating the capital resources necessary to take advantage of modern developments, whether internally or from investors. Moreover, some of the advanced techniques, although successfully employed by provincial papers, are more difficult to apply to the larger production runs of the national press.

61. There are, however, a number of developments which could have a major impact on the national press. For example:—

(i) *Typesetting* is now largely carried out on keyboard actuated line-casting machines.

Teletype setting, which separates the keyboard from the casting function, can simplify and speed up the keyboard operation by the use of a typewriter style layout and the removal of machine limitations, the keyboard work involved being akin to that of a skilled copy typist. The keyboard has a perforated tape output which can accelerate the casting operation and, further, can be transmitted to distant locations in order to activate remote linecasters. A further refinement is the interpolation of a computer between keyboard and linecaster which can eliminate almost all decision making on questions, for example, of spacing, justification and hyphenation, by the keyboard operator. Rarely, however, can this method in its simplest form fully utilise a computer's capacity. The increase in output per man hour available from the use of such methods is estimated at about 60 per cent.

(ii) *Preparation of the printing surface.* Film setting and cathode ray tube setting—the latter system is still in the process of development—obviate the need for line-casting machines and the handling of large amounts of heavy metal. Both methods offer increased operating speeds and flexibility, while the cathode ray tube system is capable of using the maximum available speed of a computer. A change to film setting can offer about 95 per cent increase in the rate of output over the conventional linotype method, although it has limitations in dealing with corrections, etc.

(iii) *Printing the web of paper.* Recent developments affecting letterpress printing have concentrated on the replacement of type metal plates with lighter and more flexible materials, and the preparation of the printing surface by photographic means. However, photographic preparation though offering some advantages, is at present slower and offers a shorter plate life than the use of metal plates.

62. Most of the publishing departments still employ manual methods for many operations, with very noticeable overstaffing. Finished newspapers are received from the printing machines, made up into bundles, wrapped, tied and conveyed to the waiting delivery vans. Mechanised publishing equipment, which is now well advanced has been available for some years, but it has been introduced only slowly and the adjustment of manning levels which should have accompanied its introduction has been even slower, although some progress has now been made in this respect as a result of productivity bargaining. There appear to be considerable economies available from the extended use of mechanised equipment, provided that it is accompanied by appropriate reductions in manning levels.

63. Present methods of production are thus well behind currently available technology, and yet further developments are on the way, albeit involving large capital investment in complex electronic equipment. Even in the short term there are many possible changes that would offer substantial economies in unit labour costs, given the necessary resources for investment and given full co-operation from trade unions and employees. The benefits would be nullified, however, if existing manpower practices were simply taken over in the new technological conditions. Provincial newspapers are leading the way in technological advance and what they are doing could also be achieved by the national press if the constraints in terms of finance and industrial relations could be overcome. Some managements have been giving serious attention to technological development and, coupled with this, to the possibilities for decentralised printing arrangements. In general, however, the industry needs in our judgment to do more and this requires a joint effort by management and unions both to improve profitability and to create an industrial relations climate suitable to the industry's needs for change.

SOURCE: PIB Report No 141. *Costs and Revenues of National Newspapers* (Cmnd. 4277, 1970, paras 57–63)

## 16B PIB AVERAGE DAILY CIRCULATION—A CHART

*National daily newspapers—Average daily circulation*

| Newspaper | 1958 | 1959 | 1960 | 1961 | 1962 | 1963 | 1964 | 1965 | 1966 | 1967 | 1968 | 1969 |
|---|---|---|---|---|---|---|---|---|---|---|---|---|
| | '000s | '000s | '000s | '000s | '000s | '000s | '000s | '000s | '000s | '000s | '000s | '000s |
| *Quality* | | | | | | | | | | | | |
| Daily Telegraph | 1,117[1] | 1,155[1] | 1,191[1] | 1,250[1] | 1,261[1] | 1,305[2] | 1,319 | 1,344 | 1,353 | 1,392 | 1,393 | 1,380 |
| The Guardian | 178 | 186 | 206 | 240 | 263 | 264 | 275 | 273 | 281 | 285 | 275 | 291 |
| The Times | 248 | 254 | 262 | 257 | 254 | 254 | 256 | 256 | 282 | 349 | 408 | 432 |
| Total quality | 1,543 | 1,595 | 1,659 | 1,747 | 1,778 | 1,823 | 1,850 | 1,873 | 1,916 | 2,026 | 2,076 | 2,103 |
| *Popular* | | | | | | | | | | | | |
| Daily Mirror | 4,527 | 4,521 | 4,607 | 4,578 | 4,610 | 4,737 | 5,018 | 4,988 | 5,132 | 5,252 | 4,992 | 4,964 |
| Daily Mail | 2,105 | 2,078 | 2,445 | 2,649 | 2,548 | 2,476 | 2,412 | 2,444 | 2,318 | 2,168 | 2,067 | 1,976 |
| News Chronicle | 1,255[1] | 1,207[1] | 1,162[1] | — | — | — | — | — | — | — | — | — |
| Daily Herald/Sun | 1,513 | 1,466 | 1,412 | 1,407 | 1,348 | 1,311 | 1,265 | 1,317 | 1,238 | 1,146 | 1,038 | 951[3] |
| Daily Sketch | 1,213 | 1,154 | 1,096 | 991 | 954 | 928 | 885 | 835 | 857 | 879 | 900 | 871 |
| Daily Express | 4,063 | 4,091 | 4,206 | 4,321 | 4,288 | 4,271 | 4,233 | 3,984 | 3,978 | 3,955 | 3,820 | 3,732 |
| Total popular | 14,676 | 14,517 | 14,928 | 13,946 | 13,748 | 13,723 | 13,813 | 13,568 | 13,523 | 13,400 | 12,817 | 12,494 |
| Total all dailies | 16,219 | 16,112 | 16,587 | 15,693 | 15,526 | 15,546 | 15,663 | 15,441 | 15,439 | 15,426 | 14,893 | 14,597 |

[1] Source: Economist Intelligence Unit Survey   [2] 2nd half year only   [3] 1st half year only

Source: Audit Bureau of Circulation

SOURCE: as Document 16A, Appendix C

## 16C PIB THE OWNERSHIP OF NEWSPAPERS—A CHART

*Ownership of national newspapers with other interests of proprietors*

| Proprietor | National daily newspapers | National Sunday newspapers | Newspapers sharing production facilities with nationals | Other group activities sharing administrative or marketing facilities with nationals | Other interests |
|---|---|---|---|---|---|
| *Quality Newspapers:* | | | | | |
| Thomson Organisation Ltd | Times | Sunday Times | Times Lit Supp<br>Times Educ Supp<br>Daltons Weekly | Provincial newspapers | Magazines<br>Printing<br>Television<br>Travel |
| Manchester Guardian & Evening News Ltd | Guardian | — | Manchester Evening News<br>Weekly Guardian | — | Newspapers<br>Television<br>Property |
| Daily Telegraph Ltd | Telegraph | Sunday Telegraph | — | — | — |
| Observer Ltd | — | Observer | — | — | — |

| *Popular Newspapers:* | | | | | | |
|---|---|---|---|---|---|---|
| IPC Ltd | Mirror | Sunday Mirror<br>People | Reveille<br>Sporting Life | Magazines, Trade journals etc | | Provincial newspapers<br>Magazines<br>Publishing<br>Printing<br>Advertising<br>Television<br>Paper |
| Associated Newspapers Ltd | Mail<br>Sketch | — | Evening News<br>Weekend | Exhibitions | | Provincial newspapers<br>Magazines<br>Paper<br>Television |
| Beaverbrook Newspapers Ltd | Express | Sunday Express | — | Evening Standard<br>Evening Citizen | Printing ink<br>Paper<br>Television |
| News of the World Organisation Ltd | Sun | News of the World | — | — | | Provincial newspapers<br>Magazines<br>Paper<br>Engineering |

SOURCE: as Document 16A, Appendix B

## 16D PIB
## THE CHAIN OF DISTRIBUTION—A CHART

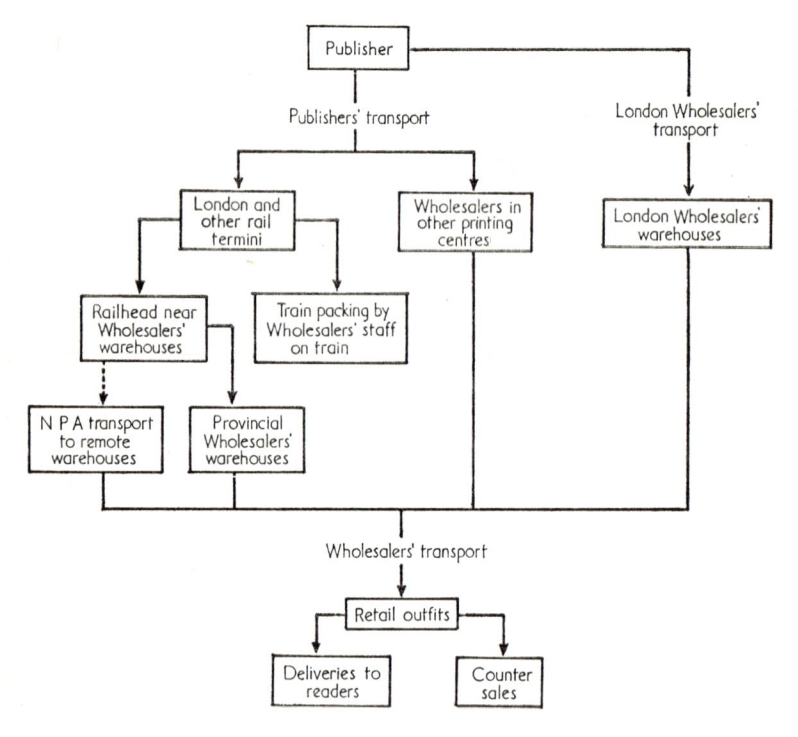

```
                        Publisher
                    /      |       \
      Publishers' transport          London Wholesalers' transport
         /     |        \                    |
   London   Wholesalers in          London Wholesalers'
   and other  other printing              warehouses
   rail termini  centres
    /    \
Railhead   Train packing by
near       Wholesalers' staff
Wholesalers' on train
warehouses
    |          |
NPA transport  Provincial
to remote      Wholesalers'
warehouses     warehouses
              |
       Wholesalers' transport
              |
         Retail outfits
          /        \
    Deliveries    Counter
    to readers    sales
```

SOURCE: as Document 16A, Appendix J

## 17 International Publishing Corporation Staff
## AN ATTEMPT TO PREVENT THE MERGER WITH REED

*The merger of Odhams Press with Daily Mirror Newspapers had produced a new giant company, the International Publishing Corporation, in which Sir Hugh Cudlipp and Cecil King were the principal figures (until the ousting of the latter). In early 1970 the Reed Paper Group announced a takeover of the whole of IPC, which later took place. Early in March a group of IPC managers and journalists, acting on their own group initiative, wrote and distributed a letter asking the staff of IPC to subscribe cash for a campaign to persuade the shareholders to reject the Reed bid. Their efforts did not prove fruitful.*

It is because we believe that our feelings are shared by the majority of our colleagues that we have taken the extreme step of issuing this letter and launching the appeal that it contains. It has been sent to as many IPC executives as we could identify in the time available.

At least for the moment, we wish to remain anonymous, and at heart that leaves us all a little ashamed. Nevertheless we have wives and families, and such is the nature of IPC and the world that we are not yet prepared to suffer the economic penalties of speaking our minds.

*The reasons*

Some of us once had a vision—no more than that, and perhaps that is a pretty unpractical thing to say. But it was a vision that we cared for, and that we tried to make IPC see. We saw, and we tried to create, a powerful, growing, international company that would span all the fields of mass and specialised communication, across as much of the world as was open to us.

We wanted to create a company that would be big enough, strong enough, to fight off the pressures of big business, of governments, of any other power groups, whenever those pressures threatened to divert it from its primary and vital role of making sure of preserving, in the new world that is emerging, the integrity and freedom that Britain at least has always demanded of its Press.

And that dream was shattered when Hugh Cudlipp and most of the IPC Board went running to Reed for help because it looked as though the penalties of their mismanagement were finally coming home to roost. It's as if a British Prime Minister, faced with losing an election, were to go to America and say: 'Please make us your 51st State—and let me keep my job.'

Nobody's trying to kid anyone in this letter. That shattered dream is the main reason we feel as we do, and we know that everyone doesn't share it. But we have faith that many of you do, and that, like us, you realise that under Reed that dream is not worth tuppence.

But there are other reasons for fighting the Reed bid, and these are just some of them:

Ever since Jan. 23, praise has been heaped on the Reed management, and abuse on IPC's—which of course means on you. Yet Reed's performance, even over the last few years, is no better than ours. Its profitability by any criterion is much lower, and its earnings per share have shown an even more marked decline than ours.

Immediately the bid was announced, Hugh Cudlipp and Don Ryder took the unprecedented step of speeding straight round to Downing Street.

What was actually said, no one knows who wasn't there; but many people in Fleet Street and Parliament were and are convinced that it was a subservient attempt to swop Government support for the merger for unconditional support of the Government by the *Mirror*.

It does Mr Wilson credit that he appears to have given the decision long and serious consideration. But the whole incident must leave a sour taste in every journalist's mouth.

The threat of take-over has been hanging over IPC for over a year. The board knew that, and knew what needed to be done to make IPC into a viable and independent entity.

They knew but they did nothing—and then, when the position became too extreme, when they knew that this year's published accounts would reveal the extent of their incompetence, they threw in the towel, and gave Reed the company for a song. Plus of course the assurance that they would keep their jobs.

The man above all most responsible for IPC's plight is

Hugh Cudlipp, who, once he had succeeded in supplanting Cecil King, had a glorious opportunity to reshape the Corporation, to give it the purpose and leadership it so sorely needed. He had, we all know, neither the experience nor the ability to do the job.

But from the debacle of this merger he comes out as deputy chairman of Reed, chairman of IPC, chairman of IPC Newspapers. We know the world is an unjust place; but that hardly seems a fair reward for the man who has let down 30,000 employees and 60,000 shareholders.

What has most persistently plagued IPC over the last few years, what has stopped most of its managers and editors from doing the competent jobs they are capable of, has been its unwieldiness; its top-heavy organisation, its bureaucracy, its elephantine lethargy—all the faults that arise when men too small for the job are trying to satisfy their own egos.

Now we are confronted with being made part of a group that is even larger, even more alien, even more autocratic. And one with a man at the top who is apparently so overwhelmed by his job already that he has to slog 18 hours a day to keep up.

Although we might not agree entirely, we can understand those IPC people who would like to see the whole corporation broken up. But the Reed deal threatens to make the whole thing three times as big, five times as inefficient, and ten times as frustrating.

Finally, and above all, we believe that the managers and editors of IPC—you—have been betrayed. Betrayed by a top management most of whom have thought of nothing in the past couple of years but their own personal machinations, their own intrigues, their own status and authority. And who have finally deserted the Corporation in the interests of their own safety.

We believe too that we have been let down by the big shareholders. By the financial institutions who saw (or should have seen) that things were going wrong, and did nothing.

We realise that IPC is in a mess. Of course we do. But we believe that in the present ranks of its management there is enough ability, knowledge, and drive to put things right. So far we have been denied that opportunity, because we have been let down by the people who should have been leading us.

And now, in a final spasm of self-preservation, those same people have denied us for ever the chance to prove that we could have made IPC strong—on its own. That is the ultimate betrayal.

*The action*

As a group, we can at least try something. We can try to force the hands of the institutional shareholders, by persuading the great bulk of small shareholders to say 'No' to the Reed bid.

They feel pretty hard done by anyway. They have been as badly let down as we have, and there will be very few of them who will be accepting the Reed offer anything but reluctantly. But they have no alternative—at the moment.

Present them with one, or the possibility of one, even present them with the facts of the case against Reed, and they will not take much persuading to ignore the Reed offer.

Since we think that you should remain anonymous, this is how it can be done. We collect money, from all over the company, in small donations, that goes into a special, safe account. And we use that money to buy ad space, say, as a target, a half-page in the *Times*.

And through that ad space we tell the shareholders the truth. We tell them what has gone wrong and we tell them what can be done to put it right. We show them how, by doing the right things, IPC is worth far more than the puny offer Reed is making.

SOURCE: *Daily Telegraph* (2 March 1970)

## 18 James Curran
## THE IMPACT OF TELEVISION ON THE AUDIENCE FOR NATIONAL NEWSPAPERS

*The reason frequently given by members of the public, and by many inside the newspaper industry, for the financial problems of the Press in the postwar period is that competition by radio and television news has deprived newspapers of some of their readers. One independent investigator, a researcher at the Open University, has produced an important argument against this widely held assumption. He argues that in pages sold, newspaper circulation has in effect risen and that there is no direct link between reading and viewing habits.*

In short, the notion that television viewing has displaced the press merely derives from a deep-rooted statistical fallacy about the significance of newspaper circulation statistics. The newspaper is not a standardized unit of measurement and should not be treated as such in analysing newspaper consumption trends.

In fact, gross newspaper consumption in the United Kingdom has risen very substantially during the age of television. The public is buying more pages of newsprint per head of the population. Public spending on national newspapers had increased significantly as a percentage of total consumer expenditure. The amount read in national newspapers also appears to have increased considerably. And while the national newspaper press has sustained the high level of readership achieved in the 1940s, the number of national newspaper readers has substantially increased. Yet all this has occurred at a time when economic forces within the press industry have artificially depressed newspaper consumption.

It should perhaps be pointed out that the findings for the United Kingdom may well apply to other countries where newspaper circulation *per capita* has fallen during the period of growth of television. Not merely are circulation statistics in themselves inadequate to measure the level of newspaper consumption, they may well also be misleading for the very same reasons that obtain in the United Kingdom. The trend towards larger and more expensive newspapers and the reduction in the number of newspaper publications is not unique to the British press, and it would therefore seem reasonable to assume that the trend towards falling newspaper duplication, and therefore falling newspaper circulation, is not confined to the United Kingdom. Future studies which distinguish between changes in newspaper buying and reading habits and changes in the level of newspaper consumption, and which assemble supplementary evidence on the demand for newspapers, may well arrive at conclusions very different from those suggested by circulation and television ownership *per capita* trends.

The world trend in newspaper consumption requires clarification in the light of further research. What is clear, however, is that television has not displaced the press in the United Kingdom. Every meaningful index of demand for national newspapers registers the success of the press in retaining the interest and loyalty of the public during the age of television. There is nothing to justify the pessimism among journalists, induced by the economic insecurity of the press industry and steadily falling newspaper sales. Nor is there a shred of evidence to support Professor McLuhan's sweeping assertion that television viewing, by changing our sensory equipment, has eroded the need for the printed word.

This is not to suggest, however, that television viewing has necessarily reinforced public demand for newspapers. A larger number of factors other than television viewing may explain the enduring appeal of the national newspaper press. Space does not permit a detailed correlational analysis between press and television media and the results of such an analysis must necessarily be inconclusive. It should be pointed out, however, that there appears to be very little connection between the growth in the size of the television audience and changes in the size of the newspaper audience. Nor does there appear to be a close connection between changes in the level of reading and viewing intensity. Nor does television viewing appear to have substantially influenced the type of features read in national newspapers. Indeed what is remarkable is how little the pattern of feature readership has changed not merely during the period of growth of television but since the pre-television era. What was read in national newspapers more than thirty years ago is remarkably similar to what is read today.

In view of the apparent lack of connection between reading and viewing trends it is difficult to suppress the conclusion that the newspaper has an independent life and distinctive appeal of its own. Unfortunately, investigations using a matched sample technique are no longer possible in the United Kingdom since the pre-conditions of research, representative samples of viewers and non-viewers, no longer obtain. A new approach is needed to investigate the interrelationship between press and television; an approach, moreover, which conceives of the differences between press and television not merely in terms of information content or communication form, but, more important, in terms of *the relationship of the audience to the medium*. What is needed is not a rationalistic appraisal of the manifest functions fulfilled by press and television but an understanding of their *latent* functions—the needs satisfied by the two media and the gratifications derived from media use. A fund of insights are available in extensive and largely untapped research. These provide a foundation from which it should be possible to explore the reasons for the enduring appeal of the press medium.

SOURCE: James Curran. 'Impact of Television 1945–1968', in *Media Sociology*, edited by Jeremy Tunstall (1970), 129–31

PART TWO

# The Press and the Law— the Erosion of Newspaper Freedom

*'If the freedom of the Press in Britain perishes'* said one chairman of the Press Council in his retiring speech, *'it will not be by sudden death. There will be no great battle in which leader writers can win imperishable glory. It will be a longtime dying from a debilitating disease caused by a series of erosive measures each one of which, if examined singly, would have a good deal to be said for it'*. The purpose of this section is to examine each of these areas of erosion and to show the extent to which editors, reporters and writers find themselves less well able to discharge their functions in this period when the laws relating to the Press have become gradually enlarged by reinterpretation in such a way as to increase the collective constraints within which the Press operates.

Before World War II British society was far more homogeneous. The links which bound the prevailing Establishment to the Press, national and provincial were complex—social, educational, corporate and financial. Though the Press carried out a traditional function of confronting the decisions and personalities of government and criticising them, it did so on the whole from a series of standpoints which both sides found acceptable. A minister could telephone an editor and feel that his point of view would be understood. In the clubs of St James's not *only the Press, but the dominating power-holders of society as a whole could meet and feel their priorities were shared—perhaps even without discussing them. The war brought about a great self-abnegation of power by the Press. A censorship of sorts was instituted and imposed upon a Press willing to shoulder the burden. After the war, however, governments experienced something of a shock as gradually the Press broke the invisible bonds of the preceding half-decade. British society as a whole lost its central moral, ethical coherence; the Press stood midway between a public which had lost its awe of the natural governing class and the forces of authority. Journalists became objects of greater fear in politicians; moreover the path between a career in journalism and one in politics became more easily trodden. The dividing lines and the points of connection both became lost.*

*In America the rift between Press and government became very serious in the late years of Lyndon Johnson's administration and the early years of Nixon's. In Britain a series of running problems, which had begun in the late 1950s, reached various points of crisis as the Macmillan administration began to run into severe difficulties. One of a series of 'affairs' which brought the workings of the Press into national prominence was the Vassall case, which resulted in two journalists being imprisoned for refusing to reveal the sources of information they had published to the discredit of the Admiralty's security arrangements. The real Press issue at stake at the Vassall Tribunal was whether newspapers had published reports which were fully or partly fabricated, and as a consequence the Press lost public support in this particular stage of the developing tension between government and Press which has continued until the present day.*

*The struggle has only in part involved measures taken directly by government, ministers or governmental agencies against newspapers. There have been very few cases of deliberate personal harassment of journalists—the notorious* Railway Gazette *affair of 1972 (when a reporter was persecuted by the authorities for revealing secret government plans for curtailing certain railways) is a very rare instance. Far more, Press freedom has been affected through an accumulating series of developments on the periphery, affecting the problems of official secrets, contempt of court, libel, obscenity, Parliamentary privilege, etc. Collec-*

tively the inhibiting aspects of these laws have increased through the accretion of precedents to the point at which any editor of a British newspaper finds it necessary to ask himself whether his freedom is as great as it should be. Certain elements of the public interest have to be protected by the state, others by a free Press; the question is only where the point of balance should be found. In the 1960s the Press came to feel that the balance was weighted too heavily on the side of secrecy, making for ease of government.

Press freedom cannot be measured by any eternal yardstick; a newspaper is free only if it is able to publish that which it feels it wants and ought to publish at a given time. Newspapers have not lost any of the specific privileges won in previous generations—they can report the affairs of Parliament, they can interview ministers, they do not have to submit their copy to an official censor; but, as this section will show, there is a series of specific issues which they cannot any longer deal with in the way they may want to and at the moment at which they may want to. Successive interpretations of specific laws, some of which have existed for centuries, are beginning to interfere with the intangible asset of Press freedom. Successive governments, at the same time, have not found it expedient or possible to alter those laws in a way which would suit the Press. Indeed, in many cases no one is certain what new measures should be enacted to re-enhance Press freedom; in other cases there is official unwillingness to give up positions gained through decisions of the courts.

## A  CONTEMPT OF COURT

'*I probably spend more time worrying about the possibility of contempt of court than I do about all the other legal restrictions put together*', Charles Wintour, Editor of the London Evening Standard has written.\*
'Contemptus curiae' is an ancient provision of English law which dates back to the twelfth century, but in recent years its implications and consequences have fanned out through a considerable area of contemporary life, protecting and sheltering the activities of authority in many guises.

Oswald's Contempt of Court (*1910*) defines it in these terms: '*To speak generally, contempt of court may be said to be constituted by any conduct that tends to bring the authority and administration of the*

\* In *Pressures on the Press—An Editor looks at Fleet Street* (1972), 129

*law into disrespect or disregard, or to interfere with or prejudice parties litigant or their witnesses during the litigation.'* For the last century there has been an almost constant stream of public complaint that the power of the courts to convict for contempt has become excessive and at one point Gladstone made efforts to reform the law. Between his attempt and World War I there were no fewer than four private bills designed to change the law (especially in regard to the Irish courts). In 1906 the House of Commons resolved that *'The jurisdiction of the judges in dealing with contempt of court is practically arbitrary and unlimited and calls for the action of Parliament with a view to its definition and limitation.'*

In the late 1950s there was a new wave of complaint after some specific cases which affected the Press. Journalists argued that in contempt cases a man was convicted by the same court which claimed it had been offended by him and could be imprisoned by that court without the intervention of a jury nor the right of appeal, for unlimited periods of time, or fined heavily. The legal profession itself has also been the origin of much complaint that the procedures involved contain inbuilt forms of injustice. However, there is virtually no section of British public or professional legal opinion which wishes to remove the law of contempt in its entirety; nor would any section want to grant the Press any total freedom to criticise courts or trials nor to anticipate their findings. Indeed, lawyers and journalists, in discussing the problem, tend to agree that some of the most appalling abuses of Press freedom occur in countries where newspapers enjoy the right to conduct their own public investigations of cases, publish the evidence and virtually hold their own trials.

There are two broad categories of offence under the heading of 'contempt': a civil contempt involves a wilful disobedience of any order of a court or the breach of an undertaking given to a court (including disobedience to a subpoena); a criminal contempt can be an insult to a judge, interference with any person attending court, a libel on a court officer, interference with juries or witnesses, creating a disturbance in court or publishing anything which assails the dignity of the court or prejudices justice in any way.

Only certain areas of the law affect the work of journalists. In recent years judges have been more tolerant of editorials attacking their decisions and have chosen to ignore where their predecessors a generation ago would have imprisoned. But editors have been sent to gaol, sometimes for many months, in the last two decades and newspapers have been heavily fined for publishing material directly involving the work of a judge or jury. Journalists have been imprisoned for refusing to reveal in court the sources of information they have published. The law of contempt has been found to apply to tribunals of inquiry investigating matters of national concern. Areas of life such as industrial relations, which formerly operated outside the law, have been made the province of special courts which function with many of the privileges of normal law courts. Journalists find themselves, more often than in any previous generation, dealing with urgent public issues which have suddenly become sub judice, because a writ has been flung, a tribunal has been set up, an inquest is pending, a judicial decision is to be made. The more work there is for lawyers, the wider the embrace of the law of contempt.

## 19 'Justice' Report
## THE LEGAL PROFESSION PLEADS FOR REFORM

*In 1959 a committee of 'Justice' under the chairmanship of Lord Shawcross, considered the law of contempt and concluded that the substantive law 'is chaotic and a serious handicap to free discussion'. The 'Justice' report saw no need for reform through legislation but felt that in due course 'the decisions of the Court of Appeal and the House of Lords will establish a fair balance between the needs of the administration of justice and other elements of the public interest'. These were their conclusions.*

### (1) Basic Principles

Every case should be governed by three basic principles: (a) that the court should retain a residuary power in all cases effectively to prevent interference with the course of justice by punishment for contempt; (b) that proceedings should be instituted only if the Attorney-General in his discretion considers them necessary; and (c) the court should not convict unless it considers that some substantial and unjustifiable interference with the course of justice has occurred. The first principle might, for instance, make it necessary to put a particularly heavy duty on distributors of foreign publications to avoid prejudicing proceedings here, where they are the only persons who can be made responsible for avoiding prejudice. On the other hand, the law of contempt should not be invoked in the case of comment before the arrest of a suspect in such a way as to reduce the likelihood of his arrest; nor should it be invoked in the case of comment on sentences in such a way as to discourage public discussion on this matter. In all cases of alleged contempt the element of prejudice to the due administration of justice should be weighed against any other public interest which might be affected by treating the act complained of as contempt of court.

(2) *Publications Prejudicial to Pending Proceedings*
The following general rules should all be considered as subject to those basic principles:

(a) *Unintentional Contempt*
In general it should be a defence to any charge of contempt on the ground of matter being published which is alleged to prejudice any judicial proceeding that the alleged contemnor neither knew nor had any reason to suspect that such proceeding had begun.

Similarly, in general, it should be a defence to any charge against a distributor of published matter alleged to prejudice any judicial proceeding that he had not examined the contents of the publication and had no reason to suspect that it contained matter in contempt of court. However, in certain cases distributors should be astute to suspect contempt, particularly where those responsible for the publication in question are not amenable to English law.

(b) *Contempt before Arrest of Suspect*
Published matter relating to one suspected of crime should be capable of being treated as contempt of court although it

is published before his arrest where (i) it is a matter of which the law forbids evidence being given at the trial, and (ii) the alleged contemnor knew that an arrest was imminent.

### (3) *Criticism of Judges*

No criticism of a judge should be capable of amounting to contempt of court unless prejudice, corruption or other improper motive is alleged against him.

### (4) *Proceedings in Chambers*

No publication of anything relating to proceedings in chambers should ever by itself constitute a contempt of court, unless it is in breach of an order of the court prohibiting publication (a) in a proceeding relating to an infant, lunatic or secret process; or (b) in interlocutory proceedings where publication might prejudice a fair trial.

## SUMMARY OF PROCEDURAL PROPOSALS

We summarise our main proposals in what we consider to be their order of importance.

1. A right of appeal to the Court of Appeal should be given immediately against any conviction or sentence by the High Court for contempt of court. This can be done by adding the five words '(other than contempt of court)' after the words 'in any criminal cause or matter' in section 31 (1) (*a*) of the Judicature Act, 1925. We would consider it unfortunate were this simple piece of remedial legislation to be held up by controversy as to other reforms relating to contempt of court. In due course the right of appeal to the Court of Appeal should also be provided for in the case of summary convictions for contempts before quarter sessions or county courts.

2. No prosecution for criminal contempt outside the court should be initiated except by or with the consent of the Attorney-General.

3. Any application for attachment or committal for civil contempt should be heard in public.

4. Every person charged with contempt should be entitled to give oral evidence in his defence.

5. The power of the Court of Appeal, the High Court and quarter sessions to punish summarily for contempt committed in face of the court should be limited in a way similar to that of county courts.

6. The Court of Appeal and any judge of the High Court should be empowered to certify contempt in face of the court for trial by another judge of the High Court.

SOURCE: 'Justice'. *Contempt of Court—a report* (1959), 40–2

## 20 Sir Elwyn Jones, QC, Attorney-General
## THE ABERFAN TRIBUNAL EXTENDS THE CONCEPT OF CONTEMPT

*On the morning of Friday, 21 October 1966, the coal-tip overhanging Aberfan collapsed and avalanched into the village below, killing 144 people. Within hours the Prime Minister, Harold Wilson, announced a high-level independent inquiry, which would be held in public in Merthyr Tydfil under Lord Justice Edmund Davies (who was born two miles from Aberfan). Within a few days the public was deluged with information by Press, radio and television on the origins of the disaster: warnings had been given, they were told, two years before that the tip was unsafe. The Chairman of the Coal Board, Lord Robens, said that much of the reporting was callous and cruel, making a spectacle of private grief. The BBC and the ITA defended themselves against such charges. Lord Hill, Chairman of the ITA, said: 'We would have been guilty of falsifying events if we had tried to prevent the reality from coming through.' On Tuesday, 25 October, Parliament approved a motion establishing the inquiry but two days later a storm of anger broke out in the Press after a further statement made in the House by the Attorney-General, which was widely interpreted as an attempt by the government to gag journalists by extending the provisions of the laws relating to contempt of court to tribunals of inquiry. This is the relevant passage.*

## ABERFAN DISASTER (TRIBUNAL)

*The Attorney-General (Sir Elwyn Jones):* Mr. Speaker, with permission, I should like to make a statement concerning the Aberfan Tribunal of Inquiry.

The Tribunal having been established with wide terms of reference, it is highly undesirable that any comments should be made either in the Press or on the radio or on television on matters which it will be the express function of the Tribunal to investigate.

Apart from their manifest undesirability, such comments may have legal consequences which are, perhaps, not at present appreciated. Just as comments on the subject matter of a pending trial may constitute contempt of court, so, also, the Tribunal would have to consider whether such comments amounted to such an interference with their highly important task as to necessitate the Chairman certifying that it called for an investigation by the High Court as to whether there had been contempt of the Tribunal. The possible consequences call for no elaboration by me.

I should like to add that I am authorised by the Lord Justice Edmund Davies, the Chairman of the Tribunal, to say that all who have relevant information will be afforded the fullest opportunity of submitting this to the Tribunal.

*Sir J. Hobson:* Will the Attorney-General reconsider whether his statement does not go too far and that an attempt should not be made to stifle all comment of every sort by Press and public on this matter, provided that it is reasonable and relevant to the inquiry, because such comment may very well lead to a new line of inquiry by the Tribunal?

Secondly, could the Attorney-General tell us whether he himself will be appearing at the Tribunal, or who will represent the public interest at it? Thirdly, would he agree that it is highly unlikely that any comment, however wide, would have the slightest interference with or effect on the very powerful and robust Chairman of the Tribunal and his fellow members, and that that is the test of what is a contempt or not? While, naturally, we want to give what protection we can to the Tribunal, it is fairly well able to look after itself.

*The Attorney-General:* Now that the Tribunal has been set up and its quality has received the aproval of the House, it is desirable that the issues which it is now charged with investigating should be considered and decided by it. The Tribunal will be anxious to receive any views, any information and any suggestions relevant to the issues it has to decide, but there is a certain danger in examination of potential witnesses on television and in the Press when the best means of ventilating opinion and passing on information now if we are to get the most effective result from this inquiry is by communication with the Tribunal itself.

Representation at the Tribunal is a matter which is receiving consideration and an announcement will be made shortly.

*Mr. Alexander W. Lyon:* Is my right hon. and learned Friend aware that this announcement will be received by many both inside and outside the legal profession with great regret? The whole pattern of events within the law over the past few years has been to limit the area of contempt of court for the obvious reasons which have just been stated by the right hon. and learned Member for Warwick and Leamington (Sir J. Hobson), that where a jury is not involved the kind of comment that might be made in the Press or television is unlikely to sway those who have to make the decision. In an area where the decision will be made by a member of the judiciary and two assessors of outstanding merit the law of contempt should surely not be extended still further.

*The Attorney-General:* I have said that there are dangers of comment and examination of witnesses and such other procedures interfering with the Tribunal's work, forestalling evidence that witnesses might give and producing results which could make the Tribunal's work more difficult. It is because we are anxious that the Tribunal should be assisted in its work and not impeded that the announcement has been made.

*Mr. Hooson:* I welcome the Attorney-General's announcement which, I think, was necessary, for it is obvious that, if there is to be examination by television or in newspapers of evidence not properly examined, people's hopes may be wrongly excited or their beliefs wrongly induced. It is very necessary with a Tribunal of this kind to have a limitation of public discussion while the Tribunal is considering it.

Can the Attorney-General say what consideration has been given to the representation of the parents of the deceased children at the Tribunal, as I understand that legal aid is not available for them?

*The Attorney-General:* On the second part of the hon. and learned Gentleman's question, my right hon. Friend the Secretary of State for Wales will make an announcement in the very near future and I do not think that the hon. and learned Gentleman will be disappointed with the answer.

I am grateful to him for the first part of his question. I am sure that the radio, television and Press authorities will have a full appreciation of the kind of consideration that the Government have in mind and will respect the approach which I have recommended to them in my statement.

*Mr. C. Pannell:* I can understand what the Attorney-General has said about radio and television and the heavier organs of the Press, but I hope that he will say a few words now which will not appear to muffle the normal discussion going on in the neighbourhood on the various courses of action which might lead to a satisfactory outcome. I can quite well imagine his statement having the opposite effect to what he wants; it might stifle discussion which would otherwise, perhaps, lead on to a useful inquiry. Although we agree—at least, I do—on the subject of television, radio and the Press, I hope that we shall not be as meticulous as all that.

*The Attorney-General:* I hope that, so far from stifling discussion, my statement will have the opposite effect by stressing the importance of all relevant information which anyone has to communicate on this grave matter, which affects the safety of many communities in our country, as I know in particular, coming from South Wales. I urge the importance of all information and all suggestions which could possibly be relevant being communicated to the Tribunal, whether this be done by scientific experts or by anyone who thinks that he can shed light upon this tragic event and, in particular, on the avoidance of a recurrence of such a thing in the future.

House of Commons, *Hansard* (27 October 1966), cols 1315–20

## 21 Press Council
## FLEET STREET EXPRESSES ITS INDIGNATION

*The* Daily Express *described the Attorney-General's statement on the Aberfan Inquiry as 'intolerable'. The* Daily Mail *thought it 'politically mistaken'. The* Sun *thought the Prime Minister should expressly state that the government was not trying to prevent free speech and comment.* The Times *said that 'there was no precedent for the Attorney General's warning and precious little authority for it; Sir Elwyn Jones' statement is basically an attempt to extend the law of contempt at a time when the legal profession itself believes it should be limited even more strictly.' The* Sunday Telegraph *went as far as to declare: 'He has brought his high office into the contempt from which he egregiously sought to protect the Aberfan Tribunal, and his statement should in turn be treated with the contempt which it deserves. If he disagrees with this verdict let him bring a test case.' The Newspaper Society, the National Union of Journalists, the Institute of Journalists, and the Leader of the Opposition all made their protests. The Prime Minister, in defending his Attorney-General later, said that certain television interviews on the night of the disaster had involved cross-examination of potential witnesses of a kind that appeared to be doing the work of the Tribunal.*

*While the work of a court of law ends with a verdict or judgment, that of a tribunal ends in a report to Parliament. A miscarriage of justice can indeed occur as a result of an unwarranted newspaper interference with its activity; but the worst that can happen if a tribunal is the victim of contempt is that its report to Parliament can be distorted, something which is in itself reparable. So great was the opposition to the government's position in the public discussion that ensued from the Attorney-General's statement that the Press Council took the unusual step of making a formal declaration of its own position; this was in conflict with the statement of the government, which the Press Council viewed 'with alarm'.*

When a great disaster occurs the public has a right to hear about it at once from the lips of those concerned. Discussion about its nature and cause cannot be stifled until after a tribunal of inquiry has issued its definitive report. Reasoned discussion and comment will assist rather than impede the task of the Tribunal.

There can be no objection to a reminder to editors of the need for exercising discretion and to the undesirability of attempting to prejudge in any way the issues before the Tribunal. Likewise, reporters can be reminded that in getting stories and information from those who may be called as witnesses they must exercise the greatest care not to colour the evidence that may be given, but the intrusion into the domain of free speech of ill-defined threats of legal proceedings is harmful to the proper conduct of public affairs in a free society.

SOURCE: H. Philip Levy. *The Press Council's History, Procedure and Cases* (1957), 451-2

*After the Aberfan Tribunal reported, the Press Council issued a much longer and more considered historical review of the issue of contempt. It wanted more detailed consideration to be given to the problem of contempt in regard to tribunals; at present, editors working in a competitive climate, were simply baffled by the state of the law on the subject. 'If to the existing uncertainty there is to be added the profound obscurity which at present surrounds the application of the law to tribunals under the 1921 Act, the editor's dilemma will become intolerable.'*

34. The Press Council submits that it would now be appropriate to give more careful and more detailed consideration than was practicable when the Aberfan Tribunal of Inquiry was set up to some of the very difficult problems indicated in this memorandum. A balance should be struck between the public interest in free speech and the public interest in the facts relating to matters of national importance being correctly made known to Parliament (a very different interest from the public interest in a fair trial and the administration of justice). Then the Press will know what rules it has to observe. The Press Council accordingly urges:
  (i) that a body—a Royal Commission or a committee—should be appointed to inquire whether it is necessary or desirable in the public interest that restrictions should be placed on the publication of comment or information on matters which are the subject of an inquiry under the 1921 Act and, if so, what clarification should be made of the existing law; and
  (ii) that consultations should take place, either as a preliminary or as part of the above inquiry, into the most appropriate methods of ensuring that evidence of potential witnesses before tribunals under the 1921 Act is unaffected by the activities of television, radio and the Press.

SOURCE: Press Council. *The Aberfan Inquiry and Contempt of Court—a statement by the Press Council*, Booklet No 1 (1967), para 34, 17

## 22 Royal Commission on Tribunals of Inquiry, 1966
### TRIBUNALS AND THE PRESS

*The Aberfan Tribunal was set up under the provisions of the Tribunals of Inquiry (Evidence) Act of 1921. Under this Act a number of celebrated* public inquiries had been held, mainly into the alleged misdemeanours of individuals holding high office. Five such inquiries had involved allegations against the police, others were the Budget Leak Tribunal of 1936, the Lynskey Tribunal of 1948, the Bank Rate Tribunal of 1957 and the Vassall Tribunal of 1962. All of these cases had by their nature been attended by very considerable publicity.

In 1966 (many months before the Aberfan disaster) a Royal Commission on Tribunals of Inquiry had been set up under the chairmanship of Lord Justice Salmon to review all the workings of the 1921 Act and to recommend any changes which the passage of time and general experience appeared to necessitate. The Salmon Commission reviewed the whole operation of public inquiries since the seventeenth century, when Pepys had been committed to the Tower for 'Piracy, Popery and Treachery' on the evidence of professional informers whom he had not been allowed to cross-examine. It was the unpleasant flavour left in the air by the Parnell Commission and the Marconi Committee (of 1912) which had given rise to the 1921 Act, which was intended to improve the procedure of the traditional Select Parliamentary Committees of Inquiry. The Salmon Commission concluded that the 1921 Act should be retained, but only for circumstances involving a 'nation-wide crisis of confidence', not for matters of local or minor importance. It recommended a large number of alterations in the conduct of tribunals and reviewed the whole question of Press publicity in regard to tribunals. It reported one month after the Aberfan disaster had occurred.

## PUBLICITY

115. As we have already indicated it is, in our view, of the greatest importance that hearings before a Tribunal of Inquiry should be held in public. It is only when the public is present that the public will have complete confidence that everything possible has been done for the purpose of arriving at the truth.

116. When there is a crisis of public confidence about the alleged misconduct of persons in high places, the public naturally distrusts any investigation carried out behind closed doors. Investigations so conducted will always tend to promote the suspicion, however unjustified, that they are not being

conducted sufficiently vigorously and thoroughly or that something is being hushed up. Publicity enables the public to see for itself how the investigation is being carried out and accordingly dispels suspicion. Unless these inquiries are held in public they are unlikely to achieve their main purpose, namely, that of restoring the confidence of the public in the integrity of our public life. And without this confidence no democracy can long survive.

117. It has been said that if the inquiry were held in private some witnesses would come forward with evidence which they would not be prepared to give in public. This may well be so. We consider, however, that although secret hearings may increase the quantity of the evidence they tend to debase its quality. The loss of the kind of evidence which might be withheld because the hearing is not in secret would, in our view, be a small price to pay for the great advantages of a public hearing. Moreover, experience shows that the Tribunals of Inquiry which have sat in public have not been hampered in their task by lack of any essential evidence.

118. We appreciate that publicity may be hurtful to some witnesses who are called before the Tribunal and indeed to some persons who are mentioned and perhaps not called to give evidence. But this is a risk which, on the rare occasions when such inquiries are necessary, must be accepted in the national interest. We have already dealt with the measures which we recommend to safeguard the interests of persons called to give evidence. Careful preparation and sifting of the statements of witnesses before the witnesses are called will do much to eliminate the risks of groundless charges being thrown up for the first time by the evidence. It may be decided to discard some witnesses altogether as being immaterial. In other cases, where there is some material evidence which the witness can give, care must be taken whilst examining him in chief not to bring out in his evidence irrelevant and groundless allegations against anyone. Nevertheless the risk remains that such allegations might be made by the witness whilst under cross-examina-

tion. This is unavoidable, but it is not a risk peculiar to hearings before a Tribunal of Inquiry. It may equally well occur in any ordinary civil or criminal proceedings.

119. It has been suggested to us that the Press should be prohibited from reporting the proceedings day by day and that the evidence should be made public only after the publication of the Tribunal's report. This would no doubt eliminate the pain sometimes caused to innocent persons by the glare of publicity. On the other hand we are satisfied by the evidence that on balance it is in the interest of innocent persons against whom allegations have been made or rumours circulated to have the opportunity of giving their evidence and destroying the evidence against them in the full light of publicity. If, as we believe, it is essential for the inquiry to be held in public, it seems to us that those members of the public who are not able to attend the hearing in person are entitled to be kept informed through the national Press of what is taking place. Moreover, if the evidence is not published daily and the public has to wait for weeks or months for authentic information about what is occurring before the Tribunal, rumours will grow and multiply and the crisis of public confidence will be heightened.

120. When the evidence is published in bulk after the report, there is perhaps only a small percentage of the reading public which embarks upon the formidable task of reading and digesting it, certainly far fewer than read the newspaper reports of the Tribunal's proceedings.

121. We have also considered the suggestion that the Press tends to highlight sensational aspects of the evidence without providing the other side of the picture. No doubt when this occurs it is largely due to the difficulties which the newspaper has in giving an accurate account of the proceedings because of the roving nature of the investigations and the consequent problem for all concerned of distinguishing between what is important and what is not. We wish to emphasise the extreme care which the Press should exercise in reporting these matters. It should be made clear, particularly in the opening stages of

an inquiry, that only one side is then being published. This is especially important in an inquisitorial inquiry when new facts may emerge suddenly during the proceedings. Care should also be taken to give the same prominence to the evidence of persons denying allegations or rumours made against them as was given to the allegations and rumours themselves. We are confident that the Press in general can safely be relied upon to be fair to all persons involved in an inquiry.

122. Although it is of the greatest importance that the hearing should be in public, it has been generally conceded in evidence that there may be most exceptional circumstances in which justice demands that the Tribunal should have a discretion to hear some of the evidence in private. Under Section 2 of the Act of 1921 the Tribunal has no power to exclude the public unless it is of the opinion that 'it is in the public interest expedient so to do for reasons connected with the subject matter of the inquiry or the nature of the evidence to be given'. These words have so far only been construed as applying to cases in which hearing the evidence in public would constitute a security risk. This is because no question has yet arisen as to whether they may confer a wider discretion. We consider that the Tribunal should have a wider discretion, certainly as wide as the discretion of a Judge sitting in the High Court of Justice. This discretion enables the public to be excluded in circumstances in which a public hearing would defeat the ends of justice, e.g. where particulars of secret processes have to be disclosed and in infancy cases. We do not think however the discretion should necessarily be confined to infancy cases or to trade secrets. It is impossible to foresee the multifarious contingencies which may arise before a Tribunal of Inquiry. We can imagine cases in which for instance a name might be required of a witness and it would be just that he should be allowed to write it down rather than state it publicly. The Tribunal might consider it desirable to exclude the public from the inquiry for the purpose of making an explanation to a witness or admonishing him. The Tribunal might consider

that the interests of justice and humanity required certain parts of evidence to be given in private. This would be only in the most exceptional circumstances which indeed may never occur. The discretion should however be wide enough to meet such cases in the unlikely event of their occurring. Clearly that discretion should be exercised with the greatest reluctance and care and then only most rarely. The words in Section 2 of the Act are very wide and should in our view be construed so as to confer such a discretion on the Tribunal.

SOURCE: Royal Commission on Tribunals of Inquiry. *Report* (1966, Cmnd. 3121, paras 115–22, pp 38–40)

## 23 Committee on Contempt in Tribunals
### LORD JUSTICE SALMON PROPOSES REFORM

*In July 1968 a special committee was set up (again under Lord Justice Salmon) to conduct the very investigation recommended by the Press Council. The previous investigation by Lord Salmon had not considered the problem of contempt because this had not been raised, in the dramatic form provoked by the Aberfan disaster, at the time the terms of reference of the Salmon Commission had been drawn up. This new committee was interdepartmental, involving the Home Secretary and the Secretary of State for Scotland, to whom the new report was addressed. Its conclusions proposed a set of changes which would go a long way towards reassuring those in the Press who had protested at the statement of Sir Elwyn Jones in October 1966.*

1. The law of contempt in a clarified and modified form should continue to apply to Tribunals of Inquiry appointed under the Act of 1921.

2. The law of contempt should apply only as from the date of the instrument appointing the Tribunal.

3. The law of contempt in its application to Tribunals of Inquiry should not prohibit or curtail any comment at any time about the subject matter of the Inquiry.

4. It should be a contempt if any person after a Tribunal is appointed says or does anything, or causes anything to be said or done, in relation to any evidence relevant to the subject matter of the Inquiry which is intended or obviously likely to alter, distort, destroy or withhold such evidence from the Tribunal.

5. The chairman of a Tribunal in his discretion may make a request that no interview with certain named persons whom he regards as especially vulnerable shall be published without imposing a legal obligation to comply with such a request.

6. Any unjustifiable attack upon the integrity of any member of the Tribunal in his capacity as a member of the Tribunal should be a contempt.

7. Anything said or done in the face of the Tribunal which would, if the Tribunal had been a court of law having power to commit for contempt have been contempt of court should be punishable as a contempt.

8. The Tribunals of Inquiry (Evidence) Act, 1921 should be amended in order to carry out the foregoing recommendations.

SOURCE: *Report* of the Interdepartmental Committee on the Law of Contempt as it affects Tribunals of Inquiry (June 1969, Cmnd. 4078, 18)

## 24 White Paper of 1973
## THE GOVERNMENT'S VIEWS ON THE TWO SALMON COMMITTEES

*It was May 1973 before the government replied in writing to the two reports prepared under the chairmanship of Lord Salmon. In the meantime a general inquiry, under Lord Justice Phillimore, into the law and practice relating to contempt of court had been set up and had not yet reported, but it was thought that its report would not render invalid the conclusions reached by Lord Salmon on the area of contempt which affected tribunals. The government's reply is designed to serve as a guide* to the setting up of future tribunals and to describe the legislation necessary for implementing the provisions of the Salmon reports. This section of the White Paper outlines the government's policy in regard to all the matters affecting the reporting of tribunals in the Press.

*Reporting of proceedings*

40. Since, in spite of this wider discretion, Inquiries will still ordinarily be held in public, it seems right that those members of the public not able to attend the hearings in person should be entitled to be kept informed by the Press of what is taking place. The Government therefore accepts the recommendation that proceedings should be conducted generally in public and reported day by day in the Press.

41. It is unlikely that anyone would dissent from the recommendation that the greatest care should be taken by the Press when reporting the hearings of the Tribunal. It is not less important that care should be exercised in Press reports during the period between the announcement of a decision to set up the Tribunal and the actual hearings, particularly in relation to the comments of persons who are likely to be asked to give evidence to the Tribunal. For in the immediate aftermath of the kind of event that leads to the setting up of the Tribunal, the persons concerned may not yet have had time to consider fully either what they are saying or the implications of saying it. The character and career of an individual may suffer irreparable damage by the publicity given to his remarks and the truth may be unintentionally concealed by an ill-considered statement to the Press that the person concerned may later find it embarrassing to retract.

42. All these considerations apply equally to the other mass media of communication, broadcasting and television. While free reporting in the Press, broadcasting or television must not in any way be fettered, those concerned in all these media should bear in mind how much harm to the individual and damage to the interests of justice can be done by carelessness and thoughtlessness when reporting events during this critical period.

*Limitations imposed by the law of contempt*

43. The Government accepts without reservation the assumption which was implicit in the report of the Royal Commission and made explicit in the first recommendation of the Interdepartmental Committee, that the law of contempt does apply to Tribunals of Inquiry. The Committee recommended however that the law of contempt should not prohibit or curtail any comment at any time about the subject matter of the inquiry. This is in keeping with the principle that there should be free reporting of the proceedings and the Government accepts it fully, subject to the two following recommendations that it should be a contempt if any person after the Tribunal is appointed says or does anything, or causes anything to be said or done, in relation to any evidence relevant to the subject matter of the inquiry which is intended or obviously likely to alter, distort, destroy or withhold such evidence from the Tribunal, and that the chairman of the Tribunal in his discretion may make a request that no interview with certain named persons whom he regards as especially vulnerable shall be published, without imposing a legal obligation to comply with such a request. As the Committee says, anyone who ignored such a request would know that he was treading on dangerous ground and legal sanctions other than those available under the law of contempt are unnecessary.

*Application of the law of contempt*

44. In the Government's view there can also be no doubt about the Committee's recommendation that the law of contempt should apply only as from the date of the instrument appointing the Tribunal. It is difficult to see how a contempt can be committed in relation to a non-existent body; and although there may be a risk of undesirable publicity between the time when the intention to set up the Tribunal has been announced and its appointment, the Government agrees with the Committee that this is a price worth paying in return for

certainty as to the moment at which commentators are at risk: a moment which, as the Committee points out, should not depend on anything so unpredictable as to whether at some future date a Tribunal will be appointed under the 1921 Act.

45. Section 1 (2) (c) of the 1921 Act provides that any person may be punished by the High Court, or in Scotland the Court of Session, as if he had been guilty of contempt of the court if he does anything which would, if the Tribunal had been a court of law having power to commit for contempt, have been contempt of that court. In view of this, the Government considers that the Committee's recommendation that any unjustifiable attack upon the integrity of any member of the Tribunal in his capacity as a member of the Tribunal and that anything said or done in the face of the Tribunal which would, if the Tribunal had been a court of law having power to commit for contempt, have been contempt of court should be a contempt, describes the effect of the existing law, having regard to the terms of section 1 (2) of the Act.

46. The Government does not share the view of the Committee that section 1 (2) of the Tribunal of Inquiry (Evidence) Act 1921 needs to be amended to put the recommendations relating to contempt into effect. One disadvantage of attempting to clarify this section as proposed by the Committee is that what is not specifically included in the section will be assumed to be excluded, which means that a Tribunal would be powerless to deal with any unforeseen circumstances which might arise. The most substantial amendment would be the proposed addition to section 1 (2) of the subsection relating specifically to anything said or done which is 'intended or obviously likely' to alter, distort, destroy or withhold evidence from the Tribunal. But the question whether any particular statement or action is intended or obviously likely to do anything is so much a matter for subjective judgment that it seems unlikely that such a provision would afford any real guidance as to the circumstances in which a contempt would be committed. If a provision could be drafted which had the element of certainty necessary

to offer such guidance, it would have the disadvantage just described; unless it introduces the element of certainty it is superfluous.

47. In these circumstances, the Government considers that the 1921 Act is better left unamended, especially since future Tribunals will have the benefit of the Committee's report to serve as a guide to them when they are considering whether any particular action should be treated as a contempt.

*Procedure for committal for contempt*

48. The Government agrees with the Royal Commission that the present procedure whereby cases of contempt are referred to the High Court or the Court of Session on the certificate of the Tribunal should continue to be followed and that questions concerning committal for contempt should in no circumstances be referred back to Parliament.

SOURCE: White Paper. *Tribunals of Inquiry set up under the Tribunals of Inquiry (Evidence) Act, 1921* (May 1973, Cmnd. 5313, pp 14–16, paras 40–48)

## 25 The Times Law Report
## THE SUNDAY TIMES AND THE THALIDOMIDE AFFAIR

*Of all the* causes célèbres *involving contempt of court and its application to the Press there has been none so far-reaching in its implications and in its ultimately inhibiting effect on the Press as the case of the* Sunday Times *and the thalidomide affair. The details of the principal judgments need reading in great detail to follow the drastic nature of their influence upon the operations of journalism.*

*The cases of 266 children who had been affected in the course of their gestation by the drug thalidomide, manufactured by the Distillers Company (Biochemicals) Ltd, were still pending when the* Sunday Times *decided to publish a series of articles of an 'exposé' nature about the drug, its consequences and the behaviour of the company towards the unfortunate parents involved.*

*The litigation had been pending, at the time of the intended publication, for 12 years. Yet on 17 November 1972, an injunction was delivered preventing the* Sunday Times *from publishing an article, then in draft, on the development, distribution and use of the drug. The ground for the order was that it would be contempt of court for a newspaper to seek to influence the outcome of pending proceedings. When the case came to appeal on 16 February 1973, The Master of the Rolls, Lord Denning, lifted the injunction, and this is his judgment.*

The MASTER OF THE ROLLS said that nearly 12 years ago an overwhelming tragedy befell hundreds of families in this country. Mothers when pregnant had taken thalidomide as a sedative. All believed it was safe. The manufacturers had proclaimed it to be so; the doctors had accepted their assurance. But, unknown to anyone, if a pregnant woman took it between the fourth and 12th weeks it would affect the limbs of the foetus. In consequence some 451 babies were born deformed, some without arms or legs, others with gross distortions.

Some of the parents were advised to bring actions for damages against Distillers (Biochemicals) Ltd, who marketed the drug. They had three years under the Statutes of Limitations to bring their actions. Only 62 did. In February, 1968, a settlement was reached under which £1m was paid to those 62. No doubt Distillers thought that that was the end of their legal liabilities, for after the expiry of three years, the claims of the remaining 389 would normally be statute-barred.

Distillers must have realized, however, that they were not altogether clear of liability. A few parents after the three years had got leave to bring actions out of time. Those were still pending when the 62 were settled. And perhaps more might follow.

Eventually 266 got leave to issue writs out of time. But another 123 did not issue writs at all. That made 389 not provided for by the 1968 settlement. Distillers, at the time of the settlement, recognized that they had a moral responsibility to those 389 who did not benefit from it. So in February, 1968, they announced that they would provide a substantial sum for the benefit of the other children. To honour that pledge, they later proposed to form a charitable trust and pay to trustees £3,250,000 for the benefit of all the malformed children.

But that proposal failed to win acceptance because Distillers insisted that all parents must agree to it. The great majority did. Many were hesitant but agreed because they thought it was the best they could get. But five stood out. The majority tried to get the parents of the five removed as next friends and replaced by the Official Solicitor, knowing that he would agree to the settlement.

The Court of Appeal on April 12, 1972, refused to remove the parents of the five: *In re Taylor's Application* ([1972] 2 QB 369). That was the turning point in the whole matter.

The editor of *The Sunday Times*, Mr Harold Evans, had told the court that the report of that case caused him great anxiety. Over 10 years had passed since the children were born and still no compensation had been paid by Distillers. He determined to investigate the matter in depth and to do all he could through his newspaper to persuade Distillers to take a fresh look at their moral responsibilities to all the thalidomide children, both those where writs had been issued and those where they had not. He had investigations made and launched a campaign against Distillers.

On September 24, 1972, *The Sunday Times* published an article headed 'Our thalidomide children: A cause for national shame.' It drew attention to the long-drawn-out legal proceedings, and said: 'It seems clear that in the new term lawyers acting for Distillers (Biochemicals) who made thalidomide, will appear with lawyers acting for the children, to seek court approval for a settlement which has been worked out in private over the last few months. Unhappily the settlement is one which is grotesquely out of proportion to the appalling injuries the thalidomide children suffered. Essentially the offer is that Distillers set up a trust for the children and their families, worth some £3¼m. This is not a large sum in the context of Distillers' commercial operations (a little less than 10 per cent of last year's after tax profits, a little more than 1 per cent of money made in the 10 years since thalidomide).'

As soon as that article was published, Distillers made a formal complaint to the Attorney General, suggesting that it was a contempt of court. On September 27 the Attorney asked *The Sunday Times* for their observations. On the 28th the editor replied justifying the publication of the article. In addition, he sent to the Attorney the draft of another article he proposed to publish.

It was the one which was in question in the present proceedings. It had not yet been published. But the court had seen it. It contained a detailed analysis of the evidence against Distillers. It marshalled forcibly the arguments for saying that they did not measure up to their responsibility—though, to be fair, it did summarize the arguments which could be made for Distillers. The editor realized that the article—with its detailed analysis—was in a different category from the article of September 24.

So he wrote to the Attorney General, asking for his observations on it, and saying: 'You may take it that we are entirely satisfied with its factual accuracy in every respect, but it is our intention to give the representatives of the parties the opportunity of commenting thereon before making a decision as to whether to publish it.'

On October 10 *The Sunday Times* delivered a copy of the draft article to Distillers and invited their comments or objections. Distillers replied that the matter was receiving consideration, but they did no more.

On October 12 the Attorney General issued a writ against *The Sunday Times* claiming an injunction to restrain them from publishing the draft article. *The Sunday Times* welcomed that step as 'both sensible and constructive'. So it seemed at the time, for it would enable the newspaper to see where they stood. But as things had turned out, his Lordship thought it was a pity.

The application was made by the Attorney General. His Lordship would himself have thought it should have been made by Distillers. After all, it was the company which would be prejudiced by the publication of the proposed article. It was their litigation which might be affected by it. Yet the court had no affidavit from Distillers telling them of the prejudice to them or of the pressures on them by reason of the article. Their Lordships had little knowledge of the state of the litigation or the negotiations for a settlement. Distillers had instructed Mr Wilmers with a watching brief. Their Lordships allowed him to address them. He pointed out the serious errors which he said were contained in the proposed article. But he did not add to their Lordships' knowledge of the state of the litigation or the negotiations for a settlement.

The Attorney General explained that he himself had made the application because of *Regina v Hargreaves-Ex parte Dill* (*The Times*, November 4, 1953). A man had been charged with conspiracy. A magazine contained an article about it. The man moved for a writ or attachment against the editor. The Lord Chief Justice, Lord Goddard, said: 'I have said on more than one occasion that it would be a good thing if such motions were made on the application of the Attorney General. . . . Such motions should only be made by the law officers'.

Those remarks were made in regard to criminal cases. But they were interpreted as extending to civil cases in the Queen's Bench Division. In 1959 a committee presided over by Lord Shawcross recommended that no proceedings for such contempt 'should be instituted except by or with the consent of the Attorney General' (Report by *Justice* on Contempt of Court (1959) p34.). Accordingly, since that time it had become the practice for the Attorney himself to institute proceedings, and that was no doubt the reason why he did it in the present case.

His Lordship thought the time had come to revert to the previous practice in civil proceedings. In the civil courts the practice for well over two centuries was for the party to the action himself to make the application. He moved the court to commit the newspaper for contempt. That had been done in every case his Lordship could discover. The notice of motion was entitled 'In the cause in regard to which the contempt had arisen' and was made to the court in which the cause was depending—to the Chancery Division, the Queen's Bench or the Divorce Court, as the case might be.

Thus in the divorce suit to which Mr Parnell was a party, Captain O'Shea, the petitioner, made the application against the newspaper and it was entitled in the suit of *O'Shea v O'Shea and Parnell* ((1890) 15 PD 50). Similarly in the civil proceedings by the claimant in the *Tichborne* suit, the application against the newspapers was made by the claimant himself. But when words were spoken to the prejudice of the criminal proceedings in the *Tichborne* case, the application was made by the prosecution: *Skipworth and Others* ((1873) LR 9, QB 230).

That was as it should be. When a man was on trial in a criminal court the Crown itself was a party and concerned to ensure the fairness of the trial. It was only right and proper that the Attorney should take the responsibility of proceeding for contempt of court.

But a civil action was different. The Attorney General would, as a rule, have no knowledge of its course—or of any interference with it—unless one of the parties to it brought it to his knowledge. If he then himself took proceedings for contempt, it meant that he was putting the authority of the Crown behind the complaint. No doubt he could do so if he thought it proper. But his Lordship ventured to suggest that the Attorney should not do so save in a plain case. When the case was open to controversy or argument, it would be better to follow the previous practice. The complainant should be left to take proceedings himself at his own expense and risk as to costs.

What did the court know about the pending actions? Their Lordships had been told that since the 62 were settled in 1968, 266 writs had been issued against Distillers. The parents must have got leave ex parte from a judge to bring those actions, no doubt with affidavits saying they did not know until February, 1968, that they had a worthwile cause of action. They had to issue their writs within 12 months of getting to know. So those 266 writs were probably issued in 1968.

But the court had been told very little of what had happened in those 266 actions. In one case there was a statement of claim, and a defence delivered in March, 1969: but nothing more had happened.

In many of the cases, by agreement, pleadings had not been served. All that had happened was the issue and service of the writs; appearances had been entered; but nothing more done in the actions. So far as the courts were concerned, those 266 actions had gone soundly to sleep and had been asleep for the last three or four years. No one had awakened them. His Lordship could see why. Both sides had been hoping for a settlement. The plaintiffs had not pressed forward in the courts because of the difficulties of surmounting the Statutes of Limitation, and the enormous expense involved in a contest. Distillers had not applied to strike the actions out because they, too, were anxious for a settlement and shuddered at the prospect of a fight.

So the litigation remained dormant. So far as appeared it was still dormant in April, 1972, when the court heard *Taylor's Application*. So far as their Lordships knew it was still dormant when *The Sunday Times* in September, 1972, started publishing its articles on the thalidomide children. It was still dormant today.

It was undoubted law that when litigation was pending and actively in suit before the court no one should comment on it in such a way that there was real and substantial danger of prejudice to the trial of the action—as, for example, by influencing the judge, the jurors, or the witnesses, or even by prejudicing mankind in general against a party to the cause. That appeared from the *St James' Evening Post Case* ((1742) 2 Atk 469) and other cases. Even if the person making the comment honestly believed it to be true, it was still a contempt if he prejudged the truth before it was ascertained: *Skipworth's Case*, by Mr Justice Blackburn.

To that rule about a fair trial there was a further rule that no one should, by misrepresentations or otherwise, bring unfair pressure to bear on one of the parties to a cause so as to force him to drop his complaint or give up his defence or come to a settlement on terms which he would not otherwise have been prepared to entertain: *In re William Thomas Shipping Co Ltd* ([1930] Ch 368); *Vine Products Ltd v Green* ([1966] Ch 484); and an article by Professor Goodhart (48 *Harvard Law Review* (1935) 895/6).

It was of the first importance that the law as his Lordship had stated it should be maintained in its full integrity. We must not allow 'trial by newspaper' or 'trial by television' or trial by any medium other than the courts of law.

But that law applied only 'when litigation is pending and is actively in suit before the court'. And there must appear to be 'a real and substantial danger of prejudice' to the trial or settlement of the case. And when considering the question, it must always be remembered that besides the parties' interest in a fair trial or settlement of the case, there was another important interest to be considered. It was the interest of the public in matters of national concern and the freedom of the press to make fair comment on such matters.

The one interest must be balanced against the other. There might be cases where the subject matter was such that the public interest counter-balanced the parties' private interest. In such cases the public interest prevailed. Fair comment was to be allowed. That had been stated in Australia in regard to the courts: *Ex parte Dawson* ((1961) 61 SR (NSW)573). It was so recommended by a committee over which Lord Salmon had presided on Tribunals of Inquiry: (Cmnd. 4078 (1969) para. 26).

Take the present case. Here was a matter of the greatest public interest. The thalidomide children were the living reminders of a national tragedy. There had been no public inquiry on how it came about. Such inquiry as there had been, had been done in confidence in the course of private litigation between the parties.

Many believed the compensation offered to be too small. Nearly 12 years had passed and still no settlement had been reached. On such a matter the law could and did authorize the newspapers to make fair comment. So long as they got their facts right and kept their comments fair they were without reproach. Our law of contempt did not prevent comment before the litigation was started, nor after it had ended. Nor did it prevent it when the litigation was dormant and was not being actively pursued.

If the pending action was one which, as a matter of public interest, ought to have been brought to trial long ago, or settled long ago, the newspapers could fairly comment on the failure to bring it to trial or reach a settlement. No person could stop comment by serving a writ and letting it lie idle; nor could he stop it by entering an appearance and doing nothing more. It was active litigation which was protected by the law of contempt, not the absence of it.

Apply those considerations to the present case. The newspapers could fairly comment on the 62 actions settled in February, 1968, and say that in making those settlements Distillers did not measure up to their moral responsibilities. Take the last 123 children in whose cases writs had never been issued. The newspapers could fairly press for compensation on the ground that Distillers were morally responsible.

That left only the 266 actions in which writs were issued four years ago but which had never been brought to trial. Did the existence of these writs prevent the newspapers from drawing attention to Distillers' moral responsibilities? If they could comment on the first 62 or the last 123, his Lordship did not see why they could not comment on the intervening 266. There was no way of distinguishing between them. The draft article commented on all the thalidomide children together. It was clearly lawful in respect of the first 62 and the last 123. So also should it be in respect of the middle 266.

His Lordship had said enough to show that the case was unique, so much so that the public interest in having it discussed outweighed the prejudice which might thereby be occasioned to a party to dispute. At any rate the High Court of Parliament had allowed it to be discussed. So why should not the courts also permit it? There was no possible reason why Parliament should permit and the court refuse it.

On November 29, 1972, there was a debate in the House of Commons on the thalidomide children. As the Attorney General had reminded the court, they must be careful in speaking of it for the Bill of Rights said: '... the freedom of speech and debate or proceedings in Parliament ought not to be impeached or questioned in any court or place out of Parliament'. Parliament had the exclusive right to regulate its own proceedings. What was said or done within its walls could not be inquired into in a court of law: *Bradlaugh v Gossett* ((1884) 12 QBD 27).

But, he hoped without giving offence, his Lordship would say that the convention of Parliament as to matters sub judice should so far as possible be the same as the law administered in the courts. The object of each was the same—to prevent prejudice to pending litigation and the parties to it. The rules for achieving it should be the same for the very good reason that as soon as matters were discussed in Parliament they could be and were reported at large in the newspapers, protected by the Parliamentary Papers Act, 1840. Comments made in Parliament could be repeated in the newspapers without any fear of an action for libel or proceedings for contempt. If it was no contempt for a newspaper to publish the comments made in Parliament, it should be no contempt to publish the self-same comments made outside Parliament.

In this very case on November 29 speeches were made in Parliament and reported in the newspapers in which Distillers were said to be gravely at fault and had not faced up to their moral responsibility. If those reports were not a contempt of court, nor should the selfsame matter be a contempt when published in the form of an article.

In view of the debate in Parliament, his Lordship felt sure that all present must have accepted that the sub judice rule did not apply to forbid discussion. The reason was no doubt because none of the actions had been set down for trial or otherwise brought before the court. It did not appear that there was a real and substantial danger of prejudice to the trial of the cases. So the discussion was allowed to take place.

If their Lordships in their court applied rules as to sub judice on the same lines as Parliament they would not go far wrong.

After the debate there was a spate of comment of all kinds, some for Distillers, others against them. In the *Daily Mail* on December 8 there was an article very critical of Distillers—on much the same lines as that which *The Sunday Times* proposed to publish. No steps had been taken against the *Daily Mail*.

Seeing that all those comments had been let through without any steps being taken by anyone to stop them, it was plain that the injunction against *The Sunday Times* could not stand. It would be discrimination of the worst kind if *The Sunday Times* was the only paper to be stopped by injunction.

But his Lordship would not rest his decision on that ground alone. He would go back to last September, when *The Sunday Times* submitted the article to the Attorney General. Even at that time his Lordship thought that its publication would not have amounted to a contempt of court.

The reason was that it dealt with a matter of the greatest public interest and contained comments which the newspaper honestly believed to be true. It drew attention to Distillers' moral responsibilities for all the 451 children, and not merely those who had issued writs. It did not prejudice pending litigation because that litigation was and had for years been dormant.

No doubt the article was intended to bring pressure to bear on Distillers to increase their offer—but that pressure was legitimate in the light of all that had happened. It would be open to Distillers to reply to it. If they had submitted their reply to *The Sunday Times*, his Lordship would have expected it to have received equal publicity. But, all in all, it was a matter which warranted debate, not only in Parliament but also in the press. He would not restrict it.

His Lordship would only add that fair comment was one thing, unfair comment or pressure another. However good the cause, and however much the sympathy for the children, no one should resort to unfair tactics to force a settlement when they did not know, and could not know, the rights and wrongs of the dispute.

But the proposed article did not come into that category. it exerted pressure, but legitimate pressure. His Lordship would allow the appeal and discharge the injunction.

SOURCE: *The Times*. Law Report (17 February 1973)

## 26 Law Lords
## FINAL JUDGMENT ON THE THALIDOMIDE AFFAIR —THE BANNING OF THE SUNDAY TIMES ARTICLE

*The Attorney-General, Sir Peter Rawlinson, QC, appealed against the Court of Appeal ruling to the House of Lords, which delivered its verdict in July. The five law lords were unanimous in supporting the Attorney-General, although settlement terms had been agreed by this time between the two sides in the substantive action. Lord Reid thought that 'anything in the nature of a pre-judgment of a case or of specific issues in it is objectionable, not only because of its effects on that particular case but also because of its side effects which may be far-reaching.' Two of his colleagues thought that an article already published by the paper in September 1972 had been in contempt although no action against the paper was proposed. The Editor of the* Sunday Times, *Harold Evans, declared that the decision was a grave blow to free speech. 'If it is not appropriate to go into the issue after 12 years when will it become so?' This was the reasoning of Lord Reid.*

Lord Reid said that in 1958 Distillers Company (Biochemicals) Ltd began to make and sell in this country a sedative containing a drug thalidomide which had been invented and used in Germany. The product, available on prescription, was consumed by many pregnant women, having been said to be quite safe for them. But soon babies were born with terrible deformities. It took a little time to prove that those deformities were caused by thalidomide in the unborn child at a certain stage of pregnancy. As soon as that was realized, Distillers, in 1961, withdrew their product.

The matter attracted some publicity and the question arose whether Distillers were legally liable to pay damages in respect of the deformed children. They denied liability. The first action against them was begun in 1962. Further publicity resulted in some 70 actions having been raised before 1968.

Claimants were faced with two difficulties—the highly debatable legal question whether a person could sue for damage done to him before his birth; and that an attempt to prove negligence by Distillers would require long and expensive inquiries.

Early in 1968, after negotiation with the claimants, a settlement was reached by which Distillers agreed to pay each claimant 40 per cent of the damages which he or she would recover if liability were established. That appeared a reasonable compromise from a purely legal point of view. Two cases were then tried by agreement to establish the proper measure of damages and ultimately 65 cases were settled, Distillers paying about £1m in all.

But many more cases gradually came to light. Leave was given to serve writs, and by February, 1969, 248 writs had been served. A few more followed. And there were many cases where claims were made but no writs served. There might still be further claims. There appeared to be more than 400 outstanding claims not covered by the 1968 settlement.

Distillers proposed to settle those claims by a trust fund of over £3m, but they made it a condition of any settlement that all claimants should agree to accept it. Five refused to do so, one because payments out of the trust fund were to be based on need, and his financial position was such that his child would get no benefit from such a settlement. An attempt was made to compel the five to agree by having the Official Solicitor appointed to look after their children's interests.

But in *In re Taylor's Application* ([1972] 2 QB 369) the Court of Appeal reinstated the five parents. In June, 1972, Distillers made some new proposals but they were not accepted. There were then 389 claims outstanding and little prospect of an early settlement.

The editor of *The Sunday Times* took a keen interest in the matter. He collected a great deal of material and on September 24 the newspaper published a long and powerful article. Two general propositions were argued at some length: first, whether those who put such drugs on the market ought to be absolutely liable for damage done by them, and secondly, that in such cases the currently accepted method of assessing damages was inadequate. But the sting of the article lay in the following paragraph:

> 'The thalidomide children shame Distillers. It is appreciated that Distillers have always denied negligence and that if the cases were pursued, the children might end up with nothing. It is appreciated that Distillers' lawyers have a professional duty to secure the best terms for their clients. But at the end of the day what is to be paid in settlement is the decision of Distillers, and they should offer much, much more to every one of the thalidomide victims. It may be argued that Distillers have a duty to their shareholders and that, having taken account of skilled legal advice, the terms are just. But the law is not always the same as justice. There are times when to insist on the letter of the law is as exposed to criticism as infringement of another's legal rights. The figure in the proposed settlement is to be £3.25m, spread over 10 years. This does not shine as a beacon against pre-tax profits last year of £64.8 million and company assets worth £421 million. Without in any way surrendering on negligence, Distillers could and should think again.'

Distillers immediately brought it to the Attorney General's attention, maintaining that it was in contempt of court. He decided to take no action. That did not prevent Distillers from bringing the matter before the court; but they took no action.

His Lordship agreed with their Lordships that the Attorney General had a right to bring before the court any matter which he thought might amount to contempt of court and which should in the public interest be so brought. The party aggrieved had the right but no duty to bring any matter he alleged amounted to contempt before the court. If the party aggrieved failed to take action either because of expense or because he thought it better not to do so, very serious contempt might escape punishment if the Attorney General had no right to act. It was for him to judge whether it was in the public interest that he should act.

The editor had in mind to publish a further article of a different character. He sent the material for it to the Attorney General, who took the view that he should intervene. He claimed an injunction by a writ of October, 1972, against *The Sunday Times*, restraining them from publishing the proposed article. The Divisional Court granted an injunction, but the Court of Appeal discharged it. The Attorney General now appealed to the House.

The whole subject of contempt of court appeared never to have come before their Lordships' House; there was no recent review of the subject in the Court of Appeal; and the circumstances of cases arising in practice were generally not such as to require any detailed analysis of the law. His Lordship could not disagree with a statement in a recent report of Justice on the Law and the Press that the main objection to the existing law of contempt was its uncertainty. Their Lordships must try to remove that reproach at least with regard to those parts of the law with which the present case was concerned.

The law on the subject was and must be founded entirely on public policy. It was not there to protect the private rights of parties to a litigation or prosecution but to prevent interference with the administration of justice. It should, in his

Lordship's judgment, be limited to what was reasonably necessary for that purpose.

Public policy generally required a balancing of interests which might conflict. Freedom of speech should not be limited to any greater extent than was necessary but it could not be allowed where there would be real prejudice to the administration of justice.

His Lordship cited a passage by Lord Atkin in *Ambard v Attorney-General for Trinidad and Tobago* ([1936] AC 322) as to the right of the public to criticize the public act done in the seat of justice, and from Lord Hardwicke's statement in the *St James' Evening Post* case ((1742) 2 Atk 469) that there were 'three different sorts of contempt', the second being 'in abusing parties who are concerned in causes here' and the third 'in prejudicing mankind against persons before the cause is heard'.

His Lordship did not think Lord Hardwicke intended that to be a universally applicable definition, though it had too often been treated as if it were. It was a good guide but must be supplemented in cases of a type he did not have in mind.

Their Lordships were particularly concerned with 'abusing parties' and 'prejudicing mankind' against them. Of course, parties must be protected from scurrilous abuse, otherwise many litigants would fear to bring their cases to court.

But the Attorney General's argument, based on a passage in Mr Justice Buckley's judgment in *Vine Products v Green* ([1966] 1 Ch 484), went far beyond that:

> 'It is a contempt of this court for any newspaper to comment on pending legal proceedings in any way which is likely to prejudice the fair trial of the action. That may arise in various ways. It may be that the comment is one which is likely . . . to bring pressure to bear on one or other of the parties to the action, so as to prevent that party from prosecuting or from defending the action, or encourage that party to submit to terms of compromise which he otherwise might not have been prepared to entertain, or influence him in some other way in his conduct of the action, which he ought to be free to prosecute

or defend, as he is advised, without being subject to such pressure.'

His Lordship thought that was much too widely stated and was not in accord with sound public policy. Why would it be contrary to public policy to seek by fair comment to dissuade Shylock from proceeding with his action? Surely it could not be wrong for the officious bystander to draw his attention to the risk that, if he went on, decent people would cease to trade with him. Or suppose his best customer ceased to trade with him when he heard of his lawsuit. That could not be contempt of court. Would it become contempt if, when asked by Shylock why he was sending no more business his way, he told him the reason? Nothing would be more likely to influence Shylock to discontinue his action. Would it make any difference if it became widely known that such pressure was being brought to bear? And though widely known, must the local press keep silent about it? There must be some limitation of that general statement of the law.

Suppose that there was in the press and elsewhere active discussion of some question of wide public interest, such as the propriety of local authorities or other landlords ejecting squatters from empty premises due for demolition. If legal proceedings were begun against some squatters by some authority already criticized in the press, must there then be silence until that case was decided? Surely public policy did not require that a system of stop and go should apply to public discussion.

His Lordship knew of no better statement of the law than that in the Australian judgment of Chief Justice Jordan in *Ex parte Bread Manufacturers* ((1937) 37 SR (NSW) 249):

> 'It is of extreme public interest that no conduct should be permitted which is likely to prevent a litigant in a court of justice from having his case tried free from all matter of prejudice. But the administration of justice, important though it undoubtedly is, is not the only matter in which the public is vitally interested; and if in the course of the ventilation of a question of public concern matter is published which may

prejudice a party in the conduct of a law suit, it does not follow that a contempt has been committed. The case may be one in which as between competing matters of public interest the possibility of prejudice to a litigant may be required to yield to other and superior considerations. The discussion of public affairs and the denunciation of public abuses, actual or supposed, cannot be required to be suspended merely because the discussion or the denunciation may, as an incidental but not intended by-product, cause some likelihood of prejudice to a person who happens at the time to be a litigant.

'It is well settled that a person cannot be prevented by process of contempt from continuing to discuss publicly a matter which may fairly be regarded as one of public interest, by reason merely of the fact that the matter in question has become the subject of litigation, or that person whose conduct is being publicly criticized has become a party to litigation either as plaintiff or as defendant, and whether in relation to the matter which is under discussion or with respect to some other matter.'

After considering other authorities his Lordship said that he would hold that as a general rule where the only matter to be considered was pressure put on a litigant, fair and temperate criticism was legitimate, but anything which went beyond that might well involve contempt of court.

In some recent cases about influencing litigants the court had accepted the law as stated by Mr Justice Buckley in *Vine Products* but—possibly to mitigate the extreme consequences of that view of the law—had held that there was no contempt unless there was a serious risk that the litigant would be influenced. His Lordship thought that test most unsatisfactory and was the cause of the Divisional Court giving wrong reasons for reaching a correct decision in *Attorney General v London Weekend Television* ([1973] 1 WLR 202), where the company had produced a television programme about the thalidomide tragedy on October 8, 1972, which appeared from the report to have had much the same object and character as *The Sunday Times* article of September 24. The Divisional Court, following the judgment in the present case, held that the programme 'bore many of the badges of contempt' and only dismissed the application on the ground that they could not say that the programme 'would result in the creation of a *serious* risk that the course of justice would be interfered with'. They had found earlier that the spoken words on the programme 'did not have that impact the producer might have hoped they would have on the viewers'. So the company only escaped because of their inefficiency. The law could not be left in such an unsatisfactory state.

There must be two questions. First, was there any contempt at all? Secondly, was it sufficiently serious to require or justify the court in making an order against the respondent? As Lord Parker had put it in *R v Duffy* ([1960] 2 QB 188), there must be 'a real risk as opposed to a remote possibility'.

The crucial question was whether it could ever be permissible to urge a party to a litigation to forgo his legal rights in whole or in part. The Attorney General argued that it could not, and the Divisional Court appeared to have accepted that view. His Lordship considered it was permissible so long as it was done in a fair and temperate way and without any oblique motive. *The Sunday Times* article of September 24 afforded a good illustration of the difference between the two views. It was plainly intended to bring pressure to bear on Distillers. It was likely to attract support from others and it did so. It was outspoken. It said: 'There are times when to insist on the letter of the law is as exposed to criticism as infringement of another's legal rights' and clearly implied that that was such a time.

If the view maintained by the Attorney General were right his Lordship could hardly imagine a clearer case of contempt of court. It could be no excuse that the passage his Lordship had quoted earlier was combined with much other totally unobjectionable material. And it could not be said that it created no serious risk of causing Distillers to do what they did not want to do. On the facts submitted to the House it seemed to have played a large part in causing Distillers to offer far more money than they had in mind at that time. But his

Lordship could not subscribe to the view that it ought never to have been published because it was in contempt of court. He saw no offence against public policy and no pollution of the stream of justice by its publication.

But it was necessary to turn to the material to which the injunction applied. If it was not to be published at this time it would not be proper to refer to it in any detail. But it could be said that it consisted in the main of detailed evidence and argument intended to show that Distillers did not exercise due care to see that thalidomide was safe before they put it on the market.

If that material were regarded solely from the point of view of its likely effect on Distillers, his Lordship did not think that its publication in 1972 would have added much to the pressure on them created, or at least begun, by the earlier article of September 24. From Distillers' point of view the damage had already been done. His Lordship doubted whether the subsequent course of events would have been very different in their effect on Distillers if the matter had been published.

But to his Lordship's mind there was another consideration even more important than the effect of publication on the mind of the litigant. The controversy about the tragedy of the thalidomide children had ranged widely, but as yet there seemed to have been little, if any, detailed discussion of the issues which the court might have to determine if the outstanding claims were not settled. The question whether Distillers were negligent had been frequently referred to but so far apparently there had been no attempt to assess the evidence. If the material were released now it appeared almost inevitable that detailed answers would be published and various public pre-judgments of the issue would be expressed. His Lordship would regard that as very much against the public interest.

There had long been and still was in this country a strong and generally held feeling that trial by newspaper was wrong and should be prevented. In the report of Lord Salmon's committee on the law of contempt with regard to tribunals of inquiry

(Cmnd 4078) there was a reference to the 'horror' in such a thing.

What was regarded as most objectionable was that a newspaper or television programme should seek to persuade the public, by discussing the issues and evidence in a case before the court, whether civil or criminal, that one side was right and the other wrong. If one were to ask the ordinary man or even a lawyer in his leisure moments why he had that feeling, the first reply might be: 'Well, look at what happens in some other countries where that is permitted.' Strong feelings were generally based on one's general experience rather than on specific reasons; but public policy was generally the result of strong feelings commonly held, rather than of cold argument.

If the law was to be developed in accord with public policy the general approach should not be too legalistic. No doubt public policy was an unruly horse to ride, but in a chapter of the law so intimately associated with public policy as contempt of court we must not be too pedestrian.

There was ample authority for the proposition that issues must not be prejudged in a manner likely to affect the mind of those who might later be witnesses or jurors. But very little had been said about the wider proposition that trial by newspaper was intrinsically objectionable.

His Lordship thought that anything in the nature of prejudgment of a case of specific issues in it was objectionable not only because of its possible effect on that particular case but also because of its side effects which might be far reaching. Responsible 'mass media' would do their best to be fair, but there would also be ill-informed, slapdash or prejudiced attempts to influence the public. If people were led to think that it was easy to find the truth disrespect for the processes of the law could follow; and if mass media were allowed to judge, unpopular people and unpopular causes would fare badly. Most cases of prejudging of issues fell within the existing authorities on contempt. His Lordship did not think that the freedom of the press would suffer, and the law would be clearer and easier to apply in practice if it was made a general rule that it was not permissible to prejudge issues in pending cases.

His Lordship considered that the law was rather too narrowly stated in the *Vine Products* case. There the question was what wines could properly be called sherry and a newspaper published an article which clearly prejudged the issue. That was technically in contempt, but the fault was so venial and the possible consequences so trifling that it would have been quite wrong to impose punishment or even to require the newspaper to pay the applicant's costs. But the newspaper ought to have withheld its judgment until the case was decided.

There was no magic in the issue of a writ or in a charge being made against an accused person. Comment on a case which was imminent might be as objectionable as comment after it had begun. And a 'gagging writ' ought to have no effect.

To prevent misunderstanding, his Lordship would add that comment where a case was under appeal was a very different matter. For one thing, it was scarcely possible to imagine a case where comment could influence Court of Appeal judges or learned Lords in the House. And it would be wrong and, contrary to existing practice to limit proper criticism of judgments already given but under appeal.

On the reasons which induced the Court of Appeal to discharge the injunction, it was said that the actions had been dormant or asleep for several years. Nothing appeared to have been done in court but active negotiations for a settlement were going on all the time. No one denied that it would be contempt of court to use improper pressure to induce a litigant to settle a case on terms to which he did not wish to agree. So if there was no undue procrastination in the negotiations for a settlement his Lordship did not see how in that context action could be said to be dormant.

Then it was said that there was a public interest which counter-balanced the litigants' private interests. But contempt of court had nothing to do with the private interests of the litigants. His Lordship had already indicated how he thought a balance must be struck between the public interest in freedom of speech and that in protecting the administration of justice from interference. He did not see why there should be any difference in principle between a case which was thought to have news value and one which had not. Protection of the administration of justice was equally important whether or not the case involved important general issues.

Some reference had been made to the House of Commons debate [on November 29, 1972]; but his Lordship thought little that was said in the House could not have been said outside if his view of the law was right.

If their Lordships were only concerned with the effect which publication of the new material might now have on the mind of Distillers his Lordship might be able to agree with the Court of Appeal decision, though for different reasons. But wider considerations were involved. The purpose of the law was not to prevent publication of such material but to postpone it. The information set before the House gave their Lordships hope that the general lines of a settlement of the whole unfortunate controversy might soon emerge. It should then be possible to permit the material to be published. But if things dragged on indefinitely so that there was no early prospect either of a settlement or of a trial in court then there would have to be a wakenment of the public interest in a unique situation.

As matters stood at present the appeal should be allowed.

SOURCE: *The Times* Law Report (19 July 1973)

## 27 Sunday Times
## REPLY TO THE LAW LORDS

*The leading article in the edition of the* Sunday Times *which followed the House of Lords judgment on the thalidomide affair stands as a most eloquently argued statement of the case of the Press on the issue of con-*

*tempt. Where does the balance of public interest lie: in the publication of facts are in protection of the procedure of justice?*

## FAIR TRIAL AND FREE SPEECH: THE PROPER BALANCE

The judgment of the House of Lords in the thalidomide case comes, happily, too late to affect the children who were the victims of the drug. Since last autumn, when The Sunday Times involved itself in a major way and the court actions against us began, Distillers have raised their offer of compensation from £3m to £20m or so. It is an offer which we have commended and it seems it will prove broadly acceptable. Publicity played a part—some might say a decisive part—in Distillers' change of course. We would say there is now a real prospect of that justice which the law, left to itself, had failed to secure over so many years. Yet the legal arguments and legal decisions about The Sunday Times' published and suppressed articles are deeply depressing.

We began on September 24, last year, with a series of articles in which we demonstrated that the thalidomide children were being treated unjustly and called on Distillers to meet their moral obligations. We proposed to publish a further article which examined how the damaging drug was made, tested and marketed in Britain. Two of the five Law Lords who have unanimously banned that further article would also have prohibited publication of our original September 24 article if they had seen it beforehand. Lord Simon in a most restrictive judgment suggests that once there is litigation there must never be any public discussion or attempt to reform the laws until the cases are concluded—until, we are tempted to say, the pound of flesh has been exacted. The reasoning of the three judges in the Divisional Court, led by Lord Chief Justice Widgery, suggests that they, too, would have banned the original September 24 article so that the campaign would have been stillborn; they did, of course, stop us publishing the draft article on the history of the drug's manufacture.

Against these judgments we have three judges in the Court of Appeal in favour of permitting the original article (and the one now banned), and three of the Law Lords (who all, however, agree in reimposing the Divisional Court ban on the history article). So it is only by one judgment—six in our favour out of a total of eleven—that the original campaign is declared legitimate. A damned close run thing. And the proposed article on the manufacture of the drug is overwhelmingly voted out by eight judges to three.

### TRUTH IS THE FIRST CASUALTY

This might seem academic in the light of all that has happened since we began our series last autumn. After all, the children have benefited, and that was a prime objective of our publication. Moreover, the public discussion created has led the Government to set up a Royal Commission on civil liability, under Lord Pearson, which is examining the wide and complex issues of law and social policy, dramatised by the plight of the thalidomide children.

What have we got to grumble about? Why don't we, it might be said, leave Distillers alone now they have done the decent thing? There are two answers to these questions. First, the banned article is germane to issues of great public importance, wider than the settlement of the thalidomide litigation itself. Secondly, the preponderant judgments have grave implications for freedom of speech and thus of the Press (for which we claim no special privileges).

The first casualty is truth. It is 12 years since thalidomide was discovered to have caused horrible deformities, and deaths, among more than 400 children. It is the biggest drug disaster that our modern times have seen. Society regards the unexplained death of one person as the fit subject for inquiry, namely an inquest. Where the human loss is greater, there is invariably a public inquiry which often ranges quite widely. One thinks immediately of the Aberfan pit disaster where the Government set up a tribunal, but a similar rigorous inquiry is undertaken for any land, sea or air disaster. There has been no such inquiry into thalidomide. The Government of the day set up no inquiry. It was negligent in this respect in a most extraordinary manner. It left the causes of the tragedy to be elucidated, if at all, by a court trial of legal negligence between Distillers and the parents. There will almost certainly never be such a trial. It is in any event an indirect and costly way of trying to get at the truth. So today, 12 years after the tragedy, we do not know why it happened. We cannot assess the lessons, if any, that there are for public policy—for attitudes to civil liability, to safety standards in drug testing and advertising.

It is true that statements have been made about the conduct of Distillers in making the drug, some way back in 1961–62 and many this year following The Sunday Times articles. These have been mostly in defence of the company. We are not particularly concerned to pursue Distillers, who no longer make drugs, as to get at the facts of the time, whatever light they shed on the narrow issue of legal liability. But these statements have been made in utter ignorance of the contents of The Sunday Times findings on the making and manufacture of the drug, and they inevitably will influence public policy. A Private Member's Bill before the House of Commons last autumn proposed a re-definition of the legal liabilities of drug companies. It was defeated. Now we have Lord Pearson's Commission and because of the Law Lords' judgment last week it will be deprived of the benefit of The Sunday Times researches on matters of fact. It is a very odd state of affairs when the air is thick with generalised opinion, but there is a legal suppression of detailed fact which alone can justify or modify opinion. We are not saying in what direction this modification might be, but it would certainly be an error to imagine it is hostile to drug companies. The information might indeed be of benefit to Hoffman-La Roche who are arguing with the Government about the justification for their drug pricing and research policy.

Nor would we limit our criticism of the evils of suppression to such acknowledged matters of public policy, for if the reasoning of the Law Lords is followed there must be an immediate stop to scientific discussion. It is almost impossible to discuss pharmacological testing without in some way touching on the legal issues of the thalidomide case; indeed there have been some broad statements in the medical Press hostile to the parents' interests, which have not excited the concern of the Attorney-General, and there has been some detailed discussion (notably in a basic reference book Embryopathic Activity in Drugs). It is unthinkable that this discussion should be fettered, yet it is just as derelict of the law, as now interpreted, as The Sunday Times article itself. Moreover, even the scientific discussion must be distorted in the absence of all the facts. No Law Lord has sought to accommodate such awkward results to their generalisations and though Lord Denning in the Court of Appeal was impressed by the absence of any public inquiry after all these years, only one of the five judges in the House of Lords even considered the implications for public policy of the restrictions on attempts to get at the truth. Lord Cross agrees that a public inquiry might have been embarrassing to legal proceedings but goes on to say that the absence of such an inquiry 'affords no justification for allowing the Press to conduct an inquiry of its own while the proceedings are still pending.' He does not say why. He is willing in his conclusions to allow pressure, possibly great pressure, on a litigant, but rules out any prejudging of the issues. Like Lord Reid he makes no comment on the possibility of legitimately presenting true facts while avoiding a legal prejudgment.

Of course, it may be objected that The Sunday Times version is not the whole truth or is inaccurate. Distillers have said that they do not accept it is accurate, but are not prepared to discuss it in detail. Our reply to this is that we honestly believe what we would like to publish would be accurate, that any comment is fair and temperate, that we are ready to publish responsible comment from any source, and that Distillers could sue us for libel. If we were wrong, we would be forced to pay damages.

There is one final point about the particular suppressed article. We recognise that our argument about the need to get at the truth would be weaker if this were 1962 and if a trial were imminent. Or even 1963. We have never argued for the right to publish information after a civil case is set down for trial. But it is a decade later than that, no trial is set down or likely, and one begins to experience an acute giddiness contemplating the legal sense of time.

There is one consistency in all the judgments, and that is the fear of 'trial by newspaper.' This is an emotive term, carrying a lot of loaded implications about what may be the entirely legitimate activities of a free Press. Does it mean the investigation of data and its publication? Does it mean the pursuit of a campaign, within the strict laws of libel, copyright, and confidence? Newspapers cannot charge, convict, punish or subpoena. They can merely present the evidence. 'Trial' by newspaper implies some impropriety in the pursuit of the newspaper's task, yet for all the possible evil consequences mentioned by the Law Lords there exist other legal defences. The use of 'trial by newspaper,' in fact, betrays a deep suspicion of the Press. More than lip service is paid to the importance of a free Press by Lords Reid and Cross, but the others seem unimpressed by its competing virtues with those of undisturbed legal processes.

### THE MOST DISTURBING FEATURE OF ALL

This reluctance to attempt a proper balance between the two is underlined by what is possibly the most disturbing of all features of the judgments—namely the failure of them to acknowledge the principal reason why The Sunday Times involved itself in the first place. This was the plain failure of the legal system to supply a remedy to the thalidomide children which was remotely acceptable. Lord Simon even says 'dwelling on the peculiar horror of this particular case is apt to cloud judgment.' That such lengthy and eminent deliberations could have concluded with barely a reference to the human realities is a measure of the insulation of the legal profession from the considerations which should now determine the making of public policy.

What is to be done? If our thalidomide case has produced confusion and regression, it has surely also produced a final decisive argument for radical recommendations from the committee on contempt now sitting under Lord Justice Phillimore. We ourselves would favour great liberalisation of contempt in civil law, with certain safeguards, and a strong, clear contempt law to protect the administration of criminal justice. We would at least expect that newspapers should have the same freedom that MPs have exercised in this case. Mr James Prior, for the Government, seemed sympathetic to the need for reform in the Commons last week; it would be an earnest of good intentions if he could make a statement before the House rises. Law reform is too important to be left to lawyers.

SOURCE: *Sunday Times* (22 July 1973)

### 28 Harold Wilson
### THE LAW LORDS' JUDGEMENT AND THE PARLIAMENTARY PROCESS

*In a letter to* The Times *during the course of the public discussion of the Lords' thalidomide judgment, Harold Wilson, Leader of the Opposition, argued that the law of contempt was operating in a manner which affected adversely not only the work of the Press but also the work of Parliament. He emphasised the need for Parliament to enjoy the benefits of a flow of public information through the Press and drew attention to the way in which the Industrial Relations Court (set up a year previously under the Industrial Relations Act) was similarly inhibiting Press comment on certain aspects of industrial relations because it operated under the same privilege of the law of contempt.*

Although Britain has survived for centuries without a written constitution, we have operated conventions designed to make effective and workable the demarcation of duties between the judiciary, the executive and the legislature. For example, the functioning of the courts is protected from parliamentary interference by Parliament's own sub judice rules, strictly enforced by the Speaker. Equally Parliament is protected by rules, and, indeed, by the Bill of Rights, ensuring that none of its proceedings can be called in question in the courts. Even the House of Commons itself appeared to be limited in its ability to discuss the thalidomide case until, following a wise ruling of the Speaker, its own select committee on procedure produced a report re-defining the sub judice rule so as to enable parliamentary discussion to take place in a manner which did not prejudice the functioning of the courts.

The most recent House of Lords judgment, reversing the decision of the Court of Appeal, means that the emphasis is now tilted in a way that affects, in a sense derogatory to the functioning of Parliament, the separation of powers between the judicial system on the one hand and Parliament, both in its legislative capacity and in its constitutional duty in acting as a check or a goad on the decisions of the executive.

Parliament is hamstrung in its discussions of, and decisions on, matters of public importance if it cannot draw both on the facts and opinions freely published in the press. In 1972, I stressed this argument on the operation of the Industrial Relations Act, following what I and other members of Parliament regarded as a threat to the freedom of the broadcasting authorities and press, namely the communication of warning messages to the media from officers of the National Industrial Relations Court. For the raw material of parliamentary debate is in fact what members read in the press.

The same inhibition would have applied in the thalidomide case, had not the House of Commons, following the select committee report, modified its own sub judice rule. In this case, the judicial process had been frozen for 11 years. During those years much had changed, including knowledge of the effects of the drug and the actions taken by other countries and governments, and there had been a significant change in public opinion on these questions, which it is Parliament's duty to reflect.

The fact is that parliamentary questions and debate forced a substantial change in the handling of the thalidomide issue. This is beyond dispute. The serious aspect of the House of Lords judicial decision in the context of the parliamentary decision is this: our debates, and the ultimate outcome, were inspired and informed by the original article in *The Sunday Times*. Without that article and the facts and arguments it adduced, Parliament would have been inhibited in a way none could attempt to justify so far as the merits of the thalidomide case are concerned.

The gravity of the House of Lords decision in respect of a further, and still unpublished, article lies in the fact that, had that decision been operative a year ago, *The Sunday Times* article which was published together with supporting evidence could never have appeared. The result would have been that the parliamentary debates, if they had taken place at all, would have been uninformed and lacking in decisive content, and the result which in fact flowed from those debates would never have occurred.

The issue therefore is that this decision, if it is from now on to condition public comment, will not only inhibit the freedom of press comment; it will equally inhibit Parliament in both its legislative functions and in its duty of holding the executive accountable to its authority.

I repeat that it is not for us to question the authority of the House of Lords in construing the law of contempt, or any other law. Accepting the doctrine of the separation of powers, what Parliament cannot accept is that such construction should be allowed to shift the balance of power against its own authority, and the fulfilment of its own duties.

Therefore, if the law is as the Lords have authoritatively stated, Parliament, the legislature, has not only the right but the duty to change it. That task must begin now.

SOURCE: *The Times* (23 July 1973)

## B OFFICIAL SECRETS

*A very large proportion of all the information used by journalists comes from official sources, that is, from members of the government, civil servants and other government employees. Information about government plans, about the operation of its services and agencies pours forth in a never-ceasing torrent. A much larger quantity of information, however, is withheld, and that proportion is frequently the most interesting and important from the point of view of the public. In an incessant struggle between the Press and officialdom in which the former endeavours to acquire or authenticate information (at points in time when government plans can still be influenced rather than at the point at which they are merely* faits accomplis), *the forces of authority may use one of the bluntest of administrative instruments with which to preserve the secrecy of the work of government—the Official Secrets Act. Section Two of this Act provides all the many elements of government with an enormous reserve power, under the threat of which the machinery of government in Britain has succeeded in remaining among the most secretive in the western world.*

*The purpose of this section is to describe the origins and working of the Act and of the D-Notice Committee which acts as a kind of buffer between government and the Press in the most important area of information affecting national security.*

*Throughout the nineteenth century there were cases of disclosure by the Press of important government papers. In 1878 a copying clerk at the Foreign Office actually helped the Press to publish the details of a secret Anglo-Russian treaty concerning the Congress of Vienna which was then in progress; the only instrument with which to deal with him was the Larceny Act of 1861—he was charged with stealing the paper on which the secrets were written. The 1880s saw the development of much of the machinery of modern government; Whitehall grew in size and so did public interest in the many matters with which the growing army of civil servants busied themselves. In 1884 General Gordon's proclamation was published before Parliament had received it. It was a period of uncontrolled 'leaks', known as 'breaches of official confidence', some of them involving the secret designs of new warships. Official interest* at first concentrated not so much on the national damage occasioned by the leaks but on the element of disobedience involved within the civil service. In 1888 a Breach of Trust Bill was therefore introduced, and in the course of subsequent redrafting the interconnected issue of spying gained greater emphasis; the Bill turned into the Official Secrets Act, 1889, and was designed to deal with a public servant who communicated official information 'corruptly or contrary to his official duty'. In the debate which surrounded the 1889 Act, MPs expressed a fear that it might impair parliamentary control over the civil service.

In the next decades fear of espionage, particularly by German agents, grew and there were various attempts to strengthen the 1889 Act in ways which protected not merely defence secrets but the whole range of governmental information. A bill introduced in 1908 had to be dropped partly because of considerable protest by newspapers, but in 1911 a new Act was passed (with very little public discussion owing to the pressing nature of other simultaneous news events), which repealed the 1889 Act and introduced a completely new concept for which the government had been pressing—Section Two of the 1911 Act embraced the receiver as well as the thief of stolen official information. The new provision was far stronger than that entailed in the abandoned 1908 Bill, and its drafters were not aware of its potential breadth.

In 1920 a further Official Secrets Act was passed which was designed to make permanent certain provisions of the Defence of the Realm Regulations which had operated during the war, and it became clear in a test case that the newly strengthened nature of Section Two went much further than dealing with German spies; a War Office clerk was convicted of the offence of discussing an official contract with a firm of tailors, and the judge pointed out that Section Two applied to any document, secret or otherwise, which happened to pass into the hands of a servant of the Crown. There have been several efforts since 1920, as the scope of governmental information has continued to grow at an enormous rate, to limit the provisions of Section Two, and some small changes were made in an Act of 1939 which limited a provision (under Section Six of the 1920 Act) which had made it also an offence for anyone (a journalist, say) to refuse to reveal to the authorities any breach of the Act which came to his attention. The intense discussion which has *surrounded Section Two in recent years indicates how increasingly intrusive the law has been in areas of otherwise normal journalistic practice, especially in regard to the operations of the D-Notice Committee, which are explained later.*

## 29 Official Secrets Act, 1911
## SECTION TWO

*It is an offence for a Crown servant or government contractor to disclose any information he has learnt in the course of his job, either orally or in writing. The category of person involved also embraces those who have had governmental information 'entrusted in confidence' to them (the term is not defined). The main classes of official referred to comprise those holding office under Her Majesty, that is, civil servants and diplomats, ministers, all members of the judiciary and the armed forces, and all police officers; employees of the Post Office and the Atomic Energy Authority are deemed to be included under other subsequent Acts. It is not clear whether the categories include employees of government bodies on the fringes of central government, but they include all direct Crown employees down to temporary gardeners at government-run tourist sites.*

SECTION 2 OF THE OFFICIAL SECRETS ACT 1911 (*as amended*)
'Wrongful communication etc. of information

1. If any person having in his possession or control any secret official code word, or pass word, or any sketch, plan, model, article, note, document, or information which relates to or is used in a prohibited place or anything in such a place or which has been made or obtained in contravention of this Act, or which has been entrusted in confidence to him by any person holding office under Her Majesty or which he has obtained or to which he has had access owing to his position as a person who holds or has held office under Her Majesty, or as a person who holds or has held a contract made on behalf of Her Majesty or as a person who is or has been employed under a person who holds or has held such an office or contract—

(*a*) communicates the code word, pass word, sketch, plan,

model, note, document, or information to any person, other than a person to whom he is authorised to communicate it, or a person to whom it is in the interest of the State his duty to communicate it; or

(*aa*) uses the information in his possession for the benefit of any foreign Power or in any other manner prejudicial to the safety or interests of the State;

(*b*) retains the sketch, plan, model, article, note, or document in his possession or control when he has no right to retain it or when it is contrary to his duty to retain it, or fails to comply with all directions issued by lawful authority with regard to the return or disposal thereof; or

(*c*) fails to take reasonable care of, or so conducts himself as to endanger the safety of the sketch, plan, model, article, note, document, secret official code or pass word or information;

that person shall be guilty of a misdemeanour.

1A. If any person having in his possession or control any sketch, plan, model, article, note, document, or information which relates to munitions of war, communicates it directly or indirectly to any foreign Power, or in any other manner prejudicial to the safety or interests of the State, that person shall be guilty of a misdemeanour.

2. If any person receives any secret official code word, or pass word, or sketch, plan, model, article, note, document, or information, knowing, or having reasonable grounds to believe, at the time when he receives it, that the code word, pass word, sketch, plan, model, article, note, document, or information is communicated to him in contravention of this Act, he shall be guilty of a misdemeanour, unless he proves that the communication to him of the code word, pass word, sketch, plan, model, article, note, document, or information was contrary to his desire.'

SOURCE: Official Secrets Act, 1911, Section 2

## 30 Radcliffe Committee, 1962
## THE D-NOTICE SYSTEM

*The main problem occasioned for journalists and editors in the 1911 Act is that it is not clear. It is so wide in its potential application that journalists often do not know when they are in breach of it. In any case it is not always clear what matters directly impinge on national security rather than merely on political convenience.*

*In order to assist editors a Committee was set up in 1912 to provide guidance to the Press on what it might publish. During World War II, there was a system of formal censorship and in the early months of peace the Services, Press and Broadcasting Committee was brought together again, with the former chief censor, Admiral Thomson, as its Secretary. He was one of the most popular government servants with whom the Press has ever had to deal; he was conspicuous for his helpfulness and for his permanent availability; most of the controversy over the work of his committee broke out after his retirement. The Committee consists of individuals representing the Armed Services, the Foreign Office, the BBC and the Press. Their work consists in issuing 'D-Notices' or brief documents warning editors about certain stories which are circulating, publication of which might prejudice some aspect of national security. For many years Admiral Thomson himself rather than the actual D-Notices was the chief authority on these matters, and journalists took to consulting him direct rather than attempting to interpret unaided the provisions of the D-Notices.*

*A D-Notice is a request to prevent publication of information; it may refer to a specific fact or to a whole subject. Occasionally the Secretary, in a moment of emergency before the Committee can be called to issue a notice formally, may telephone the editors and publishers on his list and ask them to cooperate. The whole system in fact is a voluntary one, since no penalties exist for non-observance of D-Notices. The system has always depended on the collective willingness of the Press to comply, since the breach of a notice by any single newspaper would impose an intolerable burden on its competitors.*

*Normally a D-Notice originates within a government department, which telephones the Secretary asking him to place a D-Notice on a particular piece of information. The Secretary may advise the department to withdraw the request or alter or limit it. If he wishes to go ahead, he circulates a draft D-Notice incorporating the information to the members of the Committee and, if they approve, the notice is issued. The whole system revolves around the office of a single man, who has no statutory or judicial power and whose authority is largely based on a network of personal relationships.*

*The system was reviewed by a committee under the chairmanship of Lord Radcliffe in 1962.*

## THE VALUE OF THE D NOTICE SYSTEM

133. In our view the system makes a valuable and effective contribution to protecting from disclosure 'military' information which needs to be concealed and which it would be useful to other Powers to possess. By its operation Her Majesty's Government succeeds, year in and year out, in keeping out of newspapers, radio, and television a great deal of material which, so far as we can see, could not be kept out in any other way.

134. It is necessary to ask what practical alternative there is to maintaining a system of this kind. One must begin with recognition of the fact that in this country the Press do acquire a very considerable volume of information on secret matters which, *prima facie*, is of interest and importance to their public. This information comes from a variety of sources, often unidentifiable at any one moment, but not by any means necessarily illegitimate or reprehensible. So far as legal sanctions go, there is nothing to restrict publication except the provisions of the Official Secrets Acts, 1911–39; and these provisions, though widely drawn are, generally speaking, confined to the protection of information about 'prohibited places' and information obtained through some 'wrongful communication' by or through an official. Some that comes to the Press may originate in this way, but at any rate some may not: and in any event, it must often be impossible at the critical moment of publication for the editor himself to say whether he is within or without the

provisions of the Acts. While, therefore, their existence does serve as a general restraining influence at the back of editorial life and there is always the possibility that they might be resorted to in the case of a gross breach of security, they do not on the other hand provide a working code of what should or should not be published on any particular subject nor is there a lively expectation in the Press that in any ordinary case of publication of matters which the Government wishes to keep secret publication will be followed by a criminal prosecution. It must be taken, therefore, that the Official Secrets Acts are not an effective instrument for controlling Press publication of that kind of 'military' information of some though perhaps no great individual importance which it is nevertheless most desirable to keep from hostile intelligence.

135. Such an instrument is provided by the D Notice system and, in the absence of compulsory Press censorship or voluntary censorship supported by *ad hoc* Defence Regulations (the system that prevailed in the last war), we see no alternative to it. It appears to suit the needs of both sides. It suits the official side, because it provides a centralised and quickly working means of communicating requests and warnings to the Press before the damage is done and under the authority of a Committee upon which Press representatives are known to be in a majority. It suits the Press side because, without being mandatory, it enables an editor to know before publication that a news item is regarded by the Government as unfit for use without prejudice to the national interest—a point on which the Press are sensitive where 'military' information is concerned—and it does give him the kind of guidance in respect of matters that may be affected by the Official Secrets Acts that he would have to look for somewhere, for his own protection, if there were not D Notices to rely on. According to the evidence we heard, neither side wishes to abolish or in any substantial way to amend the present system.

136. We asked ourselves whether we could detect any danger to Government security in the use and circulation of D Notices.

The existence of the Committee and the necessity of the concurrence of the Press members before a Notice is issued means that confidential or secret information has to be shared with them. But in one form or another it is a commonplace of a newspaper man's life to be a confidential recipient of secret information, and in the context of a Committee of this nature we do not see in the practice any risk that is worth attention. The official side is well aware of the importance of restricting as much as possible the positive information contributed by a D Notice; and, at the receiving end, we did not get the impression from those we asked that the Notices were carelessly distributed in the newspaper offices.

THE FUTURE

137. We feel no hesitation therefore in recommending the continuance of the D Notice system on the present lines, provided that it can be so continued. We now address ourselves to this point, which requires consideration under two different aspects.

138. First, there is the personnel and organisation of the Committee. The official representatives have been the permanent heads of the respective Departments concerned; and this, in our view, is right. The representatives of the Press have, of course, been appointed by the various Press interests concerned. It is clearly desirable that they should be of the calibre and experience that is needed for their responsibility. Apart from emphasising this fact, we have not thought it necessary to make any positive recommendation; for, although the matter would be of the first importance if the Press as a whole were prepared to regard D Notices as necessarily binding on them by the mere fact that their form had been agreed before issue by their representatives on the Committee, this is not their attitude, and we do not think that under current conditions it is ever likely to be. It must be expected therefore that rare occasions will arise upon which some newspaper will wish to criticise in public a D Notice to which it objects in principle and we do not

think that this possibility would be eliminated even by a greater strengthening of the Press side of the Committee.

139. This consideration serves to stress further the importance of what is in our view the critical question for the future—the personality of the Secretary. It is upon the work of the Secretary and not upon what can only be very infrequent meetings of the Committee that the operation of the D Notice system depends. His work involves much more than the various procedures that lead to the issuing of a D Notice. Since in most cases such notices will not be acceptable to the Press as a whole if they are intended merely as blanket stops on a particular subject—a point which we elaborate when dealing with the D Notice of 27th July, 1961—he has to provide in himself something like a continuous advisory service of voluntary censorship so as to pass, amend, or reject copy that falls within the range of subject embraced by the Notice. This is an exacting task arising at unpredictable hours and often demanding an exercise of rapid and experienced judgment on the part of the Secretary or in other cases urgent consultation with the experts in the Department directly concerned.

SOURCE: *Security Procedures in the Public Service*, presented to Parliament April 1962 (Cmnd. 1681, pp 37–9, paras 133–9)

### 31 Radcliffe Committee, 1967
### CHAPMAN PINCHER AND THE CABLE-VETTING AFFAIR

*Admiral Thomson was succeeded as Secretary of the D-Notice Committee by Colonel 'Sammy' Lohan, around whom a* cause célèbre *developed during the 1964–70 Labour administration, and much of the vicious atmosphere in which the incident was enveloped has been attributed to an alleged personal hostility between Lohan and the Prime Minister, Harold Wilson.*

*The Defence Correspondent of the* Daily Express *received information that all overseas telegrams were being collected daily by the Defence*

*Ministry from the office of the cable companies and later returned to them after being vetted. He managed to corroborate this story through the Post Office and checked with Colonel Lohan that no D-Notice existed applying to this matter. Lohan told some Foreign Office officials that the story was in the process of publication, and Lohan was then asked to prevent publication on the grounds that Whitehall wanted the article stopped. Lohan lunched with Pincher, and showed him two D-Notices, one of which they agreed was irrelevant and one of which appeared to be marginal. Lohan requested Pincher, and through him his editor, not to publish on grounds of national security, but the* Express *decided to go ahead, despite a frantic appeal made late on the evening of publication by the Foreign Secretary, George Brown, personally to Sir Max Aitken, the paper's owner.*

*On the morning of publication Wilson denounced the* Daily Express *in the House of Commons and claimed that it had contravened two D-Notices. A Committee of Privy Councillors was set up to inquire into the matter, under the chairmanship of Lord Radcliffe, and it completely cleared the* Daily Express, *on the grounds that there was no evidence of a 'deliberate intention of evading or defying D-Notice procedure or conventions'. It recommended that the Secretary be given a deputy to share his work-load and that coordination of the work of all the departments involved be improved in a number of relatively simple ways. It thought that the basic system was a good one and should not be altered.*

65. We have come to the conclusion that there is not much in the way of alteration that can usefully be recommended for the 'D' notice system. It is not that anyone familiar with its working thinks of it as perfect or as so constructed as to offer a guarantee that mistakes or breaches will never occur. It is, after all, a voluntary arrangement, embracing a very large number of independent publications, directed to securing the suppression of certain categories of news which arise, often under great pressure of handling, in unpredictable forms and combinations. But what was emphasised to us by a number of witnesses was that, despite its imperfections, it has worked effectively for a considerable number of years, and, so far as

we could learn, its working has not been a cause of any substantial dissatisfaction to those who are party to it. This is a striking fact when it is recalled that we are speaking of a free Press which is alive to the importance of asserting its independence of Government control. It indicates a sense of responsibility and an editorial care that are very much to the credit of all concerned, and we do not think that they should go unrecorded in any Report that deals with the system.

66. It is this very fact, however, of the system's proved effectiveness that makes us reluctant to recommend any alterations in it that would impose upon it a more formal or elaborate structure, because, while they might make it look more ship-shape and water-tight on paper, we think that there is a real danger that the whole thing might break down under the added strain. And, if it did, we know of no alternative that could be put in its place. It is not difficult, for instance, to see that there would be a larger margin of protection for the security interests at stake, if some scheme were introduced for holding back items of news about which a 'D' notice dispute had arisen for some agreed period of time, to allow a 'breathing space' for further consideration, or if provision were made for some regular system of appeal to an independent arbitrator for the resolution of such disputes. Ideas of this kind were suggested to us by more than one of our witnesses.

67. On the whole we do not recommend such proposals for adoption. They seem to us to contradict the underlying assumption on which the scheme has rested, that in the last resort editorial control and responsibility remain with each individual newspaper. We believe that the scheme has worked largely because of the recognition of this principle. If, at some critical point of a dispute, the decision to publish or not to publish were to be taken out of the hands of the editor and handed over to some outside person or body, with arbitral, not editorial functtions, the nature of the system would have been fundamentally changed. This is, in our view, not to its or the public's advantage. But, even putting that objection on grounds of policy aside, we

foresee very real practical difficulties in implementing such a scheme, even if it were to be favoured by both sides of the Services, Press and Broadcasting Committee. The pressure of time in what may be a matter of competitive publication tells against the feasibility of fixing an agreed period of time for the 'breathing space'; and we have not been able to arrive at any idea which seemed convincing to ourselves as to where the independent arbitrator was to be found who would be ready to carry out at very short notice the delicate work of adjudication. Certainly, as was made plain to us, such a function cannot be discharged by the Committee itself or any one or more of its members.

SOURCE: *Report* of the Committee of Privy Councillors appointed to inquire into 'D' Notice matters, presented June 1967 (Cmnd. 3309, pp 20–1, paras 65–7)

### 32A Labour Government's White Paper
### THE RADCLIFFE REPORT 'REJECTED'

*Harold Wilson refused to accept the report of the Privy Councillors as being an accurate presentation of the issue. His government produced a White Paper at the same time as the report, which continued to denounce the* Daily Express *for sensationalism, inaccuracy and damaging the national interest. In an emergency debate called by the Opposition the Prime Minister attacked Colonel Lohan for being too friendly with journalists, Chapman Pincher in particular; Colonel Lohan, he said, had never received top security clearance and would shortly be resigning. The White Paper explained that 'The Government remain of the view . . . that the article was inaccurate in matters of fact and misleading in its treatment of the story; it was also intended to convey, and did convey, the impression that the Government were responsible for introducing new invasions of privacy or for distorting existing procedures to this end.' The government, however, accepted the recommendations for changes made in the Radcliffe Report and emphasised one specific problem embedded in the existing system.*

29. Any Government is, however, faced with a basic dilemma. On the one hand, it is impossible to draft all 'D' notices in precise and specific terms without revealing far too many of the secrets which the system was designed to protect; 'D' notices in precise terms could not, in any case, hope to give comprehensive coverage; and they might well require statutory reinforcement in the long run. This is not a situation which anyone would welcome and the Government would deplore the necessity for any movement towards stricter control. Indeed, for their part, they would much prefer that the voluntary controls which have existed for so many years should be even less restrictive. But, on the other hand, 'D' notices of a general nature can only give protection if there is complete trust on both sides. Under the present system, the Press must be prepared to accept official interpretations of the applicability of certain 'D' notices to particular cases, subject, of course, to the ultimate responsibility of an editor to take the final decision. The Government, and their predecessors, have throughout recognised that a system based on voluntary self denial makes great demands on the Press. They are, however, convinced that such a system is viable: based on the essential element of mutual trust, it has operated efficiently over a long period of years. The present incident arose mainly out of a series of avoidable misunderstandings and the failure of the *Daily Express* to inform the Secretary of its final decision to publish until it was too late for any effective further steps to be taken. In accordance with the recommendations of the Committee, therefore, the Services, Press and Broadcasting Committee will now be asked urgently to consider the desirability of rewriting the 'D' notice of 27th April, 1956, to clarify its application, bearing in mind the Committee's view that some wider restriction would be justified.

SOURCE: *The 'D' Notice System*, presented June 1967 (Cmnd. 3312, p 12, para 29)

## 32B Lord Radcliffe
## GOVERNMENT AND A FREE PRESS

*In the public discussion which surrounded the 'cable-vetting' affair there was an underlying feeling that the government of the day, and perhaps governments in general, used the procedures available for protecting national defence to protect themselves, in political terms, against the disclosure of embarrassing information about their activities. On the publication of the White Paper attacking his report, Lord Radcliffe made a speech in the House of Lords in which he drew attention to perhaps the most important issues underlying the D-Notice controversy.*

... I deprecate the idea that what is called security is the only important thing in the publicity which is indulged in by this country. In my view, security is never an absolute consideration. When we have a system of our kind, with what we believe and want to be a free Press, I think we are bound to recognise that security is one of the questions, and an important one, which always has to be weighed against others, in that free dialogue between Government and Press and people out of which our public life is built up. Therefore I think that the White Paper is on the wrong foot when it suggests, as it does from phrase to phrase, that if anybody has committed what they call a breach of security, he has done wrong.

Governments always tend to want not really a free Press, but a managed or a well-conducted Press. I do not blame them. It is part of their job. It is equally part of the job of the Press to be wary about responding to these sometimes subtle, sometimes rather obvious, inducements. Do not let us think of the Government as being powerless or ill-equipped in this issue. They have all the resources of modern public relations at their beck and call. They have all the subtle acts of pressure, the nods and the winks, the joggings of the elbow, the smile at what is called the responsible reporter and the frown at the man who does not see quite clearly the Government's point of view. There is nothing evil about this. But it is one of the conflicts that goes on between the Government—whatever Government it is—and the Press who are seeking to do their duty of telling the public the news. The Government have all these resources to play on, and they have the Official Secrets Act. If anything has been done which is not covered by that diffuse and ambiguous Act, if the Government think that that Act is not sufficiently worded to cover their true national secrets, they must face the unwelcome prospect of trying to add to it or rewording it. And they have the 'D' Notices.

What I would say about the 'D' Notices is that, by accident, they have worked on the whole very well. They have given a vast amount of protection for our national interests—I am not begging the question here—that the Government could not have got in any other way without a new Act of Parliament. But it is very important that they should not be treated as if they are guns that can be fired at the Press or instruments to be discharged at them. The tendency is always to try to make more out of the 'D' Notice system than it can possibly bear or should bear.

That is why it is said that the Press, when there is doubt, should always give way to the official view on the question of interpretation of 'D' Notices. I do not see why they should at all. The 'D' Notices are not a pattern which the Government have issued or a proprietary brand of goods. They have been produced by the Services Press and Broadcasting Committee, after the official view has been put to them as to what is needed. Sometimes they reject it; sometimes they accept it; often they reword it. I see no reason why the official view on these matters should be given a certain sacrosanct priority.

SOURCE: House of Lords, *Hansard* (6 July 1967), Session 1966–7, Vol CCLXXXIV, cols 781–3

## 33 Chapman Pincher
## PRESS FREEDOM AND NATIONAL SECURITY

*At a meeting of the Institute of Journalists in November 1967, Chapman Pincher launched into a devastating attack on the abuse of the Official Secrets Act and D-Notices by a succession of governments. 'When I joined the* Daily Express *21 years ago, the late Arthur Christiansen would never allow me to mention the D-Notice system in the paper. At first I thought that this was because the mere existence of the system was secret. In fact Chris told me that it was because he was ashamed to let his readers know that he was a willing party to any form of censorship.' The speech provided a number of examples of occasions when ministers have browbeaten newspapermen into agreeing to withhold publication of important or interesting stories. In 1958, for instance, Pincher had discovered that a swing-wing aeroplane developed by Barnes Wallis was to be cancelled; officials tried to stop publication of the information, issuing threats of prosecution under the 1911 Act; the story was published when Pincher insisted that a cancelled project could not be secret. Faults in the construction of the atomic reactors at Windscale were kept from publication when a civil servant warned the editor of the* Express *that prosecution would follow; when the faults had been corrected, the civil servant boasted to Pincher that no prosecution could legally have followed. Perhaps the most important section of the speech dealt with the way in which newspapers are too easily overborne.*

The press's main weakness is its representation on the D-Notice Committee. Again there are exceptions. Lee Howard, editor of the Daily Mirror, is one. But over the last 21 years to my knowledge the press members have been far too easily overborne by the government departments. This is not just my opinion. It is the opinion of previous chairmen of the committee —given to me after their retirement—and of the two secretaries, Admiral Thomson and Colonel Lohan—given to me while they were still in office.

It has been far too easy for the high-level representatives of

M.I.5 or the Defence Ministry to insist that suppression of certain news is essential for national security. Perhaps because of their positions, their titles and their ability, they seem to meet with inadequate resistance from the press members who should be completely convinced of the validity of every demand by discussion in detail before committing the nation's newspapers to yet another D-Notice.

One former member of the committee supported D-Notices on the grounds that his newspaper was not interested in defence scoops. Some of the members representing provincial papers have taken a similar line because they have no specialists on defence work and could never get a scoop anyway. A hand-out suits them far better.

As a result the press members have accepted several D-Notices which they should have rejected or toned down. I have already mentioned the blanket D-Notice on weapons which was modified after protest. But the worst in my opinion is the latest. After all the recent battles the D-Notice press members have tamely accepted two new notices which give the Government coverage it has been trying to get for years. A requirement to get the D-Notice secretary's advice before reporting on and developing statements made in the foreign press which may be damaging to British Intelligence departments is the most outrageous.

Surely it is a basic tenet of press freedom that *anything* reported in foreign newspapers can be reprinted in Britain if editors so decide. These D-Notices argue against this on the flimsy ground that reproduction of such foreign press reports by British newspapers gives extra credence to the reports, which may have been planted for subversive purposes. Perhaps we are expected to be grateful for the compliment. But I see it as an insult to the ability of our foreign correspondents to check on these reports before filing them and to the integrity of editors in deciding whether to print them.

This Whitehall argument is by no means new. But this is the first time it has been accepted by the D-Notice press members and enshrined in a D-Notice.

Whitehall's success in achieving this must have convinced the Prime Minister that he need never be scared of newspapers. Beat them about the head enough and they will take anything.

I maintain that the onus is on those who insist on secrecy to justify *each* case completely, either to the reporter, his editor or the D-Notice press members. Instead the attitude today is, 'Its' secret because we say so.' Unless this is rigorously resisted, the 'D' for Defence in the D-Notices will soon be changed to 'G' —for Government.

SOURCE: *Journalism Today (Proc of the Institute of Journalists)*, Vol 1, No 2 (Spring 1968), 49–50

## 34 Biafran Secrets Trial
## MR JUSTICE CAULFIELD'S SUMMING UP

*Shortly before the end of the Biafran War in early 1970 a report was written by Colonel Scott of the British High Commission in Lagos which showed, among other things, how misleading the Labour Government and its Foreign Secretary, Michael Stewart, had been in their information to Parliament about the nature of Britain's supply of arms to the Federal Government. It was, in the hands of any influential supporter of the Biafran cause, political dynamite.*

*A copy of the report had been given to Colonel Cairns, who served on the international group of military observers, and he in turn had shown it to a previous member of that team who happened to live in Yorkshire close to a constituency where the prospective Conservative candidate was a journalist named Jonathan Aitken. Aitken had the document copied and sent to the* Sunday Telegraph, *which published it in early January when the Biafran forces were in their final retreat. While other newspapers dealt with the dramatic news of the day, the* Sunday Telegraph *concentrated on the details of the Scott Report, which covered the whole conduct of the war. Hugh Fraser, a Conservative MP who was a friend of Aitken and a passionate supporter of the Biafran cause as well as a former Secretary of State for Air, helped to get the Scott Report published. A year later the newspaper publisher, its* editor, Aitken and Cairns were prosecuted under Section Two of the *Official Secrets Act*; in February 1971 all were acquitted after a summing-up by Mr Justice Caulfield in which he argued for the replacement of Section Two by provisions easier of comprehension. His summing-up became a locus classicus *of the general public discussion of Section Two.*

The 1911 Act achieves its sixtieth birthday on August 22 this year. This case, if it does nothing more, may well alert those who govern us at least to consider, if they have time, whether or not Section Two of this Act has reached retirement age and should be pensioned off, being replaced by a section that will enable men like Colonel Cairns, Mr. Aitken and Mr. Roberts to determine without any great difficulty whether a communication by any one of them of a certain piece of information originating from an official source, and not concerned in the slightest with national security, is going to place them in peril of being enclosed in a dock and facing a criminal charge . . . It may well be during the course of this case you have said to yourselves, 'Well, really, we can't see the wood for the trees'. Members of the jury, you might pause and ask yourselves whether there are any trees there at all, and what you might have seen, when you look at the whole of the evidence and what you have been told in this case, is that really there is only a desert. It is a barren waste; this prosecution perhaps has been put before you in this way: that once a document emanating from an official source is stamped 'confidential' anybody who handles the document is breaking the law. I hope I have explained to you in my directions in law that that is not the law.

SOURCE: Mr Justice Caulfield (13 February 1971)

## 35 Jonathan Aitken
## AN ATTACK ON A 'LAW IN DISREPUTE'

*One of the casualties of the Scott Report affair was Jonathan Aitken's immediate political career; he had to resign as prospective Parliamentary candidate for Thirsk and Malden, and he set to work to write a book describing the origins and the increasingly hampering nature of the Official Secrets Act; he provided a detailed account of his own case, and argued that the Official Secrets Act was now a 'law in disrepute'.*

Thus by the end of the 1960s officialdom's passion for excessive secrecy was at its zenith, for by skilful use of an outdated Act of Parliament, Britain's Civil Service had developed the most enclosed system of governmental communication in the free world. This situation was particularly resented by the Press, whose journalists knew better than anyone how the Official Secrets Acts were being manipulated to thwart or stifle legitimate disclosures, and to control the flow of government information.

When it came to the enforcement of the law, successive Attorney-Generals found themselves placed in an impossible position by having to exercise a personal discretion in the dubious danger zone between prosecutions in the public interest and prosecutions in the bureaucracy's interest. Too often proceedings were instituted because the two types of interest were held to be the same, to such an extent that the Attorney-General's fiat seemed to have become the Whitehall establishment's poodle.

On a different front there were widespread anxieties about the uneven application of the law. In particular, thoughtful Parliamentarians were disturbed by the apparent immunity of politicians from Section 2 of the Official Secrets Act 1911. Above all, everyone who studied the problem of official secrecy in a democracy appreciated that the operation of Britain's law had gone too far for it was being used to prohibit activities which the original legislation had never intended to control at all.

On a ridiculous level, it could justifiably be argued that civil servants who came home to their wives and discussed what they had eaten for lunch in the office canteen were technically committing the offence of communicating official information. Another absurdity was that those sections of the 1920 Act which prohibited the 'wearing of military uniforms' were sometimes being technically infringed by teenagers buying martial finery from London boutiques such as 'I was Lord Kitchener's Valet' and wearing them (as some do and did) on political demonstrations. On a more serious level, some civil servants and politicians were certainly manipulating the law to cloak their own failures.

Mr Edward Heath summed the situation up with percipience when he said in a speech in January 1969:

> What was once a law specifically framed to counter espionage has in too many cases been used to hide facts and figures which may be inconvenient or embarrassing to the Government of the day, but which strictly speaking are not secrets at all... There is a case for a most stringent Official Secrets Act to prevent the secrets of our country being passed on to those who would make use of them to the detriment of our country. There is no case for an Act more honoured in the breach than the observance.

Yet despite such manifestations of increasing concern about the Official Secrets Acts of 1911 and 1920, there seemed little prospect of meaningful law reform in this field, for as Professor David Williams percipiently wrote in 1965: 'The irony is that while there are many people who deplore the two statutes, there are few who would repeal them.'

This seemed to be the status quo until the beginning of 1970, when there occurred an episode which was to shatter the foundations of Britain's laws on official secrecy. It was a saga which highlighted all the main grievances about the operation of the Official Secrets Acts. The threat of the law to press freedom; the inequitable abuse of the Attorney-General's discretion; the privilege of politicians; and the control of non-secret information by the Civil Service machine, all these emotive ingredients were found in abundance in the *cause célèbre* that came to be known as 'The Scott Report Affair'.

SOURCE: Jonathan Aitken. *Officially Secret* (1972), 75-6

## 36A Franks Committee
## MEMORANDUM OF THE INSTITUTE OF JOURNALISTS

*Soon after the ending of the trial of the* Sunday Telegraph *over the publication of the Scott Report, the Conservative government set up a committee under Lord Franks to explore any necessary change in the Law. The Conservative election programme of June 1970 had contained an undertaking to revise the law and the new committee had to await the completion of the trial in order to avoid prejudicing its outcome. One of the bodies which sent in evidence was the Institute of Journalists, whose memorandum describes the position of newspapers in the debate on the role of the criminal law in protecting official information.*

1. The objections of journalists to Section 2 of the Official Secrets Act 1911 are probably sufficiently well known to the Committee to need no lengthy re-statement here. Briefly they are:

(a) Any journalist who receives a piece of information—however trivial—from a public servant which he knows, or ought to know, his informant had no authority to communicate, commits a criminal offence. It follows that it is impossible for any journalist engaged in reporting or commenting on public affairs to do his job adequately without regularly committing offences—perhaps several times a day.

This is equally true of the political correspondent who ironically (in this context) is frequently the trusted recipient of ministerial confidences on matters of the gravest importance, and of the reporter on a provincial newspaper seeking information from his local police force or coastguard service. Theoretically, at least, the only way in which a journalist can avoid entirely being at peril under the Section is by relying on 'handouts' provided through the government information machine—a situation that characterises dictatorships rather than democracies.

(b) In fact, prosecution under this Section is rare and therefore a selective and—in the view of many—an arbitrary operation which can give rise to the suspicion that the Section has been invoked either to safeguard political reputations rather than the security and interests of the State, or as a vindictive act to punish unauthorised disclosures.

(c) The rarity of prosecutions was such that until the recent case involving the *Sunday Telegraph*, many journalists inclined to the view that although the Section was thoroughly unsatisfactory, administrative good sense had made it tolerable—an argument advanced for many years by successive governments to disarm criticism of the inherent defects of the Section. However, although actual prosecutions have been few, the minatory use of the Section is much more frequent and to this extent, however sensibly the Attorney General may exercise his power to authorise prosecution, it can have an inhibiting effect on the disclosure of information that the public ought to know.

(d) Officially inspired 'leaks' are now such a regular feature of governmental handling of news that the possession and use—either threatened or actual—by the government of unlimited powers to punish leaks of which they disapprove, has become even more offensive and unjust.

2. We fully accept that every government has a duty to defend the interests and security of the State and that this may be harmed by disclosure of matters other than those covered in Section 1 of the Act—obvious examples are Budget secrets, projected changes in monetary rates and certain diplomatic communications. Moreover the government is the recipient of much private information about individual citizens which it has a moral duty to keep confidential.

3. Our acceptance of the view that certain matters other than defence secrets must be protected is at first sight a justification for the all-embracing nature of Section 2, particularly

since political, economic and technological changes can produce corresponding alterations in those areas in which the security of the State may be threatened. There are, however, two objections to this argument. The first is that however hard he may try, an almost super-human detachment is needed on the part of the Attorney General not to be influenced, even unconsciously, by a regard for the convenience and reputation of his government colleagues, as distinguished from the interest of the State. The second is that however rare prosecutions may be, the mere existence of the Section in its present form makes possible its intimidatory use by officials.

4. A possible solution to the dilemma and one which would still enable a government to adapt to the changing nature of threats to security would be to amend the Section so as to permit prosecution only in cases involving 'classified' material. This is of course similar to the American system which although it may lead to the more frequent embarrassment of the government, does not appear to produce weaker State security than in Britain.

5. Obviously, for such a proposal to be acceptable, decisions on classification of material would have to be made at a very senior level and in accordance with the policy of serving the national interest rather than departmental convenience.

6. A further safeguard, and one to which we attach great importance even if no other change whatever is made to the present legislation, would be a defence available to the communicators and the recipients of information alike that the disclosure was in the public interest. We fully endorse the recommendation of the 'Justice' report of 1965: 'That it should be a defence in any prosecution under S.2 (2) of the Official Secrets Act 1911 to show that the national interest or legitimate private interests confided to the State were not likely to be harmed and that the information was received in good faith and in the public interest'. This by implication would place an onus on the prosecution to show that 'the national or legitimate private interests' referred to had been damaged and in its turn

bring into the open any abuses of the classification of material. We accept that to discharge this burden of proof adequately might entail disclosure to the Courts of legitimately secret information and it might be necessary to provide that such evidence could be heard in camera by the judge alone who would then be entitled to give a ruling to the jury on whether the prosecution had satisfactorily proved its case in this respect.

7. We accept that the government, like any other employer, is entitled to expect loyalty from its employees, that the temptations to be in breach of that loyalty and the consequences of doing so are probably greater for civil servants than for most other employees. We recognise therefore that the government is fully entitled to have a strict disciplinary machinery that it can invoke against its servants. We believe that these disciplinary powers together with the provisions of the Prevention of Corruption Act 1905 should be an effective deterrent to irresponsibility on the part of public servants.

8. Summarising, we recommend that Section 2 of the Official Secrets Act 1911 be amended so that:
  (a) It refers only to the communication or receipt of official information that is classified as secret.
  (b) Classification is to be directed solely to protecting the national interest or legitimate private interests confided to the State.
  (c) It shall be a complete defence to any prosecution under the Section to show that these interests were not likely to be harmed and that the information was given or received in good faith and in the public interest; the judge shall be empowered to hear the relevant evidence in camera and in the absence of the jury and to rule on the success of the defence.

SOURCE: Home Office Departmental Committee on Section 2 of the Official Secrets Act, 1911, Volume 2. *Written Evidence* (1972), 267–9, Memorandum of the Institute of Journalists (September 1971)

## 36B Franks Committee
## THE CASE FOR CRIMINAL SANCTIONS

*In considering the argument of the journalists the Franks Committee came down against the view that, apart from actual matters of state security, no criminal law should protect the information of government from unauthorised publication. The Committee, though deciding on the replacement of Section 2, wanted to retain certain aspects of it.*

96. The second argument for removing criminal sanctions is of a more fundamental nature. It is that the use of the criminal law to restrict the publication of matters of public interest is undesirable in principle, smacking of censorship, and something to be kept to an absolute minimum. According to this viewpoint, the use of criminal law to deal with spies and traitors, as in section 1, is legitimate. The use of a voluntary system of guidance to editors on matters affecting the defence of the nation, as in the 'D' Notice system, is legitimate. But these measures are thought to cover all that is of real importance to the nation. Over the rest of the field, it is suggested, the Government may properly protect by other means what it wishes to protect, but should not use the criminal law to deal with failures in its protective measures. Those expressing such views do not generally believe that the repeal of section 2 would in practice result in any significantly increased risk of disclosures seriously damaging to the nation as a whole. The news media, they say, have a public function as well as the Government and would act responsibly by refraining from any seriously damaging disclosures of official information.

97. It seemed to us that this second argument rested upon a number of premises of doubtful validity and we discussed it closely with the representatives of organisations holding such views who came to see us. Reliance on voluntary restraint would be unsatisfactory for several reasons. There is a danger of confusing two different meanings of the word 'responsibility' —the duty to perform a particular function, and acting with

common sense and restraint. The Government and the news media should both act responsibly, in this second sense, but their duties are distinct. The constitutional responsibilities of the Government and Parliament for protecting the nation cannot be abdicated on the basis that a failure to exercise them will be made good by the responsible behaviour of others. The same degree of responsible behaviour is not, in any event, shown by all those who may publish or communicate official information. Restraint in publication varies from one kind of publication to another. Any system which covered only one class of recipients of unauthorised disclosures—the news media—would be seriously incomplete. An effective system of protection must cover damaging disclosures to whomever they are made.

98. Most advocates of the removal of criminal sanctions, however, place their main reliance on the proposition that section 1 adequately covers all matters of importance to national security. We have described in Chapter 2 the effect of section 1 and its limitations. A conviction under section 1 requires proof that the defendant acted with a particular kind of bad intention, i.e., that he had a purpose prejudicial to the safety or interests of the State. Damage to the nation, however, is not caused by bad intentions alone. It is caused when certain kinds of official information get into the wrong hands. It makes no difference whether the information reached those hands as a result of espionage or of leakage. The damage to the nation is the same in either case. The intention of the person communicating the information is irrelevant, and in any case may be difficult to prove. It follows that, whether one takes a broad or a narrow view of the kinds of official information requiring the protection of the criminal law, section 1 does not provide full protection. Effective protection requires that the law should cover leakage of information, as well as espionage.

SOURCE: Home Office Departmental Committee on Section 2 of the Official Secrets Act, 1911. Volume 1, *Report of the Committee* (1972, Cmnd. 5104, pp 39-40, paras 96-8)

### 36C Franks Committee
### PROPOSALS

*The conclusions of the Franks Committee are extremely complex. They outline a completely new procedure and list the areas of government which should be retained within the orbit of a new act, eg defence, foreign relations, currency and the reserve Cabinet documents. They also outline an additional procedure whereby relevant ministers, by labelling a document 'Confidential' or 'Secret' can provide it with a privileged cloak of non-communicability. They proposed that the categories of officials upon whom the duty of maintaining confidentiality should be imposed should be restricted to ministers, civil servants, diplomats, officers in the forces, policemen, employees of the Post Office and the Atomic Energy Authority, former members of these groups and private citizens contracted to serve under their direction.*

*The new proposals would absolve the ordinary citizen from prosecution merely for receiving official information and no prosecution at all under the new Act could be brought without the prior consent of the Director of Public Prosecutions; certain prosecutions in fact could not be brought except with the consent of the Attorney-General or the Lord Advocate in Scotland. The Franks Committee also suggested the creation of a new committee consisting of representatives of government, the Press and broadcasting to advise on questions of classification of material and provide a forum for discussion when doubt arises on publication of official information. In Part VI the report makes these points.*

275. Our main conclusion is that the present law is unsatisfactory, and that it should be changed so that criminal sanctions are retained only to protect what is of real importance.

276. Section 2 of the Official Secrets Act 1911 should be repealed, and replaced by a new statute, called the Official Information Act, which should apply only to official information which—
    (a) is classified information relating to defence or internal security, or to foreign relations, or to the currency or to

the reserves, the unauthorised disclosure of which would cause serious injury to the interests of the nation; *or*
(b) is likely to assist criminal activities or to impede law enforcement; *or*
(c) is a Cabinet document; *or*
(d) has been entrusted to the Government by a private individual or concern.

The Act should contain safeguards relating to the classification of information of the kinds mentioned in (a) above.

277. It should be an offence under the Official Information Act—
(a) for a Crown servant to communicate information to which the Act applies, contrary to his official duty;
(b) for a Government contractor or a person entrusted with official information in confidence to communicate information of one of the kinds in paragraph 276 (a), (b) and (c), otherwise than for the purposes of the contract or for which it was entrusted;
(c) for any person to communicate information of one of the kinds in paragraph 276 (a), (b) and (c), which he knows, or has reasonable ground to believe, has reached him as the result of a contravention of the Official Information Act;
(d) to communicate or use official information of any kind for purposes of private gain.

Prosecutions should require the consent of the Attorney General in the case of information of the kinds mentioned in paragraph 276 (a), (c) and (d), and of the Director of Public Prosecutions in the case of (b) and of private gain.

SOURCE: as Document 36B, pp 101-2, paras 275-7

### 37 Editorial Liaison Committee
### OPPOSITION TO THE REPORT OF THE FRANKS COMMITTEE FROM THE PRESS

*The Franks Report was considered by an Editorial Liaison Committee of three groups involved in the newspaper industry, which had itself provided the investigation with a rival set of proposals. The ELC welcomed the proposal to abandon Section 2 and to exclude the mere receipt of information as grounds for prosecution, but argued that in any new system a defence of 'publication in the public interest' should be included. (The Franks Committee had merely wanted a procedure by which the classification of any document must be reviewed before proceedings were initiated.) It was this desire on the part of the ELC that lay behind its opposition to much of the Franks Committee's line of thought.*

4. It would be as well to spell out here our profound objection to this procedure since it is the nub of our opposition to the whole report. But for this we might have given a qualified welcome to the proposal for an Official Information Act: we would certainly not have felt it necessary to raise many of the objections listed in succeeding paragraphs, where we deal with the matters likely to be included within the ambit of such an Act.

5. The Committee is quite specific: '*No court will be concerned with the effect of a disclosure on the interests of the nation.*' However, they propose, as a safeguard, that, before any prosecution can be brought, the responsible Minister shall review the classification and decide if, at the time of the disclosure, the information was properly classified, and if unauthorised disclosure would cause serious injury to the interest of the nation. If he decides affirmatively he will issue a certificate *that must be accepted by the court.*

6. It is a denial of natural justice that any Minister can thus be judge in his own case, and that the defendant should be denied the right to argue this vital point, and secure a judgement upon it from an impartial judge.

7. We find the Committee's objection to this unconvincing. The fear that it might involve the further disclosure of classified material is surely met by the power that already exists to hear 'secrets' trials in camera. Provision could be made for this to be a decision of the judge alone, and argument could take place

in the absence of a jury. Are we asked to believe that a Judge of the Supreme Court is unfit to be entrusted with State secrets, or that he is unfitted to decide the interests of the nation?

8. Some cases will be dealt with summarily. In these circumstances, a ruling could be sought (if necessary) from the Divisional Court before the hearing of the case by magistrates.

9. We believe that this proposal—to place what is essentially a judicial function in the hands of a Minister (and a Minister with departmental responsibility for the matter being challenged)—must be resisted with all the force that we command.

10. Although we broadly agree with the degrees of classification proposed by the Committee, we must state our objection to the mechanics of the operation. We appreciate the Committee's intention to restrict the matters to which the new Act would apply, we nevertheless think it undesirable that

1. The method of application of the rules on classification is to be *determined by regulations made by the Secretary of State:*

2. The Secretary of State will also determine the *level of authority* at which decisions on classification are to be taken; and

3. He will also be responsible for *periodic reviews and declassification.*

11. We believe that, to avoid ambiguity and to ensure uniformity of practice, these matters should not be dealt with by statutory instrument but should be spelt out in the principal Act.

SOURCE: Editorial Liaison Committee of the Newspaper Society, Guild of British Newspaper Editors and Newspaper Conference. *Report on the Franks Committee Report* (1973), paras 4–11

## 38 Granada Television and the D-Notice Committee
### THE SECRECY OF SECRECY

*In August 1973 an incident occurred in broadcast rather than printed journalism that shed much light on the workings of the D-Notice system, which continues in the absence of any legislation following the Report of the Franks Committee. The incident is described in an exchange of letters in* The Times *between the managing directors of Granada Television Ltd and the vice-chairman of the D-Notice Committee.*

## D NOTICE CUT IN TELEVISION PROGRAMME
*From Mr Denis Forman and Mr Alex Bernstein*
Sir, We write this letter to clear up some misunderstandings about Granada's *World in Action* programme on the Official Secrets Act transmitted on Monday, July 30.

The programme described the feeling that Section 2 of the Official Secrets Act had fallen into disrepute and it reported the views of the Franks Committee, former civil servants, editors of national newspapers and also of the Home Secretary who recently outlined his proposals for alternative legislation.

During the preparation of the programme Admiral Farnhill, Secretary of the D Notice Committee, inquired about an interview in which Mr Geoffrey McDermott, former Foreign Office Advisor to the Head of MI6, gave details of the Government communications establishment at Cheltenham and described the nature of its work. Admiral Farnhill asked us to delete the address of the establishment and one sentence relating to its functions, but acknowledged that his role was only advisory. As this information could already be deduced from magazines and books already in print, Granada decided to go ahead.

Subsequently, this matter was discussed between the Independent Broadcasting Authority and the Secretary of the D Notice Committee and Granada were asked by the IBA to delete one sentence spoken by Mr McDermott—'They invent machines, they keep them up to date, they make codes and they break codes.' Granada were asked not to make any reference in the programme to this deletion.

Granada recognizes that often in matters of security only those in charge of the nation's security forces can be in a position to make judgments. We also accept the IBA's special responsibility as a statutory body and their right to ask for any deletion in a programme.

But isn't there a special irony in this episode? Viewers watching the programme which gave the impression that Section 2 of the Official Secrets Act was moribund were unaware that the same Section of the same Act had caused the programme itself to be censored.

Yours faithfully,
DENIS FORMAN, ALEX BERNSTEIN,
Joint Managing Directors,
Granada Television Limited,
PO BOX 494, 36 Golden Square, W1.
August 7

*From Mr Windsor Clarke*
Sir, Once again a certain amount of public concern is being generated over the question of official secrets and, in particular, over the role of the Defence, Press and Broadcasting Committee (the 'D Notice Committee') in security matters. Once again the purpose and function of the D Notice Committee is being widely misinterpreted by people who ought to know better, including some writers in national newspapers and some of their editors.

The most recent examples of this have been in the case of a cut made in the television programme, *World in Action*, dealing with the Official Secrets Act, and in the disclosure of the alleged head of Britain's intelligence services.

In the interests of accuracy, of informed public comment (which I believe to be important) and of future legislation, I hope you will allow me to dispel at least some of the worst misconceptions. Especially would I like to kill once and for all the report that the D Notice Committee 'ordered a cut' in the *World in Action* programme.

First, however, it is necessary to restate that the D Notice system has nothing to do with the Official Secrets Act. This has been made plain publicly in Parliament, and in the Franks

Committee evidence and report. It has also been made plain for editors by the current general introduction to D Notices. The subject of a D Notice may or may not be covered by the Official Secrets Act. The fact that a particular item of information is not covered by a D Notice does not mean that it is not covered by the Act. The fact that an item does not contravene a D Notice might well mean in practice that a prosecution under the Official Secrets Act is highly unlikely—but that is something the editor himself has to consider, and thank heaven we have not reached the stage in this country at which the final decision to publish or not is taken by anyone but the editor.

The essence of the D Notice system is that it is voluntary. A D Notice has no force in law. It is merely a request to editors not to publish certain items of information because to do so would be likely to harm the security of the country.

If the editor is in doubt he is invited to consult the Secretary of the D Notice Committee, who is empowered to express an opinion as to whether a D Notice applies or not, but not to give a ruling either over publication or over possible application of the Official Secrets Act.

An editor can fly in the face of advice and publish in defiance of a D Notice. That editors do not do this is a tribute to their sense of responsibility. During my association with the D Notice Committee I have (with warm approval) noted one occasion on which an editor deliberately ignored the general tone of a D Notice because the facts he was dealing with were old ones, were of legitimate public interest, and had no relevance to circumstances at the time of publication. (The D Notice, however, was still perfectly valid in an up-to-date context.)

The D Notice system being voluntary, the D Notice Committee *never* orders a cut in a broadcasting programme or anything else, for the very good reason that it has no authority to order anyone to do anything. None of us in the press and broadcasting section of the committee would accept such authority if it were offered to us, and I have never detected any inclination on the part of official members of the committee to invite such authority.

The function of the committee is limited to deciding whether an official request for the issue of a D Notice on some particular subject is valid from the national security standpoint (*not national interest, which is quite different*) and, if a notice is to be issued, how it should be phrased. In practice no one, not even the Prime Minister himself, can have a D Notice issued unless there is broad agreement by the working journalists forming the press and broadcasting section of the committee. Even at a moment of crisis, an emergency D Notice cannot be issued unless three members of the press and broadcasting section agree, and then their decision must be reviewed and, if appropriate, confirmed by the full committee as soon as possible.

Furthermore, for the benefit of those people (especially in Fleet Street) who imagine that there is a queue of senior civil servants demanding a D Notice on any subject that takes their fancy, I might add that during the eight years during which I have been a member of the committee *there has not been a single request for the issue of a new D Notice*.

It would be flattering if I could say that my press and broadcasting colleagues and I had stoutly resisted all approaches. The truth is that whatever approaches there might have been from Government departments have been rejected by the official side of the committee (*the senior civil servants, no less*) as not having strength enough to call for the full committee's consideration.

What the press and broadcasting members have done is to review every D Notice that existed up to August, 1971. The result was that the number of D Notices was reduced, and those remaining were shortened, simplified and re-written in the light of changed conditions. All, after discussion and some sensible compromise on phraseology, were accepted by the official side of the committee.

This, I submit, is an honourable record of sensible cooperation between responsible press and broadcasting organizations and those departments of government concerned specifically with national security (not national interest or the convenience of politicians).

I would therefore like to make a plea to my fellow journalists in all the media, to certain members of Parliament, and to anyone else interested, to abandon the wholly erroneous notion that the D Notice Committee censors anything. On the contrary, the existence of the committee forces officialdom to make a very convincing case indeed (a case which may be disclosed to us but which, by definition, cannot normally be made public) before we will even support a *request* to editors not to publish information which could be harmful to the actual security of this country. I am sure the press and broadcasting members of the committee would not be willing to serve on any other terms.
WINDSOR CLARKE,
Vice-Chairman: Defence, Press and Broadcasting Committee,
Spokesman: Press and Broadcasting Section,
Westminster Press Limited,
PO BOX 265, Newspaper House, 8–16 Great New Street, EC4.
August 7.

SOURCE: *The Times* (8 August 1973)

## C PRIVACY

*The question of whether the individual's right to privacy should be protected constitutionally or legally has been discussed increasingly since the 1930s, when the social implications of totalitarian forms of government in Germany and the USSR started to become apparent in the more democratic areas of the world. Instruments adopted both by the United Nations and the Council of Europe embody statements on the right of the individual to live a life that is unmolested and free from investigation by governmental or corporate agencies. British law contains many provisions which partly guarantee the individual's protection from wanton intrusion—including the laws of trespass, of libel, of* habeas corpus. *Britain, however, has no general law to protect privacy as such; in the United States and in many European countries there is a legal or con-*

stitutional guarantee of privacy as a right—and this has gradually acquired a certain amount of case law to back it up.

Modern society has evolved a considerable number of mechanical and administrative devices which involve intrusion; banks have to disclose certain information about their clients to the Inland Revenue, credit companies prepare dossiers on the creditworthiness of individuals without their knowledge. Computers store vast quantities of information which, if analysed, could enable the private lives of individuals to be pieced together. Then there are dozens of newly invented mechanical devices which can be used to pry and eavesdrop on people by their enemies and rivals, by the police, the tax authorities, social security officials. There has been a growing demand for legislative protection against the growing barrage of intrusion.

Only certain aspects of intrusion affect the Press. More than by any other single practice of newspapers, however, their gradually worsening public image has been caused by their use of techniques of intrusion. Newspapers have earned a great deal of abuse for publishing photographs of individuals taken unawares in moments of private grief or indeed in moments when they were committing crimes. The development of investigative journalism in the last decade has brought about almost as much dismay as praise; increasingly often, modern journalism has meant that reporters have deliberately listened in to private conversations, hidden themselves to take photographs by ambush, intercepted mail, bribed doormen and servants to reveal domestic information, whether in pursuit of some scandal deserving of public revelation or merely to provide a sensational scoop.

The Press Council has handed down a series of judgements which have tended to define, though very shakily, the circumstances in which 'intrusion' is legitimate, and in what forms, and the occasions when it is to be avoided. None the less there has been a growing demand in Parliament and elsewhere that there be some form of consistent and clear legislation which might help to reassure the citizens of a modern, highly technical, publicity-ridden society that they can continue to enjoy, to some extent at least, the right to live their lives in privacy.

## 39 'Justice' Report
## WHAT IS PRIVACY?

*As the issue of privacy came to be discussed in the 1960s, several sections of the legal profession began to take an interest in the problem of defining the concept of privacy; without a clear definition, it would be very difficult to proceed any further. One important attempt was made by a special committee of 'Justice', under the chairmanship of Mark Littman, QC, and Peter Carter Ruck, a solicitor with a distinguished record in the field of libel. In their report they tried to formulate the problem underlying the task of definition.*

In the course of our work, we have become increasingly aware of the difficulties which seem to beset any attempt to find a precise or logical formula which could either circumscribe the meaning of the word 'privacy' or define it exhaustively. We think that there are two underlying reasons for this. First and foremost, the notion of privacy has a substantial emotive content in that many of the things which we feel the need to preserve from the curiosity of our fellows are feelings, beliefs or matters of conduct which are themselves irrational. Secondly, the scope of privacy is governed to a considerable extent by the standards, fashions and mores of the society of which we form part, and these are subject to constant change, especially at the present time. We have therefore concluded that no purpose would be served by our making yet another attempt at developing an intellectually rigorous analysis. We prefer instead to leave the concept much as we have found it, that is as a notion about whose precise boundaries there will always be a variety of opinions, but about whose central area there will always be a large measure of agreement. At any given time, there will be certain things which almost everyone will agree ought to be part of the 'private' area which people should be allowed to preserve from the intrusion of others, subject only to the overriding interest of the community as a whole where this plainly outweighs the private right. Surrounding this central area there will always be a 'grey area' on which opinions will differ, and the extent of this grey area, as also that of the central one, is bound to vary from time to time.

SOURCE: 'Justice' Report. *Privacy and the Law* (1965), 5, para 18

## 40 Right of Privacy Bill, 1967
### AN ATTEMPT TO LEGISLATE

*There have been several private bills put before Parliament (both Houses), none of which have proceeded very far. The 'Justice' Report itself contained a draft law. One attempt, presented by Alex Lyon, MP, with a group of Labour and Liberal backbenchers in 1967, was designed to 'protect a person from any unreasonable and serious interference with his seclusion of himself, his family or his property from the public'. It leaves unanswered many major issues affecting the conduct of the Press.*

Be it enacted by the Queen's most Excellent Majesty, by and with the advice and consent of the Lords Spiritual and Temporal, and Commons, in this present Parliament assembled, and by the authority of the same, as follows:—

1. For the purposes of this Act the right of privacy shall be the right of any person to preserve the seclusion of himself, his family or his property from any other person.

2. Any person who has been subject to any serious and unreasonable infringement of his right of privacy shall have a cause of action against the offender.

3. It shall be a defence to show that—
   (*a*) the defendant did not knowingly infringe the right of privacy; or
   (*b*) where the infringement consists of any written, spoken or visual publication in a speech, newspaper, periodical, book or television or sound broadcast, the infringement was reasonably necessary to comment fairly upon a subject of reasonable public interest in which the plain-

tiff, his family or his property were directly involved; or
(c) the infringement was reasonably necessary for the conduct of the business, profession or other occupation of the defendant and he neither knew nor ought to have known that the plaintiff would object; or
(d) the plaintiff, explicitly or by his conduct, had consented to the infringement; or
(e) the defendant was acting in accordance with authority conferred upon him by statute or by any other rule of law.

4. In any action brought under this Act the Court may—
(a) award damages,
(b) grant an injunction if it appears to be just and convenient.

5. In assessing the damages which ought to be awarded for an infringement of the right of privacy, the court shall have regard to all the circumstances of the case, particularly the effect of the infringement upon the health, welfare and financial position of the plaintiff or his family and any financial gain which the defendant made as a result of the infringement.

6. Any person who knowingly derives financial benefit from an infringement of the right of privacy shall be concurrently liable with the original offender.

7. This Act may be cited as the Right of Privacy Act 1967.

SOURCE: Right of Privacy Bill, printed 8 February 1967 (Bill 181), 1–2

### 41A Younger Report on Privacy
## THE PROBLEM OF A GENERAL RIGHT

*In the early 1970s it became clear that the issues of privacy affected the work of three governmental departments more than any others—the Home Office, the Lord Chancellor's Office and the Scottish Office (the last because of the differences between the English and Scottish systems of law). These three departments accordingly set up a committee under the chairmanship of Sir Kenneth Younger, which reported in July 1972. It concluded that there would and should be no attempt to create a general right of privacy, which would have meant creating a new tort. This was one important part of its line of reasoning.*

40. It follows from this that, if a general right of privacy were to be declared, it would fall to the courts to exercise a wide discretion in applying the law. Only gradually would a body of case law grow up, giving some measure of confidence to citizens and their legal advisers about what is and what is not within the law. It is argued that the courts already exercise this sort of discretion, for instance in interpreting what is 'reasonable' in negligence cases or in assessing the defence that a statement complained of in actions for defamation is 'fair comment on a matter of public interest'. In cases of this kind where general principles are hard to lay down, trial by jury has been the traditional method of keeping the law reasonably in tune with the current values of society.

41. As against this it has seemed to us that what is 'reasonable' in respect of an intrusion into privacy may prove to involve a more complicated and subjective judgment than what is reasonable in respect of, for instance, the negligent driving of a motor car. Where in defamation cases a court has to decide what is or is not in the public interest, it is at least dealing with a situation in which a given statement is defamatory and untrue, and it is clear to the courts that such a statement will give rise to liability unless the defence of public interest is made out. But when, for instance, the right to privacy and the right to speak and publish the truth are in conflict and no guidance is given on their relative importance, it is very doubtful whether a court is an acceptable arbiter on the issue of public interest involved.

42. Even if it were, the law is a clumsy instrument for handling all but the more extreme instances of breach of privacy and it seems likely that resort to action in the courts would be fairly infrequent. While this may not in itself be a disadvantage, one result of it would be that it would take many years before

the present unsatisfactory definitions became refined by case law and in the meantime the uncertainty might lead to serious inhibitions on freedom of communication, and to the issuing of writs with the object of preventing publication, followed by the settlement of actions out of court without any clarification of the law having taken place. It is in any case questionable whether a topic which is subject to such rapid changes in social convention as privacy can suitably be regulated on the basis of case law, slowly built up, which would tend to reflect the values of an earlier period rather than of contemporary society.

43. On balance we have come to be more impressed with the risks involved in propounding a rather general law, the scope of whose impact upon other important rights seem uncertain, than we are either with the seriousness of the residual wrongs which might thereby be righted or the effectiveness of the legal remedy proposed. We are therefore inclined to rely only partly on new law and, for the rest, to count upon the varied pressures, educational, cultural and social, employed in a democratic society to persuade particular sections of the community to behave in an acceptable manner.

SOURCE: Committee on Privacy. *Report*, presented July 1972 (Cmnd. 5012, pp 11–12, paras 40–3)

## 41B Younger Report on Privacy
## PROPOSALS

*The Younger Report provided an intricate set of proposals dealing in the main with the problems of the new electronic forms of surveillance. It put forward methods for freeing people from anxiety on the grounds of intrusion into their privacy in the fields of banking, credit rating, employment, education, medicine and private detection work. In the field of journalism it placed the onus of change on the Press Council, the BBC's Programme Complaints Commission and the ITA's Complaints Review Board.*

45. The Press
   (i) One half of the membership of the Press Council should be drawn from outside the press—i.e. 'lay members'.
   (ii) The Press Council should put forward names of suitable people from whom vacancies among the lay members should be filled.
   (iii) To make the decision on who should be appointed lay members from among the names put forward by the Press Council, the Council should create an appointments commission with members independent of the press, having a varied experience of public life and enjoying good standing in the eyes of the public.
   (iv) These changes (i–iii above) should be made at an early date.
   (v) When the Press Council makes a critical adjudication the newspaper at fault should publish it with similar prominence, if possible, to that given to the original item of news.
   (vi) The Press Council should consider the possibility of providing practising journalists with a codification of its adjudications on privacy, and should keep it up to date.
   (vii) Magistrates should be readier to ask the press not to publish identities of offenders appearing before them where they are advised that the public disclosure of the offender's identity might involve a risk of severe mental disturbance to him or members of his family.

46. Broadcasting
   (i) The BBC should extend the terms of reference of its Programmes Complaints Commission to empower it to handle complaints about invasions of privacy which are alleged to have been perpetrated in the course of preparing programme material, irrespective of whether the material involved is subsequently used in a broadcast.
   (ii) The BBC should amend the procedure for the sub-

mission of complaints to the Programmes Complaints Commission by allowing it to accept a complaint if it has been raised with the Commission—and not only if it has been raised in writing with the BBC as now provided—within thirty days of the date of the programme or of the end of the series of programmes concerned.
(iii) The present members of the Programmes Complaints Commission, when making proposals to the BBC as to the mode of securing the appointment of their successors, should try to ensure a widening of the Commission's experience.
(iv) The ITA should publish the adjudications of its Complaints Review Board.
(v) The ITA should extend its Review Board procedure to commercial radio if and when the Authority takes responsibility for that new service.

SOURCE: as Document 41A, pp 13–14, paras 45–6

## 42 Harold Evans, Editor of the Sunday Times
## PRIVACY AND THE LAMBTON-JELLICOE AFFAIR

*In the summer of 1973 two ministers were obliged to resign from the government of Edward Heath because of the revelation of a number of sexual misdemeanours, involving prostitutes. The revelation was partly the work of two Sunday newspapers, the* Sunday People *and the* News of the World, *which had obtained their information in ways which had involved, among other techniques, the taking of clandestine photographs. A great deal of discussion raged around the ethics of the newspapers involved and the Editor of the* Sunday Times *published an important article which attempted to weigh the social value of the revelation of important public information against the right of every individual to a private life.*

What would the British public think of an editor who bought a girl of 13 for prostitution and took her into a London brothel where he posed as a dirty old man? We do not have to speculate because it happened and some time before double-mirrors, infra red cameras and bugging devices began to worry us. The editor was W. T. Stead and since his paper, the Pall Mall Gazette, was as like the News of the World as the Church Times of today his conservative-minded readers were appalled when they opened their paper on July 6, 1885, to find an account of Stead's experiences sensationally headed The Maiden Tribute of Modern Babylon. It was as if today, if he will forgive the comparison, Mr William Rees-Mogg of The Times and not the News of the World photographer had taken those wretched pictures.

There was the usual reaction: the cries of indignation were drowned only by a rush of the self-righteous to buy up the succeeding articles in the series. The judge who presided at Stead's trial—for he was accused of abduction—had pronounced views on how far editors should go with what we now call investigative journalism. 'I cannot forget,' he said, 'that you are an educated man and should have known that the law cannot be broken to promote any good or supposed good, and that the sanctity of private life cannot be invaded for the furtherance of views of an individual who, I am inclined to think, believes that the end justifies the means.' Stead soon found himself in convict dress at the beginning of a jail sentence of two months and seven days.

And yet Stead had performed one of the most signal services in the history of journalism. A white slave traffic was a concealed commonplace of Victorian London. Girls were sold to rich men for seduction. The day after a girl passed her 13th birthday she had reached 'the age of consent' and could easily be procured for prostitution if there was some kind of evidence that she had agreed. If she was inveigled into a brothel her consent was assumed, yet a draft Bill attacking the scandal by raising the age of consent to 16 seemed doomed in that complacent and hypocritical society. Stead decided to shock it by proving how easy procuring was (while also making elaborate plans with the Salvation Army to protect the girl). He bought a girl from her mother for £3. He went 'disguised,' as he put it, 'into the lowest haunts of criminal vice.' He succeeded. Four days after his first article the reform Bill was sped on its way to law. Only a technical error made him open to the charge of abduction which the Attorney-General seized with relish.

What Stead did disgusted the public as much as the News of the World's sneak pictures. He was denounced by the rest of the Press; W. H. Smith & Sons banned his paper; advertisers cancelled bookings; a hostile crowd threatened to storm his offices. Yet right was on Stead's side, it seems to me, as much as it is against the News of the World, and against the Sunday People to a lesser extent.

If I am correct the comparison provides us, in the confused debate about privacy and the Press, with a double test for the limits of legitimate journalism. The public good must be proportionate to the methods of inquiry and disclosure. This will disappoint those who seek a quick salve for public wounds in a new code of conduct for the Press. We can, from our experience, rough out some general principles and I will, from mine, indicate some which guide me and my colleagues. But only at risk to the value of true information in a free society could we embrace any abstract and immutable code of conduct drawn up in the heat of today's sensation. No code by-lined even by H. G. Wells and Immanuel Kant could provide an automatic censor for the infinite permutations of privacy and public interest that will occur again and again in the unimaginable circumstances of the future. *Circumstances must determine everything.*

THE THREE QUESTIONS

There are three immediate questions. Should the News of the World have taken its secret photographs? Should the Sunday People have paid Colin Levy for these pictures? Should the Sunday People—and the rest of the Press and broadcasting—have published Norma Levy's allegations against a third

Minister? Beyond these questions loom the recommendations of the Younger Committee on privacy and the Press Council is under pressure to produce a code of conduct.

Both the immediate and long-term debate is confused because two distinct, if related, topics are mixed up. They are the role of the Press, and the means by which it fulfils its role. There is a school of thought—more sincerely held the closer one approaches any centre of power—that the Press should simply act as a conduit pipe for information which others wish to see published. When the Press comes across something else it should inform 'the authorities.' It is not a view which bears much scrutiny, for a considerable part of the duties of the Press is to act as a check on the very authorities for whom it is supposed to be a lackey. The Times, for instance, rightly decided to conduct its own inquiry into police corruption because it rightly had no confidence in the official attitude then to investigation. This is one instance among hundreds yet a good deal of the criticism of Press methods comes down, on examination, to a disbelief in its duties. One is always reminded of Northcliffe's definition —that news is what someone somewhere wants to suppress and everything else is advertising.

Deciding the public good in the Lambton-Jellicoe affair is difficult. It is because it is such a complex brew of private morals and public standards, of the freedom for an individual and the wisdom of a Minister of the Crown associating with a world flecked by crime, that it is a relief to escape into a simple denunciation of the methods of the Sunday newspapers. That does not take us far. It is more helpful in defining Press standards, and fairer to editors, if we assume that the Prime Minister was right to accept the resignations. Curiously, some of those most insistent that it was a public scandal are also among the most scornful of the Press. But if this is more honest it requires a further response. The onus is on the critics to say what they would have done to ensure that the allegation was checked and the truth not suppressed. This is the heart of the matter, but though it is more difficult to practise investigative journalism than strike moral postures, it is here that the Sunday newspapers erred. They were, on my assumption, right to investigate—but W. T. Stead did better.

He was exposing an entrenched evil, which would yield only to shock. He had to raise hell. The News of the World could not even raise Lord Lambton to confront him with its evidence. Disclosing the substance of an allegation to the subject is one of the first principles of good journalism, or fair play, which can only be disregarded in exceptional circumstances. It is no excuse that the News of the World, having been willing to wound, was afraid to strike by publication, for it gave to Colin Levy the photographs it had taken which he could have used for blackmail and which he did indeed peddle in Fleet Street. Nor was it necessary, in any event, to go into this odious business of pornographic photography. A combination of surveillance of the premises and affidavits from the Levys would have been less offensive and enough for a challenge. Divorce judges settle for that. As for the Sunday People, its real offence was shared by all the daily newspapers and BBC and ITV. It was to publish in an atmosphere reminiscent of the post-Profumo hysteria, allegations about an unnamed third Minister without independent corroboration or private confrontation with the victim.

The People is also open to criticism for paying Levy, but the Press Council principle which frowns on payments to 'persons engaged in crime or other notorious behaviour,' does concede that the public interest may sometimes warrant payment.

The trouble with all this is that the public may be induced to regard investigative journalism as electronic eavesdropping, cheques for unsavoury characters, and a claim for rights greater than the ordinary citizen's. It is nothing of the kind. The Press has no greater rights than the ordinary citizen. It has no powers comparable to the police, for instance, such as the right to search. It does not claim any such powers. Because it has made investigation its business it is equipped to exercise the ordinary citizen's rights more extensively but this does not affect the principle. And there are countervailing restrictions.

There is the law of libel, which is more rigorous in Britain than in any comparable country and which punishes any newspaper if it cannot prove what it publishes to be true. There is contempt of court. There is the Official Secrets Act; various restrictions on court reporting; and the laws on breach of confidence and copyright.

NOT GOOD ENOUGH

Within these bounds, the Press does its best—which is frequently not good enough—to monitor political decision making; to expose corruption; and to alert the public to abuse in which the police either have no interest or cannot cope. There is a large area between the actionable and the questionable. The Sunday Times would not want to claim undue credit for its part, but its article on Rachmanism in 1963 was the first detailed account of the behaviour of unscrupulous landlords. The exposure of Dr Savundra in The Sunday Times and the Daily Mail demonstrated the vulnerability of our car insurance and later articles of ours warned of the dishonesty of other firms still taking money. The list of Sunday Times business and consumer investigations stretches from pyramid-selling rackets to the multi-million pound IOS swindle by Bernard Cornfeld and his Geneva syndicate, which occupied for more than a year three talented journalists and a Queen's Counsel.

We have no kind of monopoly in social and political investigation. The treachery of Philby and the blunders which permitted it were exposed in hot competition between The Sunday Times and the Observer. It was the Guardian which disclosed how commercial spies tap state records. This week the Daily Mirror has named British firms whose goods overcome the sanctions barrier to reach Rhodesia. Most recently the Sunday Times and Daily Mail investigated thalidomide.

SET OF PRINCIPLES

Not one of these investigations involved bugging or payment to criminals (though most attracted the usual crop of unsubstantiated allegations against the conduct of the reporters). Investigative journalism by and large is a hard slog of interviews and prolonged reading and checking. In all this activity a set of principles has grown up in this office which we consider with each set of circumstances. They are not a code but tests in no order of priority, which are put in the balance with the claims of privacy and the public good.

1. The matter under investigation should be of genuine public concern.

2. The reporter should not do anything illegal, such as breaking and entering, stealing documents or other property, threatening people with physical violence, demanding money with menaces, impersonating a police officer, etc.

3. When photographing people without their permission or using recording machines nothing should be done which may not subsequently be described in the published story. These methods should be considered only when no other means are available.

4. Reporters should in general identify themselves but in some circumstances it is permissible to assume unofficial roles as members of the general public, tourists or students or so on. A reporter should not, however, impersonate a public official like a gas meter reader, to gain entry.

5. Anyone investigated should be told the findings before anything is published. Where the subject has left the country or gone to ground every effort should be made to get a message to him. Where the people named have not been challenged, this fact should be included in the published report.

6. People should not be paid sums or in such circumstances as the paper is unwilling to disclose. Payment should not be made to fugitives from justice or people engaged in hostile espionage activities.

7. Under no circumstances should anybody be given any help to break the law, such as being supplied with money or implements nor furnished with any information by which he could do something a responsible reporter would not do, e.g.,

We should not give people anything which could be used in blackmail.

8. After publication, reasonable corrections of substantiated errors should be printed. In general, a newspaper should not hit people who cannot hit back.

It is true that some exposés have required bugging which the Younger Committee would ban. The Times used secret recording devices to prove police corruption and so did The People to expose football bribery. Both, I believe, were justified because of the overwhelming public good and because, given the character of the main informant, bugging of third parties was the only safe method of proof. The Sunday Times used bugging to expose the antique ring, but both past and present editors of Insight say they would not be dismayed if the Younger ban were law. There would, and should, however, be strenuous resistance to another idea in the Younger Report, which is to define a new offence that would prevent illegal disclosure of information. This is full of dangers. There are already damages and injunctions to protect copyright and to stop disclosure for spite or commercial gain. The Press now has to prove that disclosure is in the public interest and I for one am prepared to accept this.

### WANTED: MORE DISCLOSURE

The truth is that what we need in Britain is not further sanction for secrecy but more disclosure in business and Whitehall. It is comic that I should have been cautioned under the Official Secrets Act for publishing an official paper canvassing abolition of half the railway system. It is wasteful and potentially fraudulent of the public that the information filed at Companies House is laxly filed and may be years out of date. Or that nominee shareholdings are allowed.

It is ironic that those who luxuriate in the idea that Watergate could not happen here miss the point that at stage after stage the American Press disclosures would have been made inoperative here by legal or social bars.

If my plea for pragmatism and professional standards smacks of vested interest to the reader who has been so indulgent as to have stayed the course so far, let me make two final points. The first is positive and the second is a question. I would favour legal aid for libel actions or other litigation against newspapers and broadcasting. I would favour a strengthened Press Council or university centres to vet Press performance.

But if, even with this, it is thought that the public's need to know should not rest with editors and journalists, I must ask who else is to judge? The only answer is the State since no system of controls—however ostensibly self-imposed on a Press Council pattern—can work unless it is backed by the State's power.

That is the logic of the demand for greater curbs on the Press and it rests on the notion that the Government is trustworthy in a way that newspapers and their readers are not. Those were the views which have fuelled restrictions for 200 years and which persuaded Scott to write to Lockhart when he was about to enter journalism: 'I would rather sell gin to poor people and poison them that way.' It would be intolerable if we allowed ourselves to drift back to that attitude of mind by the incidental misdemeanours in photographing a tart.

SOURCE: Harold Evans. 'Privacy and Journalism—striking the balance', *Sunday Times* (10 June 1973)

## D  LIBEL

*Of all the constraints involved in the production of newspapers there is none which is, perforce, so deeply ingrained on the professional subconscious of the British journalist as the fear of uttering libel. The laws of libel in Britain do not seem to impinge to a crippling extent on the ability of newspapers to perform their function, but the consequences of infringement even by accident can be so severe and so difficult to predict that editors and journalists since the birth of the Press have had to build into their craft a wary ability to sidestep the Defamation Act (apart from the rare occasions when libel is deliberate).*

Hundreds of years ago libel was simply a criminal offence, but compensating the victim became a regular custom and the offence gradually became the subject of mainly civil actions. Criminal libel is still an offence on the statute book and can be committed when the libel is such as to occasion, or to threaten, a breach of the peace. In practice, however, libel suits are now all civil suits. In the 1840s a Select Committee of the House of Lords considered the law of defamation and its report led to an Act of 1844 which bears the name of Lord Campbell, who has provided us with as good a definition of libel as exists, namely that it is committed when a writer publishes something which tends 'to injure or degrade the character of the person who is the object of it'. In a celebrated case of 1840 Baron Parke had provided the classic though narrower definition that libel was 'a publication without justification or lawful excuse which is calculated to injure the reputation of another by exposing him to hatred, contempt or ridicule'.

In the last century there has been only one large-scale effort to reform the law, which was when the Porter Committee was set up in 1939; this committee reported finally, after its work was interrupted by the war, in 1948 and its recommendations led to the Defamation Act of 1952. This Act brought radio and television broadcasting into the scope of libel rather than slander (which meant that a victim could claim damages without having to prove special actual damage) and made one or two changes to reduce the liability for damages of persons who commit libel innocently.

In British law anything which defames can be the subject of litigation, but journalists are free to report material severely critical of an individual if it is covered by absolute privilege, that is, if it is a fair report of something which has occurred in a judicial proceeding within this country. The journalist enjoys qualified privilege if his report accurately represents a proceeding in Parliament or in one of the international organisations such as the United Nations, or if he is reporting a public inquiry or even a public meeting; so long as the newspaper prints the material without 'malice' and is willing to print a letter or statement 'by way of explanation or contradiction', then a journalist is safe in reporting defamatory matter which has been originally presented in a forum eligible for qualified privilege. In any case a newspaper can claim 'justification' of a statement or that a particular passage is 'fair comment', if it contains no errors of fact and has not been motivated by malice and deals with a subject of genuine public interest. Journalists have to beware of libelling through innuendo, that is of describing someone in terms which, though harmless, can carry some special additional meaning for readers who are aware of some additional set of facts.

Despite the safeguards which protect a journalist, in many areas of work there are subjects which it is very difficult to tackle in British newspapers; businessmen can sue successfully if their interests are materially damaged even by material which is true in fact, and great care has to be taken in describing faulty merchandise or bad building, even if it has led to a disaster of some kind. People in public life cannot be attacked on the grounds of their constitutional unfitness to hold a specific office, although their conduct of that office is of course fair game for comment. (Lord Goodman, and the New Statesman magazine, have been pressing for specific reform of the defamation law to remove public figures from its purview.) The real difficulty with the laws of libel, as far as the Press is concerned, is the uncertainty of the jeopardy involved in any particular publication; a newspaper and its owner may be prepared to risk an action for publishing material which they believe the public should know, but in the event of their losing any action which results, the damages, which are fixed by the jury and not the judge, can sometimes be cripplingly high, sometimes surprisingly small. Northcliffe once had to pay £50,000 for libelling a soap manufacturer. The record sum awarded is £100,000. Small publications can sometimes face ruin after libel actions. It is a professional hazard, which newspaper owners try to guard themselves against as best they can, but face, occasionally with great courage, when they know it cannot be avoided. Every jury chooses its own method for assessing, in terms of cash, the intangible value of an individual reputation.

## 43 Cecil King
## NEWS AND ABUSE

*Cecil King, who was formerly Chairman of IPC, has contributed an essay to a symposium on the laws of libel in which he tries to describe the extent and nature of the restraint imposed in practice by the British libel laws.*

It is not generally understood how far-reaching the law of libel is. You may not say a subject is being held by the police: you have to say a man is at the police station 'helping the police' when in most cases he is of course doing his best not to help the police. You may not say a company is badly managed or you will be sued, probably successfully, by the managing director or chief executive. So you have to say the figures are disappointing, which is far less effective. You may not say the teachers at a school are not good enough. This may often be true but it is safer to say the classes are too big and the buildings out of date. You may not say a football team is badly trained: you have to say their performance this season has been disappointing. You may not say a professional musician is a bad violinist. You have to say he gave a disappointing performance last night. If a building falls down you may not say it was the architects' fault, however obvious this may have been. You may not hold people up to ridicule and contempt and this serves to protect from comment the monsters who appear from time to time in the news—doctors who, by over-prescribing, provide the black market with their supplies: parents who kill or maim their small children by savage beatings and so on. The mealy-mouthed reports of such events must sometimes give the impression the newspaper is sympathetic to such people. Forthright comment on men in jail is also risky. Whatever crimes a man may have committed he is deemed to have a reputation that can be damaged. If the newspaper fails to prove its case, and as I have said this is often very difficult, the damages even for a man serving a long jail sentence will be far from derisory. In book publishing the law is of course the same; yet, unlike a newspaper publisher, a book publisher has time to check his facts, eliminate defamatory adjectives and so on. On the other hand, with fiction the danger is that someone may claim to recognize himself in some disreputable character in the book and sue. Or the villain in a novel may bear some resemblance to someone the author once knew, or by pure coincidence the story of the villain may coincide with that of a man the author never knew. But the author and publisher are in trouble.

In the literature of the past open reference in unflattering terms was often made to living people and the world's fiction abounds in characters clearly based on actual living persons. If Dickens were to write his novels today he would be crippled with libel actions and injunctions. If he clearly drew his characters only from his imagination they would lack the convincing verisimilitude which is so important a part of his books. The same is true of foreign authors from Dante to Proust. If they wrote in England today they would either have to water down their creative talent or alternatively maintain a discreet silence on the living and only base their characters on persons now dead. Our libel laws have turned the old maxim on its head *de mortuis nil nisi bonum*. It is now not the dead but the living about whom only good may be said.

SOURCE: *Wicked, Wicked Libels*, edited by Michael Rubinstein (1972), 98–9

## 44 Porter Committee
## THE EXTENSION OF QUALIFIED PRIVILEGE

*The laws relating to libel are among the least frequently reconsidered provisions of British law. Between 1888 and 1952 there was no legislation in the field of libel and only one major official investigation. During this time radio and television had come into existence and the production of newspapers and the social conditions in which they are produced had changed very considerably. The composition of the reading public and its habits had also undergone a transformation. The Porter Committee's report in 1948 led to the reforms of 1952, but many of the recommendations in its thorough and extensive survey have remained the subject of continuing public discussion. It wanted to extend qualified privilege to cover all societies and associations connected with academic, artistic, professional, and commercial activities, as well as all court reports within the Commonwealth, all legislative assemblies in the world, all the new international organisations, meetings of registered companies, and meetings of committees and councils at every level of local government. The 1952 Act dealt only with certain of these. This was how the Porter Committee considered this area of the law.*

95. The defence of 'qualified privilege' which is liable to be defeated by proof that the defendant in publishing the defamatory matter complained of was actuated by malice, exists partly at common law and partly as a result of statutory provisions.

96. Speaking very broadly 'qualified privilege' at common law exists wherever the person publishing the defamatory statement (whether libel or slander) is under a duty to, or has an interest in, publishing it, and each person to whom it is published has a corresponding duty or interest in receiving it. In the course of the evidence submitted to us, little or no criticism has been directed towards this branch of the law of defamation—which is of vital everyday importance to all members of the community—and we do not recommend any change.

97. 'Qualified Privilege' as a creation of Statute exists by virtue of Section 3 of the Parliamentary Papers Act, 1840, and the Law of Libel Amendment Act, 1888.

98. Section 3 of the Act of 1840, which extends its protection to all members of the public and is not limited to 'newspapers' deals primarily with Parliamentary proceedings and Parliamentary papers. It appears to work satisfactorily in practice; it has not been the subject of any criticism in the evidence tendered to us, and we do not recommend any alteration.

99. The Law of Libel Amendment Act, 1888, applies only to 'newspapers' as defined in that Act, and has been the subject of a considerable amount of comment and criticism. The criticism, however, has been directed not to the actual opera-

tion of the Act in those cases to which it applies, but to its limitations. The consensus of opinion is that the principles and procedure laid down are satisfactory. All the proposals which have been made relate to an extension of the provisions of the Act to classes of periodicals and to categories of reports which do not at present fall within its scope.

(1) *The Definition of 'Newspaper'*

100. For the purposes of the Law of Libel Amendment Act, 1888, a 'newspaper' is defined as—

> 'any paper containing public news, intelligence, or occurrences, or any remarks or observations thereon printed for sale, and published in England or Ireland periodically, or in parts or numbers at intervals not exceeding twenty-six days between the publication of any two such papers, parts or numbers.'

101. This definition, while it includes daily, weekly and fortnightly periodicals, excludes monthlies and quarterlies as well as annuals. The purpose of the Act as a whole is to provide protection for reports of current news of public interest which may be published before its accuracy can be ensured. In limiting the protection provided by the Act to periodicals published at less than monthly intervals, it was, no doubt, assumed by Parliament in 1888, that monthlies and quarterlies would have sufficient opportunity to sift the accuracy of the facts contained in any reports published by them.

102. In our opinion, the changes in publishing methods since 1888, and the practice of monthly publications to include the most recent news falling within their sphere, have made it desirable that the protection of the Act should be extended to them. We understand that, for technical reasons in connection with dates of publication, there may at times be a five weeks' interval between two consecutive numbers of a monthly periodical.

103. We accordingly recommend that the protection given to a 'newspaper' by the Law of Libel Amendment Act, 1888,

should also be given to periodicals published at intervals not exceeding 36 days.

(2) *Reports entitled to Privilege*

104. Section 4 of the Law of Libel Amendment Act, 1888, grants qualified privilege to a fair and accurate report published in any newspaper of—

(*a*) a public meeting, i.e. any meeting *bona fide* and lawfully held for a lawful purpose, and for the furtherance or discussion of any matter of public concern, whether the admission thereto be general or restricted;

(*b*) any meeting (except where neither the public nor any newspaper reporter is admitted);

(i) of a vestry, town council, school board, board of guardians, board or local authority formed or constituted under the provisions of any Act of Parliament, or of any committee appointed by any of the above-mentioned bodies;

(ii) of any commissioners authorised to act by letters patent, Act of Parliament, warrant under the Royal Sign Manual, or other lawful warrant or authority;

(iii) of any select committees of either House of Parliament;

(iv) of justices of the peace in quarter sessions assembled for administrative or deliberative purposes.

The Act also extends qualified privilege to—

'the publication at the request of any Government Office or Department, officer of state, commissioner of police or chief constable of any notice or report issued by them for the information of the public.'

105. Apart from the fact that such privilege is liable to be defeated by malice, the Act contains the further safeguard that the defence shall not be available to a newspaper if it is proved that the defendant has been requested to insert in the newspaper in which the report or other publication complained of appeared, a reasonable letter or statement by way of contradiction or

explanation of such report or other publication, and has refused or neglected to do so.

106. The list of reports entitled to privilege which has been set out above reflects the matters which were of interest to the public at the close of the Nineteenth Century when the **Law of Libel Amendment Act, 1888**, was passed. It has been urged upon us on behalf of the Press that changes in social and administrative conditions since that date, and the increasing interest in foreign affairs, have rendered inadequate the categories of reports entitled to privilege, and that the time is now ripe for a considerable extension.

107. We agree with this suggestion. Moreover, we consider that the right to the insertion of a statement in contradiction or explanation—which corresponds to the *droit de response* existing under many Continental systems of law—is one which, though valuable in the case of reports of meetings of a local or limited character, is unsuitable and liable to abuse in the case of reports of such bodies as the United Nations or a foreign Parliament.

108. Had not the practical difficulties proved insuperable, we should have desired to add to the list of reports entitled to qualified privilege, reports of proceedings in some foreign courts. But the legal systems of the different countries of the world vary considerably and drastic changes in the character of their judicial tribunals may occur with little previous warning. Legal proceedings may be of a political character, and may take place *in absentia*. We have found it impossible to put forward any criterion of general application which could be adopted to limit and define such foreign courts as maintain a standard of justice and a method of procedure which would justify our recommending that reports of their proceedings should be entitled to qualified privilege without any *droit de response* on the part of the person defamed. Equally, we feel that it would be objectionable to grant a *droit de reponse* in such cases since, in effect, this could lead to a 're-trial' of foreign legal proceedings in an English newspaper upon necessarily inadequate material and without any of the safeguards which legal pro-

ceedings should ensure. We have accordingly felt reluctantly compelled to omit reports of foreign legal proceedings from our recommendations for the extension of the classes of reports entitled to qualified privilege.

SOURCE: *Report* of the Committee on the Law of Defamation (October 1948, Cmnd. 7536, pp 24–6, paras 95–108)

## 45 'Justice' Working Party
## THE DEFENCE OF QUALIFIED PRIVILEGE, AND THE ADMISSIBILITY OF EVIDENCE OF BAD CHARACTER

*One of the most comprehensive sets of proposals for reforming the entire range of legal restrains upon the Press is contained in the report of the joint working party of 'Justice' and the British committee of the International Press Institute, under the chairmanship of Lord Shawcross. The report came down in favour of retaining the jury system in libel cases, but proposed that the Court of Appeal be given the power to vary the amount of damages awarded. It argued that the judge should not decide whether the words in question are capable of bearing a defamatory meaning, as is the case at present, but that the jury should decide this issue without a ruling. It suggested that reports of foreign courts and parliaments should be the subject of qualified privilege. Its most important recommendations, as far as the practice of the Press is concerned, were its suggestions on extending the provisions of qualified privilege and changing the rules concerning the production of evidence of the past character of a plaintiff.*

*Special defence of qualified privilege*

119. We are concerned with the number of occasions on which newspapers have refrained from publishing matters of public interest and importance because of the fear that they might not be able to prove in a court of law what they believed to be the truth. At common law where one person, who has a recognised duty to do so, publishes a defamatory matter to a recipient, who has a recognised interest in hearing it, qualified

privilege attaches to the publication. The law does not, however, recognise that newspapers have a duty to publish matters which are of public interest and importance. Nor does the law recognise that the public has a legitimate interest in learning of such matters. We consider that the law should recognise such a duty and such an interest. *Accordingly we recommend that there should be a statutory defence of qualified privilege for newspapers in respect of the publication of matters of public interest where the publication is made in good faith without malice and is based upon evidence which might reasonably be believed to be true, provided that the defendant has published upon request a reasonable letter or statement by way of explanation or contradiction and withdrawn any inaccurate statements with an apology if appropriate to the circumstances.*

120. A somewhat different difficulty arises where, criticism not involving allegations of fact having been made of a person or institution, a newspaper feels inhibited from publishing such matter for fear of becoming liable for the repetition of a libel. The fact that such criticism has been made, irrespective of the merits of the criticism, is often a matter of public interest. Yet the plea of fair comment is not always available to a newspaper in such circumstances, for if the initial critic was actuated by malice a newspaper repeating the criticism will be liable in defamation, even though acting with the utmost responsibility and good faith in repeating the criticism. We consider that it is sometimes desirable that publicity should be given to such criticism. Where the public interest justifies publication, newspapers should be free to publish, but the person or institution criticised must be given the opportunity to reply to the criticism, and any such reply must also be published. *Accordingly we recommend that there should be a statutory defence of qualified privilege for newspapers in respect of publication of criticism made of a person or institution if the subject matter of the criticism was one of public interest, and the newspaper made the publication in good faith, provided that the newspaper if requested to do so by the person or institutions criticised has published a reasonable letter or statement by way of explanation or contradiction.*

*Offer of amends*

121. We agree with the criticism that witnesses have made of the operation of section 4 of the Defamation Act, 1952. *Accordingly we recommend that this section be amended to provide that where a defendant relies on the defence that an offer of amends was made in accordance with section 4 of the Defamation Act, 1952, the court should have power to rule that an apology made before the rejection of the offer of amends constituted satisfaction of that part of the offer which requires publication of an apology.*

*Admissibility of evidence of previous bad character*

122. We have considered the suggestion made by certain witnesses, and also by the Porter Committee, that evidence of previous bad character should be admissible in an action for defamation. We feel that it is unjust that the defendant is never entitled to adduce evidence of the plaintiff's previous bad character in mitigation of damages. The Porter Committee recommendation that a defendant upon giving due notice to the plaintiff should be entitled to rely in mitigation of damages upon specific instances of misconduct on the part of the plaintiff was not enacted in the Defamation Act, 1952. There is certainly an argument against permitting evidence of past instances of misconduct where such evidence has no relation in time or substance to the subject matter of the libel. For example, it should not be permissible having made an allegation of rape in 1965 to tender evidence in mitigation a conviction for burglary in 1947. Nonetheless we take the view that some provision should be made for such evidence to be tendered where there is a contiguity in time or substance. *Accordingly we recommend that evidence of specific known past conduct of the plaintiff, which is connected in time or substance to the statements of which the plaintiff complains, should be admissible in evidence in mitigation of damages.*

SOURCE: 'Justice' and International Press Institute: *The Law and the Press* (1965), 38–9

## 46 Lord Thomson of Fleet
## ON REFORM OF THE LIBEL LAWS

*In May 1966 Lord Tangley introduced a debate in the House of Lords on the subject of the Press and the law. During the course of this debate Lord Thomson put forward a set of proposals for reforming the libel laws in such a way as to retilt the balance towards ease of publication.*

The trouble, my Lords, as I see it, is that the law of libel too often hinders newspapers in doing their public duty, which is to make facts of public importance public knowledge. There is always a narrow balance to maintain between public duty and private right. It is fair and proper that honest individuals should have their reputations and their private lives protected from undue exposure. I am not interested in loosening the law of libel to the point of licence. I have always insisted on decent standards and fair play in my own newspapers, and I would not be speaking here to-day if I thought that anything was proposed here to-day which might enable unscrupulous people to make money out of pure sensationalism.

But, my Lords, this is not the real issue, not the real danger, to-day. It is not that we know too much about private people, but frequently we know too little about public affairs. That balance between the individual's right to privacy and the public's right to know has been tilted too far to privacy. The caprices of the law as it is administered to-day mean that too often it is not the honest man but the scoundrel who is protected —the crooked salesman, the Rachman, the fraudulent speculator, the tax evader. Newspapers have, in my view, a positive public duty to uncover facts in such instances and to make them public knowledge. The law does not recognise that duty.

Of course, a good newspaper will continue to try to do that duty, despite the difficulties and perils; and we should not exaggerate the hindrances that exist. They did not prevent the *Sunday Times*, for instance, exposing the antique dealers' ring or, more recently, the affair of the cooker that did not cook.

However, I believe there are reforms that we could safely make that would assist the newspapers to do their public duty while preserving the private individual's right to his reputation.

I will confine myself to two small reforms which could help. First, the method of trial. Again in this connection I am repeating something I have said before, but I hope with a little more emphasis. Libel actions should be tried by a judge alone. Jurors may be excellent for criminal trials where they have to give simple 'guilty' or 'not guilty' verdicts. The law of libel is, however, different. It has become so technical that it is asking too much of juries to cope with its complexities. We have recently had the celebrated case of the 'Three Little Pigs' in which the jury's verdict resulted in a judgment they had not intended. I do not want to comment on the rights or wrongs of that case; but there is no doubt that it dramatically demonstrated that even the most conscientious jury cannot grasp the technicalities of a libel case even after a fifteen-day trial and a summing-up, which ran to 26,000 words, of a judge who is an expert in the libel field. In the words of one of the jurors: 'I did not know whether I was on my head or my heels.' In the words of another: 'I think the legal mumbo-jumbo beat us'.

The result, my Lords, is that libel actions are a lottery and are apt to be decided other than on their true merits. A judge is much better qualified to deal with the technicalities, and a judge, I submit, is certainly in a much better position to fix a proper figure for damages. Juries are given no guidance at all on this in terms of actual figures. As your Lordships will know, previous awards in comparable cases cannot be mentioned to them during the course of the trial. It is not surprising, though very inhibiting for public-spirited newspapers, that in a number of cases juries have gone wildly wrong on damages. A number of them, of course, have had their awards set aside by the Court of Appeal. But this is not the answer. Since we are making judges (in the Court of Appeal) the ultimate arbiter of the rightness or wrongness of a verdict, why do we not do this in the first place? What objection can there be to that?

The consistency and fairness which should result would help newspapers without threatening anyone's rights.

The other day a libel case was brought to my notice in which damages were awarded and the foreman of the jury was asked how he had arrived at the figure for damages. He said: 'I had each member of the jury write a figure on a piece of paper; I added them up and divided by twelve—and that was the figure.' That is not a very scientific way of meting out justice.

My second point is one on the question of privilege. The Press should, in my opinion, be given clear protection for fair and accurate reports of all foreign Parliamentary and judicial proceedings. The noble Earl pointed out the dangers that that might involve; but I submit that if anyone really wanted to do something against an enemy in this country he need only sit in the House of Commons or in your Lordships' House or in a court of law and make those remarks. He would then be quite privileged. Why would he have to go to a German court or a French court? If proceedings in a foreign Parliament or foreign court are to be properly reported, surely it should be a matter of privilege for British newspapers to quote them on the same basis as they can quote proceedings in this House.

We should also consider extending that protection in a qualified way to other matters of legitimate public interest. In this country, of course, newspapers are protected from libel when they give fair and accurate reports of our courts and Parliament. With a world that is getting smaller every day I find it incredible that the same protection does not extend to reports of foreign proceedings. It is true, and I concede it, that since the case against *The Times* in 1960 these reports can be privileged in certain circumstances. But that is not enough. The privilege should be automatic. Surely it is wrong that a newspaper might have to fight an expensive action right up to this House to establish that it could safely publish fair and accurate reports of, for example, the United States Senate. Those are two reforms that I feel sure we could safely make.

My Lords, there are other areas that we should explore.

There is a case for qualified privilege for other reports of legitimate public interest. For instance, it was something of a shock for me to be told the other day that newspapers in this country might have had to pay out some thousands of pounds, or perhaps hundreds of thousands of pounds, in damages for their reports of the assassination of President Kennedy if it had ultimately turned out that Lee Oswald had survived and was innocent. Your Lordships will remember that at the time that was a question which arose; though later, I think, it was resolved to everyone's satisfaction. We published the reports that came across to us at that time, but if Lee Oswald had survived, and had been proved innocent, he could have sued all the newspapers in this country who published those reports and could have been awarded substantial damages. Surely that is not a situation which should be perpetuated. I believe—and I am sure your Lordships will agree—that the newspapers were justified in carrying that news as they did. They did not suppress the news; but they were taking a deliberate and unnecessary risk.

Whether we should go on from this, and say that newspapers should have qualified privilege for other reports published in good faith and without malice on matters of true public interest is a more controversial point. It would have to be made conditional upon publishing a reply in equal prominence; and such a change in the law would need the most careful drafting to see that we did not tilt the balance too much against the individual. At the moment, on the broad issues, I am convinced that the balance is too much against the members of the public who have a right to know.

SOURCE: House of Lords, *Hansard* (25 May 1966), Vol CCLXXIV, cols 1386–90

### E  PARLIAMENTARY PRIVILEGE

*The House of Commons enjoys an ancient right to act as a kind of supreme court of judgment on individuals (sometimes its own members) who have* been held to have jeopardised the dignity or rights of the House. Parliament (and its members when acting in that capacity) insists that it requires certain privileges, if it is to discharge its duties. An infringement of these privileges constitutes a species of contempt of Parliament analogous to contempt of court, and the House of Commons, in circumstances of alleged infringement, itself acts as judge and jury in the case. A contempt of the House can be committed simply by a member or a stranger bringing it into disrepute by appalling public behaviour, or by deliberately telling lies at a meeting of the House. Newspaper editors can be summoned to the Bar of the House and reprimanded by the Speaker if the Committee of Privileges (which holds hearings and produces recommendations on every case) finds them guilty of publishing reports of the proceedings of a committee before the official date of publication, or of misreporting a debate, or of publishing material which insults the House in such a way as to lower its credibility in the eyes of the public.

Individuals brought before the Committee of Privileges (which meets in private) can bring no legal representatives with them, nor are they allowed to cross-examine their accusers or witnesses. The sentence passed can be influenced by the general comportment of the accused when he faces the Committee. If the Committee decides a breach of privilege has been committed, the guilty individual can be obliged to appear at the Bar of the House to be publicly admonished; he can then even be imprisoned; a member of the House so summoned can be suspended or expelled from membership.

## 47 Committee of Privileges
### THE GARRY ALLIGHAN CASE

The operation of the privilege system can aptly be illustrated by a case of a fairly extreme and unusual nature which occurred in 1947. A Labour member who had formerly been news editor of the Daily Mirror published an article in World's Press News claiming that every newspaper in Fleet Street kept a list of contacts who were MPs and supplied those papers with information on private party meetings held within the precincts of the House. Some of those contacts were on retainers, some received specific sums for individual pieces of information, and others were paid in personal publicity. Allighan then wrote that the London *Evening Standard* *often carried verbatim reports of Parliamentary party meetings, supplied by such a contact.*

*The Speaker of the House decided that there was a* prima facie *case of breach of privilege and the matter was referred to the Committee of Privileges; Allighan apologised to the Committee and said that in his time as news editor of the* Daily Mirror *he had not in practice ever paid a sum of money to an MP for betraying the confidence of his colleagues. The editor of the* Evening Standard, *however, under pressure from the Attorney-General (who said that a refusal to provide full information would have to be referred to the House) agreed to reveal the name of his paper's secret contact, who was employed through a news agency; the name was Garry Allighan, who was then recalled and admitted that he himself received most of the profits of this agency and benefited to the tune of £120 per month for acting as the* Evening Standard *contact. Another member admitted to the Committee that he had supplied confidential information to the rival evening paper in London, the* Evening News.

*When the Committee's report was duly debated by the House, Allighan was expelled and the other MP reprimanded; the editors involved delivered apologies at the Bar of the House. The Committee had decided that publication of information about private party meetings was a serious breach of confidence but not of privilege. The paying of a member for information, however, was bribery and therefore a breach of privilege. In its report the Committee of Privileges endeavoured to separate the two issues of contempt of the House and breach of privilege; technically and historically these are separate offences (the latter originally involving physical molestation of members) which have become partly confused in modern times.*

14. On any view this is a case of great seriousness. It is also one of much difficulty from the point of view of the law and custom of Parliament . . . Your Committee are very mindful of the fact that Parliament has no right to extend its privileges beyond those to which recognition has already been accorded and they believe that it would be contrary to the interest both

of Parliament and of the public so to do. On the other hand the absence of an exact precedent does not in itself show that a particular matter does not come within some recognised principle of Parliamentary privilege.

15. Moreover, it is to be remembered that the right to punish for contempt is by no means restricted to the case where some actual privilege has been infringed. The two matters are distinct.

16. Whether or not the matter has by analogy some relation to the privilege that Members are entitled to be free from molestation, it has long been recognised that the publication of imputations reflecting on the dignity of the House or of any Member in his capacity as such is punishable as a contempt of Parliament. It is true that the imputation upon a Member to come within this principle must relate to something which he has done as such, that is to say incidentally to and as part of his service to Parliament. Thus in an extreme case concerning the Times in 1887, an allegation that certain Members 'draw their living . . . from the steady perpetration of crimes for which civilisation demands the gallows' was held not to constitute a contempt in that it did not refer to the action of the Members concerned in the discharge of their duties as such. Reflections upon Members, however, even where individuals are not named, may be so framed as to bring into disrepute the body to which they belong, and such reflections have therefore been treated as equivalent to reflections on the House itself. It is for the House to decide whether any particular publication constitutes such an affront to the dignity of the House or its Members in that capacity as amounts to a contempt of Parliament.

17. In modern times the practice of holding private meetings in the precincts of the Palace of Westminster of different parties has become well established and, in the view of Your Committee, it must now be taken to form a normal and every-day incident of parliamentary procedure, without which the business of Parliament could not conveniently be conducted. Those meetings held within the precincts of the Palace of

Westminster during the parliamentary session are normally attended only by Members as such and the information which is given at such meetings is, in Your Committee's view, given to those attending them in their capacity as Members. Your Committee therefore conclude on this matter that attendance of Members at a private party meeting held in the precincts of the Palace of Westminster during the parliamentary session, to discuss parliamentary matters connected with the current or future proceedings of Parliament, is attendance in their capacity of Members of Parliament. It does not, of course, follow that this conclusion attracts to such meetings all the privileges which are attracted to the transactions of Parliament as a whole.

18. It follows that an unfounded imputation in regard to such meetings involves an affront to the House as such. Your Committee consider that an unjustified allegation that Members regularly betray the confidence at private party meetings either for payment or whilst their discretion has been undermined by drink is a serious contempt.

19. Where, as here, the contempt alleged is the making of such a charge against Members, proof that the charge was true would not, in Your Committee's view, of necessity provide a defence. If the publication were intended to bring to light matters which were true so that an end might be put to them, then, however discreditable the facts, Your Committee consider that such a publication, for such a high purpose, would constitute a defence. It was not suggested the article in question here was published with any such object.

20. Whether the actual betrayal of information about a private meeting of Members held in a Committee Room of the House or its publication in the Press constitutes a distinct breach of privilege is a separate and very difficult matter. Although the publication of reports of debates is technically a breach of privilege (May 117) this rule is not now enforced in the case of *bona fide* reports. It would, it is true, be different if the House had resolved to sit in secret session; and if a Committee had resolved to transact its proceedings behind closed

doors, this decision, although it does not exclude the right of other Members of the House to attend, would no doubt result in the publication of what had taken place constituting a contempt. If the real basis of this latter rule is not that the publication involves a breach of confidence but that it involves a premature disclosure before the Committee has reported to the House, it would be difficult to draw any analogy with the private party meeting, since in the latter case no report to the House is involved and no question of premature disclosure arises. On the other hand it appears to be clear that the orders against publication of debates can be enforced where the publication is made in bad taste. Where a Member publishes confidential information to a newspaper for reward, or where a newspaper pays a Member for betraying confidential information which it proceeds to publish, it could hardly be said that either publication had been made in good faith. It is arguable, therefore, that the publication of confidential information given for or obtained by payment, about the transactions at a private party meeting, could by analogy be treated as a breach of the rule against publication of Parliamentary proceedings. In Your Committee's view, however, this would be straining the rule and this they are not inclined to do. They content themselves with observing that publication of information about secret meetings of his party by a Member clearly involves a gross breach of confidence but is not in itself a breach of privilege.

21. This, however, does not dispose of the matter. It is clearly a breach of privilege to offer a bribe or payment to a Member in order to influence him in his conduct as a Member. An obvious case would be to vote in a particular way. It would be unobjectionable to persuade a Member to exercise his vote in a particular way: it is the element of payment which gives rise to the offence. Once it is conceded, as Your Committee think it must be, that the information which Members obtain at private party meetings held as aforesaid is obtained by them in their capacity as such, it seems to Your Committee to follow

that if they sell such information, or others buy it, the transaction is still with a Member as such and the payment relates to the Member's conduct in his capacity as a Member. The information has come to him confidentially as a Member; it is only as a Member that he can part with it. In Your Committee's view, therefore, the making of a payment in order that a Member should specially note what took place at the meeting and should disclose information about it, or the acceptance of such a payment, constitutes a transaction in the nature of bribery of a Member in regard to what is part of his work in Parliament and is a breach of the privileges of this House.

SOURCE: *Report* from the Committee of Privileges (23 July 1947), pp ix–xi, paras 14–21

## 48A Select Committee on Parliamentary Privilege, 1967
### HISTORICAL ORIGINS OF PRIVILEGE

*The nature of the concept of privilege has long been subject to public and indeed Parliamentary criticism. There is a general agreement that Parliament requires special forms of protection, but many questions have been raised about the procedure involved and the extent of the privilege accorded to members in the conduct of their business. A Select Committee considered the whole system in the light of postwar practice and current discussion and reported in December 1967. The passage that follows is part of its account of the origins of the system, which goes back ultimately to the medieval unitary parliaments which operated as a kind of High Court; when the House of Commons emerged as a separate House it was not clear what 'privileges' it inherited from the former unitary Parliament. In the early fifteenth centvry the Commons demanded from the king the services of a royal serjeant of the kind who attended powerful individuals and corporations; a serjeant, bearing a mace as the symbol of his authority, had special power to arrest without warrant, collect taxes, impress men for ships etc, and the power of the Commons' Serjeant was gradually increased when Henry VIII tried to increase the status of the*

*Commons vis-à-vis the Lords. The Commons could use its Serjeant to enforce its special rights, such as protection from arrest in civil suits (which was one of the privileges of members until very recent times).*

31. The Serjeant and his mace became the authority of the Commons to commit for misconduct which the House thought worthy of punishment. It became the practice to designate those misconducts as 'breaches of privilege' and hence to invent a 'privilege', analogous to that of freedom from arrest in civil suits, the breach of which was the subject of punishment. But, as John Selden said, 'In plain truth breach of privilege is only the actual taking away of a Member of the House; the rest are offences against the House; for example, to take out process against a Parliament-man or the like'.

32. What Selden described as 'an offence against the House' is in modern terminology a 'contempt'. It is for the House to determine what is an 'offence against the House' or a 'contempt'. Having so determined, it is at liberty to send out its Serjeant to arrest the person deemed to be guilty. The Serjeant requires no authority other than his mace.

33. In more modern times the Serjeant's mace has come to be accepted as the formal corporate symbol of the authority of the House and accordingly, in order to avoid the removal of the mace from the House and hence the disruption of the proceedings of the House, the system grew up of the use of Mr. Speaker's Warrant, addressed to the Serjeant at Arms, requiring him to take persons into custody, bring them to the Bar of the House or commit them to prison.

34. On 11th December, 1962, Mr. Harold Macmillan, as Prime Minister, reported to the House that Her Majesty had informed him that in future the Crown's prerogative of appointing Serjeants at Arms would be exercised only after informal soundings had been taken from Members and their sense conveyed by Mr. Speaker to the Crown. Thus the House for the first time achieved a recognised voice in the selection of the Serjeants at Arms. However, the terms of their appointment

by the Crown require them, today as in former days, to attend upon Mr. Speaker at the time of every Parliament, but to attend upon Her Majesty's person when there is no Parliament. Accordingly, on prorogation or dissolution the Serjeant returns the mace to the Jewel House. The power of the Commons to punish by imprisonment lapses during the absences, however fleeting, of the mace, e.g. on prorogation; it is for this reason, so it has been suggested, that the period of committal by order of the House extends only to the end of the Session current at the time of committal.

35. Mr. Speaker's warrant requires all civil authorities to assist the Serjeant in executing the warrant. So far as the courts are concerned, the authorities appear to be clear that they will not interfere with the execution of a Speaker's warrant except in the unlikely event of its disclosing on its face a purported justification for its issue which could only be regarded as an arbitrary abuse of power. In other words the courts will not normally interfere with the decisions of the House as to what conduct amounts to contempt of the House. These decisions are for the House and for the House alone.

SOURCE: *Report* from the Select Committee on Parliamentary Privilege (1 December 1967), pp xii–xiii, paras 31–5

### 48B Select Committee on Parliamentary Privilege
### THE JURISDICTION OF THE HOUSE

*The Select Committee recommended that the term 'privilege' should be abolished and that in future the House should speak of its 'rights and immunities' and of 'contempt' rather than breach of privilege. Although the Committee wanted the House to retain an ultimate power to punish the obstruction of its functions, it thought that wherever a member has a possible remedy through the courts, he should no longer be allowed to use the penal jurisdiction of the House. The freedom from arrest in civil actions which members had traditionally enjoyed should be abolished.*

*In future, the Committee recommended, reporting the proceedings of the House or a committee of the House should not be capable of being a contempt if the Press (or 'strangers') have been admitted. It also wanted to remove from contempt the premature publication of how a member voted, and the contents of a Parliamentary question or notice, as also the publication of the expressed intention of a member to vote in a particular manner. This was how the Committee considered the issue of the House of Commons' future area of jurisdiction on its rights and immunities.*

36. At the commencement of each Parliament Mr. Speaker declares to the Commons: 'I have in your name and on your behalf made claim by humble Petition to Her Majesty, to all your ancient and undoubted rights and privileges, particularly to freedom of speech in debate, freedom from arrest, freedom of access to Her Majesty whenever occasion may require, and that a most favourable construction may be placed on all your proceedings.' Apart from the specific rights and freedoms referred to by Mr. Speaker, other rights and immunities have come to be recognised as part of the law and custom of Parliament, and hence of the law of the land. In some cases these rights and immunities rest upon a basis of statute, in others of custom and common law. These rights and immunities will be discussed later in this Report.

37. Your Committee commence this section of their Report by emphasising that the rights and immunities referred to in paragraph 36 should be clearly and carefully distinguished from the penal jurisdiction of the House which enables it to commit for contempt. Your Committee have already shown in paragraph 31 how the confusion between 'contempt' and so-called 'breach of privilege' arose. The confusion has continued because the breach of any of the recognised rights and immunities of the House and of its Members is capable also of being a contempt of the House; but contempts can extend far beyond the boundaries of these recognised rights and immunities.

38. Your Committee consider that the simplest and safest way of distinguishing between these two concepts is by reference

to the remedy in each case. The rights and immunities of the House and its Members will and must be enforced by the courts as part of the law of the land. Thus the right of freedom of speech with the correlative prohibition, embodied in Article 9 of the Bill of Rights, 1688 (1 Will. and Mary, Session 2, c. 2), 'that the freedom of speech and debates or proceedings in Parliament ought not to be impeached or questioned in any court or place out of Parliament' will be enforced by the courts by the grant of 'absolute privilege' in respect of words uttered by Members in debates or on other occasions which the courts hold to be 'proceedings in Parliament'. Similarly, the courts will provide remedies for the protection of each of the other recognised rights and immunities, subject to interpretation by the courts of the relevant statutory or common law provisions. The power to punish for contempt, however, is a power exercisable only by the House and it is for the House and the House alone to determine whether conduct is contemptuous. Save possibly in the exceptional case referred to in paragraph 35, the courts have no power to pronounce upon the boundaries of contempt of Parliament; they cannot punish it.

SOURCE: as Document 48A, pp xiii–xiv, paras 36–8

## F  OBSCENITY

*The development of an 'underground' Press, mainly appealing to a younger generation, has brought about a considerable literature on the subject of obscenity. A series of celebrated trials of editors of 'underground' publications and a number of publicised police actions in this field have helped to emphasise the imprecise nature of the existing legislation on obscenity. As far as the ordinary Press is concerned, however, the laws of obscenity very rarely impinge; journalists are constrained far more by the anticipated susceptibilities of their readers than by the arm of the law when they come to deal with descriptions of sexual matters.*

*The Obscene Publications Act, 1959, states in its first section: 'An article shall be deemed to be obscene if its effect or (where the article* comprises two or more distinct items) the effect of one of its items is, if taken as a whole, such as to tend to deprave and corrupt persons who are likely, having regard to all relevant circumstances, to read, see or hear the matter contained or embodied in it.' No one is clear, including the judiciary, whether depravity and corruption should be defined in terms of the effect of the material or in terms of whether it simply shocks or disgusts a significant group of citizens. The law allows the defence of justification in the public good 'on the grounds that it is of interest to science, literature, art or learning or other objects of general concern'.

In 1971 there occurred the celebrated trial of the magazine Oz in which a number of expert witnesses were called, in a (fruitless) attempt to prove that issue number 28, which had been produced by a group of schoolchildren, was not obscene. In the appeal case the Lord Chief Justice ruled that expert witnesses could only testify on the issue of public good, not on the issue of whether an article was obscene. The overall effect of the Oz case was a tightening of the law in that the final judgment included a ruling that the Press was to be separated from ordinary literary works in obscenity cases; a magazine (or newspaper) could and should be submitted to an item-by-item consideration while a book was to be treated as a whole. The Oz case also left the definition of obscenity in some confusion: a subjective definition of obscenity was upheld (in that something offensive to someone could be obscene) and this could mean that descriptions or photographs of distressing material taken from real life (e.g. pictures of warfare in newspapers) might be deemed to be obscene by some court at some future time.

## 49 Select Committee on the Obscenity Bill of 1958 SIR ALAN HERBERT'S EVIDENCE ON THE DEFINITION OF OBSCENITY

The present Act was designed in the late 1950s when the onslaught on traditional values and morals of the following decade had only just begun to evidence itself. The issue of how to separate pornography with a deliberate commercial intention from work of a literary intention was, however, even then an important one. Sir Alan Herbert, who had submitted a long memorandum to the Select Committee set up to consider the new bill, appeared in person before the committee to give verbal evidence. This was part of his questioning.

### Mr. *Simon*

744. The case as put to you, I think is where the defendant says: 'I sold this to a prostitute. I know her to be a prostitute'? ——Yes. (Sir *Alan Herbert*.) May I say, Sir, I am interested to hear these questions about 'deprave and corrupt' because I have been taking a lot of trouble in the last two days drafting a memorandum, and the main subject is these words 'deprave and corrupt' which, I think, are ridiculous, unpractical and unreal. I think my friends here have perhaps followed too dutifully the legislation of the past, and perhaps here is an opportunity for this committee to break out anew. By the way, we must not be blamed because we have followed the wording under which literature has suffered for 100 years, but let us forget that. I am anxious that the mind of the party charged should be taken into consideration, whether it is intention or knowledge, but I do not see how you can harness that in any way to 'deprave and corrupt.' Nobody ever thinks about depraving and corrupting. When I write a book I do not think: 'I am not going to corrupt.' I write a book saying: 'I must do my love scenes and my sex scenes truthfully and sincerely,' taking care, of course, and using artistic restraint, but I certainly do not think whether I am going to corrupt or deprave anybody. The thought never enters my mind or the publisher's. It is the other man you want to get after, the man who sits down and thinks—and in this memorandum I have used a good old English expression, but I am sure you will pardon it—'I want to make my readers as randy as I can, as often as I can.' That is the man you are after always. He is not bothering whether he corrupts anybody. He is frankly marketing lust, he is marketing something he knows he can sell. The problem you have to face in clause 2 is to distinguish, shall we say, between myself and the other fellow. Mr. Stevas has not had a chance to con-

sider this, so I am only committing myself. I suggest we leave out altogether in clause 2 this business about 'deprave and corrupt.' If the avoidance of corruption is the ultimate end of such legislation it might well find its place in a Preamble, but is it? Surely society, rightly or wrongly, wishes to suppress and to prevent the traffic in pornography whether the customer is already corrupt or not, as it refuses drink to a drunken man. Should we not therefore try to define obscenity, or as I prefer, pornography—and, by the way, I should like to see this Bill called the 'Pornographic Publications Bill'—by saying exactly what we mean, as the Americans do? The Americans, you see, talk about 'promoting lust' and 'appealing to prurient interest,' and Scotland talks about 'creating inordinate and lustful desires.' Very tentatively, I would suggest that 2 (a) might read thus: 'Any such matter shall be deemed to be obscene or pornographic,' and so on, 'if its dominant purpose or effect is to excite prurient interest, to provoke lustful desires' and, there if necessary you might get in 'common decency,' but I know what Mr. Stevas means. That would be a simple thing and then, of course, you could add, or not, the words about the persons to whom it is addressed. That, it seems to me, would be a simple objective test which would distinguish chaps like me from the chaps in Soho. At the moment I could be brought into the same net. This is all at the moment very tentative. I will leave this document with you. I did not mean to show it to you but Mr. Nigel Nicolson was asking questions about these particular words.

SOURCE: Minutes of Evidence taken before the Select Committee on The Obscene Publications Bill in session 1956–7, printed 20 March 1958. Evidence of 15 July 1957, 107–8

## 50 Select Committee on Obscene Publications, 1958 RECOMMENDATIONS

*The final conclusions of the Select Committee of 1958 give a good idea of the intentions behind the Act which now governs obscene publications in Britain. It was an attempt to liberalise and to clarify, which in the context of the social climate in the decade which followed the 1959 Act led inevitably to confusion and conflict.*

42. Our recommendations are:—
  (i) The test of obscenity to be applied in any statutory definition should begin with the words 'whether the matter tends to deprave and corrupt'.
  (ii) The class of persons liable to be depraved and corrupted should be defined in accordance with the explanation of the law contained in R. *v.* Secker.
  (iii) The effect of a work as a whole should be considered.
  (iv) A defence of literary or artistic merit should be afforded.
  (v) An author should have a right to be heard in criminal proceedings if he is not already a party; he should have a similar right, and a right of appeal in proceedings under the Obscene Publications Act, 1857.
  (vi) A defence should be afforded to booksellers on the lines of the proviso to section 2 (i) of the Children and Young Persons (Harmful Publications) Act, 1955.
  (vii) Penalties for a statutory offence of obscene libel.
  (viii) The consent of the Director of Public Prosecutions should be required for the initiation of proceedings.
  (ix) The trial court should be empowered to make the necessary destruction orders in the case of a successful prosecution.
  (x) The Obscene Publications Act, 1857 should be amended by omitting the requirement of proof of sale.
  (xi) Warrants under the Obscene Publications Act, 1857, should give power to seize documents relating to the business.

(xii) Warrants under the Obscene Publications Act, 1857, should enable stalls and vehicles to be searched.

(xiii) The law relating to obscene publications should be consolidated incorporating the preceding recommendations.

SOURCE: *Report* from the Select Committee on Obscene Publications, printed 20 March 1958, p xi, para 42

PART THREE

# The Principles and Practice of the Press

*It is possible to trace a continuous line of journalism in Britain for three and a half centuries; during that time journalists in each generation have been taught by journalists of a previous generation. The traditions in the printing room can even be traced visibly throughout that period. In the field of editorial practice, the professional attitudes and unofficial codes are identifiable for at least a century. Yet until modern times there has been very little codification of the rules and principles by which journalists work. A general ethic has been handed down from the grand period of Victorian journalism and a collective mythology has grown up in the newsrooms of Fleet Street, but until the last quarter century there has been no professional court, no obligatory set of rules and no special status in law for journalists. They have neither acquired special privileges as a profession nor imposed stringent requirements upon themselves, as other professional groups have done. In fact, journalism, strictly speaking, is hardly definable as a profession at all. The purpose of this section is to show how the Press Council has evolved a set of specific policies on the practice of journalism and to indicate the kind of public pressures which have led to this development.*

    *It is impossible to separate the whole area of journalistic ethics from the problems involved in the handling of sources. Does the journalist have an overriding moral duty to protect a source of information rather than assist the public processes of law and Parliament? If he does, then should he enjoy some special privilege? Is he entitled to any privilege in society not enjoyed by any other citizen?*

*If anything has enabled journalism to become a profession in the twentieth century, it is the highly organised nature of the regular sources of news; the growth of the public relations industry and the proliferation of Press officers and government information officers has made it necessary for society to acquire a specialist quasi-professional group of information sifters and recorders; journalists have in a sense become brokers between the creators of information and the public. They have become collectively an organic element in modern society; the entertainment element in journalism sustains an industry whose task it is to enable the complex governmental processes of a modern mass society to be carried on. At least, that is one theory which can be advanced to describe the role of the Press in our era, and it is a theory which explains the contemporary demand for the imposition (from within) of specific rules of professional conduct so that the public, as much as the profession, can feel its interests are protected. The public which buys newspapers is no longer choosing from an array of glittering commodities in a market place profuse with choice; in buying its newspapers the public is participating in the political and economic work of the society. If the public did not imbibe this information, the society could not function. If it ignored the advertisements, the economy could not function. The demand for the creation of a Press Council, the constant complaint against the Press for invasion of privacy, cheque-book journalism, inaccuracy, sensationalism, harassment and trivialisation is a demand for wider forms of public accountability. The purpose of this section is both to show the evolution of that demand and the steps which have been taken to meet it.*

## 51 Cecil King
## THE BEHAVIOUR OF THE PRESS

*In a lecture entitled 'The Press, the Public and the Future' given at the University of Liverpool, Cecil King set out to describe the new public demand for a 'responsible' Press and the tension which exists between Press and government in the process of acquiring the information the public needs to know.*

## THE PRESS, THE PUBLIC AND THE FUTURE

The public is rightly concerned today not only about the concentration of newspapers but also about their behaviour. Yet there is danger to the public interest arising out of this very proper concern. Because national newspapers belong to large commercial concerns, because intense competition has led some newspapers into practices which have ceased to be tolerable, because of the efforts of the press lords of the past to exceed the role they should play in society, the responsible public tends to forget today that its own liberties are bound up with the liberties of the Press.

Yet the truth of the matter is, that though newspapers may be concerned to maximize their profits, and willing to devote much of their contents to entertainment, they nevertheless retain their primary function: with all their defects, they are still the voice of the governed, the voice of the people. The instinct of government, no matter how benevolent and democratic it may be in intention, is still to conceal its blunders, to hide its scandals, to mask its inefficiencies. And what applies to government, applies to every public body down to the humblest rural council.

'Let's hope', they say, 'that the Press does not get hold of this'. Fortunately the Press often does. Without a fearless, probing, exposing, independent and uncorrupt Press, we should be far worse governed than we are. The Press may exaggerate, and, faced with official silence and obstruction, get its facts a bit wrong or out of balance; but it does bring things into the open and often compels the disclosure by authority of the inconvenient truth.

You may say that we have Her Majesty's Opposition to do just that. So we have. But the press reports are the starting point of perhaps most of the probings of the Opposition. The knowledge of 600 M.P.'s of what is going on in our society is immensely enriched by the activities of the twenty odd thousand working journalists in Britain. Without a free Press, Parliament would be gravely hampered in its attempts to keep a vigilant watch on the Executive.

Yet the Press in Britain labours under restraints, greater in their effect than those of any other democratic society. It may be that as a people we are more naturally reticent than the peoples of Western Europe and the U.S.A. It may be that we have had an hereditary establishment—of which the civil service is part—undisturbed by revolution. The fact is that British journalists have always had to fight authority to get at the facts the people are entitled to know.

There is today, it is true, an army of press officers in Whitehall. But their job is to provide the facts that the governors wish the public to know and these are not always the facts the public need to have.

This is not however to decry the government's press services. There is a vast amount of orthodox information which must be efficiently distributed. There are many routine questions to which the information officer can get a speedy answer. The provincial press and the trade press which before the war often found it impossible to penetrate civil service reserve even on orthodox regional or trade matters now receive a courteous and prompt service. The difficulties of newspapers begin when they ask for information which departments feel they would prefer to remain undisclosed. Then the information officers can become a departmental shield.

## *The Specialists*

Around some of the Ministries are clusters of specialist journalists. There is for example a corps of labour specialists who watch the activities of the Ministry of Labour and the D.E.A. Financial editors may see the Treasury collectively. The diplomatic correspondents gather around the Foreign Office. And so on. It is a convenience to the minister if he can talk, sometimes in confidence, to men who may know as much as and even more about the subject than he does himself.

But there are dangers in the system too. Though specialist journalists will defend it, their colleagues back in the office may feel that the system is too cosy and that the convenience of the group may be put before the needs of the individual newspaper. Collective newsgathering can dull individual enterprise. There is another problem the specialist has to face. If he wishes to write a bitter criticism of a department, should he stay his hand because he is dependent on the department for a flow of information obtainable nowhere else if he becomes persona non grata? That is a recurrent problem.

The most criticized institution among journalists is the Parliamentary Lobby. Before the war it was a small elite group which made severe rules for itself to ensure that ministers and members could talk in confidence about the way their minds were working. Their confidences 'in lobby terms' were printable but not attributable. In those days there was less governmental action than there is today and there were few political specialists operating on a departmental level. Today the lobby is vast—it has about 70 members, because the smaller newspapers have won the right to be represented. Individual enterprise in the lobby is practised intensively and yields valuable results. But when a minister sees the lobby collectively he has the whole of the Press at his disposal. He may send up a kite and the Press will fly it for him without involving him in any public commitment. The device has its uses. But it can be, and today often is, carried to excess.

The lobby correspondent is essentially a general practitioner of political journalism at the highest level and every specialist journalist, every commentator is dependent upon him for his essential general knowledge of what is going on at the centre. The lobby man cannot possibly have more than a general knowledge of finance, economics, defence and foreign affairs. Yet often he has to cope with specialist subjects calling for expert treatment, simply because they are the subject of a lobby confidence to which none but he or his deptuy may go.

Shrewd as he may be, he may swallow a ministerial interpretation of the facts which would make his specialist colleagues shake with cynical laughter. Worse, he cannot always effectively challenge the minister because he lacks the expert detailed knowledge which would enable him to put the critical questions. Mr. Ian Waller of the *Sunday Telegraph* writing in *Encounter* has argued that the coverage of Whitehall and politics is too diffuse and takes too little account of the post-war extension of governmental activities. He proposes that Whitehall and Parliament should be covered by teams of highly qualified specialists working together under a political editor who himself would have access to the lobby and the essential close contact with policy that this provides.

There is one more important information gap. The theory that only ministers make policy and that their civil servants are merely advisers is wearing very thin. In fact a great deal of policy is made by high civil servants who are shielded by convention from public responsibility and public criticism.

Ministers accept the praise or the odium which is the result of the acts of their chief officials, although everybody inside the Establishment knows who is really responsible for them. Has not the time come to change this convention?

SOURCE: *The Cecil King (Granada) Lectures* (1966), 96–101

## 52 National Union of Journalists
## CODE OF PROFESSIONAL CONDUCT

*The demand for a professional code originated in the National Union of Journalists in 1934. At the annual meeting of delegates of branches the Hartlepools representative submitted a motion instructing the executive to prepare a code which would be binding on members of the Union 'on the lines of those codes of behaviour enforced by other professions and trade organisations'. There was a great deal of opposition to the idea, and the Glasgow representative demanded to know whether there was any form of unprofessional conduct which could not in any case be dealt with under existing union rules. Several prominent members of the Union, however, supported the idea and a year later a draft was prepared, but referred back by the 1935 annual meeting for alterations. The version debated in 1936 was the one which eventually emerged as the official code of the NUJ. It has appeared ever since as an appendix to the Rule Book of the Union.*

Like other trade unions, formed for mutual protection and economic betterment, the National Union of Journalists desires and encourages its members to maintain good quality of workmanship and high standard of conduct.

Through years of courageous struggle for better wages and working conditions its pioneers and their successors have kept these aims in mind, and have made provision in Union rules not only for penalties on offenders, but for the guidance and financial support of members who may suffer loss of work for conforming to Union principles.

While punishment by fine, suspension or expulsion is provided for in cases of 'conduct detrimental to the interests of the Union or of the profession' any member who is victimised (Rule 20, clause (*f*)) for refusing to do work . . .'incompatible with the honour and interests of the profession,' may rely on adequate support from Union funds.

A member of the Union has two claims on his loyalty—one by his Union and one by his employer. These need not clash so long as the employer complies with the agreed Union conditions and makes no demand for forms of service incompatible with the honour of the profession or with the principles of trade unionism.

1. A member should do nothing that would bring discredit on himself, his Union, his newspaper, or his profession. He should study the rules of his Union, and should not, by commission or omission, act against the interests of the Union.

2. Unless the employer consents to a variation, a member who wishes to terminate his employment must give notice, according to agreement or professional custom.

3. No member should seek promotion or seek to obtain the position of another journalist by unfair methods.

4. A member should not, directly or indirectly, attempt to obtain for himself or anyone else any commission, regular or occasional, held by a freelance member of the Union. A member should not accept a commission normally held by a freelance member of the Union without reasonable cause.

5. It is unprofessional conduct to exploit the labour of another journalist by plagiarism, or by using his copy for linage purposes without permission.

6. Staff men who do linage work should be prepared to give up such work to conform with any pooling scheme approved by the National Executive Council, or any Union plan to provide a freelance member with a means of earning a living.

7. A member holding a staff appointment shall serve first the paper that employs him. In his own time a member is free to engage in other creative work, but he should not undertake any extra work in his rest time or holidays if by so doing he is depriving an out-of-work member of a chance to obtain employment. Any misuse of rest days—won by the Union on the sound argument that periods of recuperation are needed after strenuous hours of labour—is damaging to trade union aims for a shorter working week.

8. While a spirit of willingness to help other members should be encouraged at all times, members are under a special obligation of honour to help an unemployed member to obtain work.

9. Every journalist should treat subordinates as considerately as he would desire to be treated by his superiors.

10. Freedom in the honest collection and publication of news facts, and the rights of fair comment and criticism, are principles which every journalist should defend.

11. A journalist should fully realise his personal responsibility for everything he sends to his paper or agency. He should keep Union and professional secrets, and respect all necessary confidences regarding sources of information and private docu-

ments. He should not falsify information or documents, or distort or misrepresent facts.

12. In obtaining news or pictures, reporters and Press photographers should do nothing that will cause pain or humiliation to innocent, bereaved, or otherwise distressed persons. News, pictures, and documents should be acquired by honest methods only.

13. Every journalist should keep in mind the dangers in the laws of libel, contempt of court, and copyright. In reports of law court proceedings it is necessary to observe and practise the rule of fair play to all parties.

14. Whether for publication or suppression, the acceptance of a bribe by a journalist is one of the gravest professional offences.

15. A journalist shall not, in the performance of his professional duties, lend himself to the distortion or suppression of the truth because of advertising considerations.

SOURCE: *NUJ Rule Book*, Appendix A, 36–7

### 53 Vassall Tribunal
### PROTECTION OF THE CONFIDENTIALITY OF SOURCES

*In 1963 it was discovered that an agent of the Russian Secret Service had been working as a clerk in the Admiralty for seven years; Vassall was convicted and imprisoned, but in the course of the case a considerable number of imputations circulated in the Press of neglect or breach of duty against Admiralty officials and senior politicians. After the trial a Tribunal was held under the 1921 Tribunals of Inquiry (Evidence) Act to inquire into the whole case and to investigate all the Press reports (of which there were 250 in all). Many of the allegations turned out to be mere expressions of criticism and comment. Some were traced to their source and found to be lacking in fact. But a few remained which could not be cleared up without the Tribunal knowing the sources of the information on which they appeared to be based. 'It was to these statements that we resolved to direct our attention' said the final report (para 4, p 4) 'and to endeavour by questioning the makers as to the basis and source of their information to measure for ourselves the validity of what was said and to assess its possible implications.'*

*The investigations which followed resulted in a situation in which two journalists, by refusing to reveal their sources, ended up in gaol; their refusal was reported by the Tribunal to the High Court, the men were imprisoned but continued to withhold the names of their informants. In this section of the report, the Tribunal's reasons for its insistence on being given the evidence are set out.*

... Our only function, as we have seen it, is to try to report on the facts coming before us in the course of our inquiry, and for this purpose to examine and to accept or to reject any relevant allegations or assertions that have been brought to our attention.

15. There remained, however, certain statements of fact that had appeared in Press publications, which proved on inquiry to have been based on material supplied to reporters by their own independent sources. As to these some obstacles were presented to the full prosecution of our inquiry by the fact that, as a general rule, the journalists to whom the reports were traced objected to identifying their informants on the ground that to do so would be contrary to the dictates of their professional conscience. Since, without being able to know who these informants were and thus to examine them for ourselves, we were unable to obtain direct information and so to satisfy ourselves as to the truth or falsity of the statements made, we could not accept these claims to professional privilege except so far as the law governing the proceedings of our Tribunal would itself admit them, and this, as we understood the matter, it did not do. Consequently we were obliged to require witnesses to answer questions on these points wherever it appeared to us necessary for the purposes of our inquiry that an answer should be given.

16. We did not, however, think that we were called upon to require answers unless the situation we were faced with satis-

fied this test. Thus in a few cases we felt confident that the information we had already obtained from other reliable sources was such as to make further inquiry of no value; in others, the source which the witness was anxious to conceal appeared, when his statement was scrutinised, to have contributed nothing that could be described as information of any substance at all; or again, in one or two cases, the subject dealt with appeared to be beyond the fringe of what was relevant to the scope of our inquiry. We did not require answers in any of these cases, thinking it a proper exercise of our discretion not to do so.

17. There were in the result three journalist witnesses only who refused to give the names of their informants or, alternatively, to answer questions as to the type of source that they represented and from whom we decided that it was necessary to require answers. To be precise, one (Mr. Foster) told us that he did not know and never had known the names of the persons of whom, he said, he had made inquiries, but he refused to answer questions directed to ascertaining what type of informant they were. One (Mr. Mulholland) refused to give the names of, as we understood, two different persons of whom, he said, he had obtained information. The third (Mr. Clough) similarly refused to name the person from whom, he said, he had received material for his story.

18. All three of these gentlemen persisted in their refusal. In the case of the third (Mr. Clough), however, after proceedings in the High Court for punishment of the offence constituted by the refusal, he later identified for us the person whom he had spoken of as his informant. This was after the man in question had come forward voluntarily and been examined before us. He proved to be one of the officers employed in the Information Department of the Admiralty. We were unable to conclude from what he told us that he had in fact given Mr. Clough any confirmation of or contribution to the story we were inquiring into.

19. We have received no answers from either of the other two. Our investigation has been brought to a close therefore without

exhaustion of the lines of inquiry to which the questions put to them were directed and to that extent remains incomplete. We must record that the allegations involved which we desired to follow up were not supported by any other acceptable evidence which came into our possession and some of them were in fact contradicted by other evidence that we did obtain and are prepared to accept. Although, therefore, everything that we know of points to the conclusion that the allegations were not true, it is just because they conflict with what we have learnt that it remains of some importance to probe them and try to measure what weight, if any, can be attributed to them.

SOURCE: *Report* of the Tribunal appointed to inquire into the Vassall Case and Related Matters (April 1963, Cmnd. 2009, pp 5–6, paras 14–19)

*The report provides a verbatim account of the questioning of the journalists concerned. In this passage from the questioning of Mulholland he is asked about allegations he published concerning knowledge in the Admiralty of the homosexual practices of Vassall.*

2221. The same source told you about his career in the R.A.F., told you that he had flunked a moral leadership course, told you that his colleagues in the office knew him as 'Auntie' and told you that several of his colleagues in the office recognised him as a homosexual?——Yes.

2222. Was that in answer to questions by you?——Partly, I think.

2223. And otherwise a disclosure of information which I have just mentioned was spoken to you by the preson whom you were interviewing?—I was not interviewing him. I was just asking for information.

2224. Was it somebody at the Admiralty?——I am not prepared to say where it was from at all.

2225. Have you asked the person who appears to be a man

whether he is willing that his name should be disclosed?——
No, I have not.

2226. You realise, of course, that what you are saying affects considerably persons employed in the Admiralty and their care and knowledge? Is it not a reflection on the Admiralty generally to say that persons in the Admiralty recognise and know homosexuals and leave them in positions of trust and that a person of that sort is continued to be employed in the Admiralty, despite this knowledge of the persons working there?——I did not say anything about the people in authority in the Admiralty knowing that this man was a homosexual. I am talking about his colleagues.

*Attorney-General*: We cannot tell, can we, unless we know exactly who told you and what was the information?

My Lord, in my respectful submission, this is a material question which ought to be answered in order that proper enquiries can be made as to the extent of knowledge on this subject within the Admiralty.

*Chairman*: Yes. Mr. Cusack, you may, if you wish, say anything that suggests I should not direct the witness to answer the questions that have been put to him. I will tell you quite frankly I am proceeding on the basis that, if I had the name of this informant, it is a subject upon which I should think it proper and necessary to send for him and ask him questions about his information.

*Mr. Cusack*: My Lord, I am not going to repeat submissions which I have made when similar matters have occurred earlier. I fully appreciate the position of the Tribunal, as I am sure the Tribunal in its kindness, appreciates the position of witnesses. My Lord, I do not think that there is anything I can usefully say. It is a matter for your Lordship.

*Chairman*: I ask you because as I think you quite rightly said when a similar question arose before, each one is an individual case in which the witness has to make up his own mind.

*Mr. Cusack*: Also this, that appearing as I do for these witnesses, I have taken the view, and indeed it accords with my instructions, that each one must make up his mind as to what he says and it is not a matter for me to place before the Tribunal, even if I was in a position to do so, or place any pressure in the individual witnesses.

*Chairman*: I quite appreciate that.

*Mr. Cusack*: It is essentially, if I may say so, a matter between the Tribunal and the witness.

*Chairman*: As there is legal representation, I wanted to give you an opportunity of saying anything that you might wish to say.

*Mr. Cusack*: My Lord, I am most grateful to your Lordship for giving me this opportunity.

2227. *Chairman*: Mr. Mulholland, I direct you, therefore, as Chairman of the Tribunal, to answer the question as to the name of this informant which was put to you by the Attorney-General.——I am sorry, Sir, I am unable to do that.

*Chairman*: I shall have to indicate later what line I think it necessary to take in respect of your refusal. For the time being your cross-examination should go on.

*Attorney-General*: My Lord, perhaps it could be suggested to him that he should ask the source, who may be perfectly willing that his name should be disclosed.

2228. *Chairman*: Are you prepared to do that? I cannot make an Order on that, but are you prepared to ask this informant whether he is willing for his name to be disclosed?——No, I am not prepared, Sir; it would be a waste of time.

2229. I did not ask you whether you thought it would be a waste of time. I asked you whether you were prepared to do it.——No, I am not.

2230. *Attorney-General*: Was it the same source as the one from which you obtained the information about the girl typist and the keys?——It was one of them.

SOURCE: *Report* of the Tribunal appointed to inquire into the Vassall Case and Related Matters (April 1963, Cmnd. 2009, pp 157–8, paras 2221–30)

## 54 Scotsman
## HOW MUCH PRIVILEGE FOR THE PRESS?

*There was considerable public controversy at the time of the imprisonment of the journalists following the Vassall Tribunal. Few cases in recent years have so dramatised the problem of the confidentiality of sources and the resultant dilemma of journalists towards their apparently conflicting duties. This is a section of an article in the* Scotsman *which discussed the problem of whether journalists should enjoy special professional privilege to protect their sources.*

Though in Britain newspapermen are in no worse position than are members of other professions in regard to confidences, things are different in many other countries. The United States has no general privilege for professional secrecy, except in the relations of a lawyer and his client, but many of the individual states recognise the right of doctors and clergymen to withhold information.

Most European countries, however, specifically protect what the French call 'necessary confidants,' like doctors, public health officials, pharmacists, clergymen and others to whom secrets are entrusted because of the nature of their vocations. Indeed, it is sometimes an offence for them to reveal confidential information.

TOO LARGE A CLAIM

Should journalists be put in the same position as 'necessary confidants'? The weakness of such a claim is that journalists acquire information for a different purpose. Others have to protect the privacy of their patients, spiritual or physical. The Press seeks information to publish it, or perhaps the substance of it, for newspapers do exercise discretion. It can hardly be put on the same footing as professions which could not be exercised without uninhibited confidences.

Hard cases do not make good laws. Sympathy for journalists who follow the tradition of their profession that confidences should be preserved, whatever the consequences, is not a sufficient reason for demanding statutory protection. It would, in any event, be hard to draft a Bill, even if Parliament were willing, without making exceptions that would exclude the cases most likely to arise.

An absolute privilege against disclosure of information, even if it had a direct bearing on questions of national security, would be too large a claim. A limited privilege would be of little use, for courts rarely demand breaches of professional secrecy.

Perhaps the question of professional secrecy should be looked at like the matter of Press freedom in general. The freedom of the Press is not a privilege; it is not something which the Press as such enjoys and which is denied to ordinary persons. It is a fundamental freedom which journalists exercise in the name and in the interests of the public and which depends on the support of individuals. The abuses of Press freedom are also partly the blame of the public, who have it in their power to censure these by the effective way of ceasing to buy offending newspapers.

MUST BE EARNED

The standard of the Press depends on the tastes and interests of the public, and its rights, too, depend on public esteem. If it does its work properly and gives people the information about public affairs which they are entitled to know, even at the cost of embarrassing those in high places, it need not fear that it will be crippled by invasions of professional secrecy, even though this is not protected by law.

Confidences will be respected in practice by the discretion of courts who recognise that it is essential for the Press as an instrument of public enlightenment. For this reason the Press as an instrument of public enlightenment. For this reason the Press can claim almost complete protection for its confidential relations, without asserting that the principle of professional secrecy should override every citizen's duty to promote the security of the state.

In other words, the journalist's right of secrecy must be earned by constant proof that it is necessary for the public good as a means of exposing misgovernment, official mistakes or administrative waste and arrogance and not merely as a cover for spreading scandal and frivolous gossip.

SOURCE: *Scotsman* (9 March 1963)

## 55 John Whale
## THE PARLIAMENTARY LOBBY AND ITS SYSTEM

*One of the most important groups of journalists in the country are those who work inside the building of Parliament; their task is to report on the political affairs of the country and to do this they are given special privileged access to senior politicians, alongside whom, in a sense, they are allowed to work. Although their loyalties are to the papers they serve, they also have a collective loyalty to the organisation of the lobby, to which they must belong and to whose rules they must adhere if they are to retain their special privileges. The role of the lobby in British political journalism is subject to a certain amount of criticism. John Whale, a political journalist who has experience both of Fleet Street and broadcasting, has described the Parliamentary lobby in a book which deals with the mutual influences of newspapers and politicians.*

The clasp sometimes known as the establishment embrace is easily enough shrugged off. It gives, in any event, diminishing returns; even the most impressionable new editor realises in time that the information to be had at the dinner-tables of the great, to say nothing of the food, seldom repays the time spent taking it in. But there is a group of journalists, and not the least important, who live their whole professional lives within the arms of that embrace. They are the Lobby: the corps of political correspondents at Westminster.

All specialist correspondents are to some extent smothered by their sources. Many of them—specialists in defence, or the environment, or education, or the welfare services—get by far the largest part of their information from a single department of state. They are therefore very well aware that if they gave offence to that department, their work would become very difficult. They are susceptible to official suggestions that in the general interest a certain piece of information would be better unpublished. The more useful an acquaintance within the department, the less they will be inclined to use what he tells them, in order that he shall feel free to tell them more. But they are at any rate not generalists: they concentrate their knowledge on a given field; and they therefore have certain sieves through which to pass the official information they are fed.

Lobby men are specialists who are also generalists. They are the top generalists in the trade. Politics covers the whole of human life, and they cover politics. All reports made to the Government, all legislation promulgated by the Government, all parliamentarians and their rise and fall and their private causes, all Whitehall, all party activity—they have a big bag to rummage in. And they seldom have time to travel more than two hundred yards from New Palace Yard.

They are probably the hardest-working journalists in Fleet Street. On the rare occasions when they have nothing else to do, they stand about in the members' lobby which gives them their name—the stone-flagged ante-room to the Commons chamber, where MPs pause to collect documents and messages, and to gossip. Sometimes the lobby men have no-one to talk to except each other and the policemen: sometimes the place is like a cocktail party without the liquor, with people's eyes flickering over each other's shoulders to see who else is there. The lobby men may learn here of an early-day motion by one group of back-benchers, or an approach to the Chief Whip by another; but the real stuff of their work is not here. Increasingly, they get the word from Downing Street.

Every morning at a fixed time, and sometimes every afternoon too, they wander across Whitehall to the Prime Minister's house; and before the first hand falls on the knocker the door opens, and the doorman bows them in, and they file into the

Press Secretary's rounded office overlooking the street. He tells them the Prime Minister's engagements, and then there is a half-hour exchange of loaded badinage. On afternoons when the House is sitting, to save them the walk, the Press Secretary comes across to a little turret room in the Palace of Westminster, high above the river, with the names of past chairmen of the Lobby inscribed on the wall; and on Thursdays he brings the Leader of the House with him, and sometimes the Prime Minister; and later on the Leader of the Opposition clambers up; so the Thursday night news bulletins, and the Friday morning papers, are full of strangely concordant speculation about the Government's legislative plans and the Opposition's schemes for opposing it. It may be no more than the mechanics of political life, but lobby men have a delightful sense of being in on the marrow of it.

SOURCE: John Whale. *Journalism and Government* (1972), 77–8

## 56 THE RULES OF THE LOBBY

*The daily rules by which the Parliamentary lobby operates have been published in a study of their role by Jeremy Tunstall. Some would argue that adherence to this very strict set of all-embracing precepts tends to deprive the members of the lobby of their 'teeth', that the rules in effect 'sanitise' the lobby; on the other hand the evolution of the lobby system enables newspapers to obtain far more information about the operation of Parliament and far better access to politicians than would be possible if the politicians had no certainty that their confidence would be protected.*

*Private and confidential*
*Notes on the practice of lobby journalism.*

July 1956

LOBBY PRACTICE
The technique of Lobby journalism can be fully acquired only by experience. It is a technique which brings the journalist into

close daily touch with Ministers and Members of Parliament of all parties, and imposes on him a very high standard of responsibility and discretion in making use of the special facilities given him for writing about political affairs.

The Lobby journalist's authority to work in Parliament is the inclusion of his name in a list kept by the Serjeant at Arms for the Speaker.

There is no complete guide to Lobby practice. This book is designed to help the journalist coming into contact with Parliament for the first time, and sets out the general principles which should guide him.

*Individual lobbying*
Over a period of seventy-five years the Lobby has been under an obligation not to name informants. Moreover, experience has shown that Ministers and M.P.s talk more freely under the rule of anonymity. In any case, members of the Lobby should always take personal responsibility for their stories and their facts.

It is the Lobby correspondent's primary duty to protect his informants, and care must be taken not to reveal anything that could lead to their identification (though there are occasions, especially in connection with constituency affairs, when no objection is taken to quoting an M.P., so long as permission has been given).

Sometimes it may be right to protect your informant to the extent of not using a story at all. This has often been done in the past, and it forms one of the foundations of the good and confidential relationship between the Lobby and members of all parties.

Above all, do not use information, even if given unconditionally, if you have reason to believe that its publication may constitute a breach of Parliamentary privilege.

Again, all embargoes, whether openly stated or merely understood, must be observed. This is important. Where the embargo is an explicit one, no difficulty can arise. Where it is merely implied it is equally important there should be no breach of confidence.

Remember always that you hold a responsible office, and that Ministers, Members and officials have a right to rely on your tact and discretion.

Keep in mind that: (1) while you have complete freedom to get your own stories in your own way, and while there are no restrictions of any kind of personal initiative, you have a duty to the Lobby as a whole; (2) you should do nothing to prejudice the communal life of the Lobby, or the relations with the two Houses and the authorities; (3) this is in your interest and that of your office, as well as in the general interest of the Lobby.

*Collective lobbying*

It has become common practice for Ministers and others to meet the Lobby collectively to give information and answer questions.

Members of the Lobby are under an obligation to keep secret the fact that such meetings are held, and to avoid revealing the sources of their information.

The Chairman of the Lobby will, during the course of the Parliamentary session, remind members of this all-important rule, which has, as its main purpose, the safeguarding of informants.

It is recognized, however, that a correspondent has a special responsibility to his editor. The following resolution was therefore passed by the Lobby in July, 1955: 'That it is consistent with Lobby practice that members of the Lobby may tell their editors, or acting editors, the sources of their information at Lobby meetings on the rare occasions that this may be vital, but must, on every occasion that such information is passed on, explain to their editors, or acting editors, that the source is strictly confidential.'

Do not talk about Lobby meetings BEFORE or AFTER they are held, especially in the presence of those not entitled to attend them. If outsiders appear to know something of the arrangements made by the Lobby, do not confirm their conjectures, or assume that, as they appear to know so much, they may safely be told the rest.

Steps have been taken to prevent leakages of information about Lobby meetings through Departmental officials and others.

Do not make political or debating points at Lobby meetings.

Stay to the end of meetings. This rule should always be observed, unless there is some compelling reason to the contrary, in which case an officer of the Lobby must always be informed. If it is impossible to stay, you are under an obligation not to make use of anything that has been said at the meeting before the meeting ends.

When meetings are arranged on behalf of the Lobby, it is your duty to attend, even if the subject to be discussed is not of first-class importance to you. Important news stories sometimes develop unexpectedly at such meetings.

The Lobby's machinery cannot operate effectively unless the courtesy and co-operation shown by Ministers and officials are reciprocated.

*General hints*

Do not 'see' anything in the Members' Lobby, or in any of the private rooms or corridors of the Palace of Westminster. You are a guest of Parliament, and it has always been the rule that incidents, pleasant or otherwise, should be treated as private if they happen in those parts of the building to which Lobby correspondents have access because their names are on the Lobby List. This rule is strictly enforced by the authorities.

Do not run after a Minister or Private Member. It is nearly always possible to place oneself in a position to avoid this.

When a member of the Lobby is in conversation with a Minister or Private Member, another member of the Lobby should not join in the conversation unless invited to do so. Nor should the Lobby activities of any colleague ever be the subject of published comment.

Do not crowd together in the Lobby so as to be conspicuous. Do not crowd round the Vote Office when an important document is expected. In general, act always with the recollection that you are a guest of Parliament.

Do not use a notebook, or, as a rule, make notes when in private conversation, in the Members' Lobby.

NEVER, in ANY circumstances, make use of anything accidentally overheard in any part of the Palace of Westminster.

*Parliamentary privilege*

Inform yourself, as fully as you can, on the law of Parliamentary privilege. Erskine May's 'Parliamentary Practice' is the standard work, and the officials of both Houses are always most helpful when consulted.

In particular, great care should be taken in writing about the proceedings of any Select Committee of either House.

Items dealing with Select Committees which are published in the Votes and Proceedings of the House of Commons, and the Printed Papers of the House of Lords, may always be quoted.

But references to the findings of Select Committees before their reports are available to Members of Parliament are governed by a ruling given by Mr Speaker on July 27, 1948.

He said then that, once a report had gone to the printers (in other words, had been 'laid on the Table'), it had technically been laid before the House, and no breach of privilege was caused by publication.

But he thought it 'a wholly undesirable principle' that Press accounts of a Select Committee's report should be published before M.P.s had themselves had a chance to read it. Such accounts, he said, would, 'call for my displeasure'.

It seems therefore desirable to err on the side of caution in handling such reports.

If you are in any doubt as to whether or not a Parliamentary Committee is a Select Committee, ask and make sure. For instance, the Kitchen Committee *is* a Select Committee of the House of Commons.

Finally, if you are in doubt about ANY point of the Lobby etiquette or practice, consult the chairman or the honorary secretary of the Lobby. They have special facilities for clearing up doubtful points with the Authorities

They will be glad to help and guide all newcomers to the Lobby, especially in identifying those parts of the Palace of Westminster which are in or out of bounds.

NOTE—You should ensure that a deputy acting in your absence understands Lobby practice.

SOURCE: Jeremy Tunstall. *The Westminster Lobby Correspondents*, Appendix, 124–8

## 57 Anthony Lewis
## AN AMERICAN CRITICISM OF THE PARLIAMENTARY LOBBY SYSTEM

*In a lecture to the Institute of Journalists Anthony Lewis, the Chief London Correspondent of the* New York Times, *delivered a vigorous criticism of the Lobby system as it operates in Westminster. In the American system there is far more open conflict between the politicians as a group and the correspondents who operate in Washington.*

When all of us—reporters, editors and others who make journalism their life—think about these problems of restraint on publication, we should not omit to look at our own failings. I occasionally felt in the United States that the press would accomplish more if it stopped moaning about the government secrecy and did a little more hard work itself, and I am not sure that the picture is altogether different here. I think the news columns of the national newspapers—I do not refer to leaders—take too much for granted what the politicians say and do not sufficiently dig underneath for the facts. The Prime Minister is given to complaining about the hostility of the press toward him. To the contrary, I think the press is too much of a conduit for the government, conveying its version of events to the reader without the necessary scepticism.

*Abuses of the Lobby System*

It is doubtless presumptuous of a foreigner to say so, but I think the central mechanism of political reporting in your newspapers has gone wrong. I refer to the lobby system. That a selected group of trusted correspondents should have access to the leaders of government on a confidential basis sounds wise, but all too often the result is only to make captives of the reporters. Without any attribution whatsoever they write that such and such a glorious event is about to happen, when in fact that is only the opinion of someone in the government.

Just the other day, for example, I noticed a Press Association lobby story on the background of the government's decision to devalue sterling. The story said, among other things, that the long silence following the Thursday cabinet decision to devalue 'was due entirely to technical considerations and the time required to complete consultations with the other financial powers in the world.' The story also said that there had been no question of foreign banks 'seeking to impose conditions' unacceptable to Britain. That was written as an absolute truth, unchallengeable by mortal man. But it was really the government's version, to say the least a highly arguable version, of events. Others might say—they have said—that the delay in devaluation was caused by the government's incompetence and that the government well knew that any further foreign loan without devaluation would have carried with it severe conditions, even though no banker had been so crude as to state that out loud.

At the risk of offence I must say that I think that kind of reporting is a disservice to the country and an outrage to our profession. No newspaper or news agency should carry such statements without a clear indication that they are just one view of controversial matters—the government's view. If the lobby system results inevitably in such abuses, it should be abandoned. I suspect that those most unhappy to lose it would be not the press but the politicians.

SOURCE: *Journalism Today*, Vol 1, No 2 (Spring 1968), 59–60

## 58 Royal Commission on the Press, 1947–9
### LORD KEMSLEY'S FEARS ABOUT THE EFFECTS OF A PRESS COUNCIL

*The Royal Commission of 1949 recommended the creation of a Press Council but four years passed before the Council came into being. The idea of any central system of supervision was abhorrent to the traditional world of Fleet Street where, it was felt, the liberty of expression which had been fought for over three centuries could be undermined by such an institution. A Council would be pointless without sanctions, some thought, and with sanctions it would be intolerable. In 1952, however, a private member's bill was introduced in the House of Commons to set up a Press Council by statute, but the attempt failed; the newspapers agreed a year later to set up their own body, although the chairman (contrary to the recommendation of the Commission) was not an independent layman.*

*The Press Council used and uses no sanction other than the publicity which ensues from its adjudications. Its purpose is to preserve the freedom of the Press by preserving its good name. The nature and extent of the original opposition to the idea of a Council can be gauged from the evidence of Viscount Kemsley to the Commission in May 1948.*

### PRESS COUNCIL

I have studied carefully the questions asked by the Royal Commission on the subject of the Press Council. The essential character of such a Press Council as seems to be in mind is that it might be a body whose membership extends beyond those directly concerned with the production of newspapers and that its function should be either directly (if endowed with statutory powers) or indirectly in the nature of a censorship. I cannot believe that such a body would serve a useful purpose but foresee that it might be extremely dangerous in action. Although I regard with repugnance all unwarranted intrusions into private life, I would rather rely on the reaction of public opinion than on the endowment of such a body as the Press Council with statutory powers. No less do I think it would be undesirable for a Press Council to be so constituted as to be able to influence editorial judgment on the method of presenting the news or of expressing views, or in the allocation of their space between particular interests.

Moreover, the establishment of such a body for journalists is not comparable to the case of other professions. It seems to me that the incorporation of other professions has really been based on the fact that by law a recognised professional qualification is required for certain acts to be performed. For example, a death certificate can be given only by a qualified doctor; certain pleadings can be made only by a qualified solicitor or barrister. But editors are not licensed in this sense, nor, therefore, can any sanctions be imposed on them by the withdrawal, or the threat of withdrawal, of their licence.

Apart from the initial difficulties of constituting a Press Council, I find it impossible to see how it would work. If it is to become a tribunal for the examination of alleged false reports or misrepresentations, is the Council to act as an initiating body or is it to consider only those complaints which are brought to its notice? If it is to avoid the charge of partiality it could not initiate action without covering the whole field of journalism and closely studying all the morning, evening and weekly newspapers published throughout the country. Even if it deals only with cases brought to its notice, a great deal of work would be involved and the same charge of partiality will be levelled against it if it rejects some complaints and accepts others.

I cannot believe that such a tribunal, even were it possible for it to be established, would be able to enforce its findings or have behind it any strength of professional, or public, opinion.

So far, therefore, as my own views go, I am bound to object to the idea of a Press Council.

SOURCE: Minutes of Evidence taken before the Royal Commission on the Press, 36th day, 27 May 1948 (Cmnd. 7503, p 5)

## 59 Press Council
## CONSTITUTION

*In February 1953 a joint committee of newspaper proprietors, unions and editors which had been meeting for many months finally produced an agreed draft of a plan for a Press Council. The meeting had been greatly influenced by the House of Commons debate of November 1952 which resulted from the private member's bill which would have obliged the newspaper industry to set up a council. The body which now emerged was composed entirely of individuals from various parts of the newspaper world, with no lay members and no independent chairman. When the second Royal Commission forcibly repeated the need for a lay element, the Council reconstituted itself, in 1963, under the chairmanship of Lord Devlin and with five other representatives of the public. This is the first section of the 1953 constitution.*

Terms for the constitution finally adopted were:
 1. *Constitution.*—The General Council of the Press, hereinafter called the Council, is constituted, on and from the first day of July, 1953, by the organisations named in the Schedule hereto, hereinafter referred to as the constituent organisations, as a voluntary organisation of twenty-five members.
 2. *Objects.*—The objects of the Council shall be:—
   (i) to preserve the established freedom of the British Press.
   (ii) to maintain the character of the British Press in accordance with the highest professional and commercial standards.
   (iii) to keep under review any developments likely to restrict the supply of information of public interest and importance.

(iv) to promote and encourage methods of recruitment, education and training of journalists.
(v) to promote a proper functional relation among all sections of the profession.
(vi) to promote technical and other research.
(vii) to study developments in the Press which may tend towards greater concentration or monopoly.
(viii) to publish periodical reports recording its own work and reviewing from time to time the various developments in the Press and the factors affecting them.

3. *Procedure.*—The Council is empowered by the constituent organisations to regulate and control all its procedure and action for the furtherance and attainment of the objects defined in Clause 2 hereof as the Council may decide, provided that in dealing with representations which it may receive about the conduct of the Press or of any persons towards the Press, the Council shall be required to consider only those from complaints actually affected, and shall deal with such in whatever manner may seem to it practical and appropriate.

4. *Membership.*—
(i) The Council shall consist of fifteen editorial representatives and ten managerial representatives, elected or nominated as provided in this Clause.
(ii) Membership of the Council shall be restricted to persons who have the qualification of being full-time directors or employees on the editorial or managerial staffs of newspapers, periodicals, or news agencies supplying a regular service of news to daily newspapers, which qualification shall also include full-time professional free lance journalists regularly engaged in supplying news or articles to such newspapers, periodi-

Note on Paragraph 3.—While the Council is 'required' to consider only complaints from complainants actually affected it may, at its discretion, consider complaints reaching it from any source.

cals, or news agencies. Any member ceasing to be so qualified shall notify the secretary or acting secretary of the Council within one month and shall terminate his membership of the Council within three months of such cessation of qualification.

(iii) The fifteen editorial representatives shall comprise:—

| | |
|---|---|
| National newspaper editors elected in accordance with the provisions of section (vi) hereof ... | 3 |
| *Provincial newspaper editors elected in accordance with the provisions of section (vi) hereof ... | 2 |
| *Provincial newspaper editors nominated by the Guild of British Newspaper Editors ... ... | 2 |
| Scottish newspaper editor elected in accordance with the provisions of section (vi) hereof ... | 1 |
| Nominees of the National Union of Journalists ... | 4 |
| Nominees of the Institute of Journalists ... ... | 3 |

(iv) The ten managerial representatives shall comprise:—

| | |
|---|---|
| Nominees of the Newspaper Proprietors Association | 4 |
| Nominees of the Newspaper Society ... ... | 4 |
| Nominee of the Scottish Daily Newspaper Society | 1 |
| Nominee of the Scottish Newspaper Proprietors Association ... ... ... ... ... | 1 |

(v) The method of selecting nominated members of the Council shall be left to the discretion of the organisations by which their nominations are made but in deciding upon their nominees the organisation concerned shall have regard to the desirability of ensuring as wide a representation of the categories of morning, evening, Sunday and other weekly newspapers as possible.

(vi) The national newspaper editors shall be elected by the editors of newspapers in membership of the Newspaper Proprietors Association; two provincial newspaper editors shall be elected by the editors of newspapers in membership of the Newspaper Society; and the Scottish

* The term 'Provincial newspaper editors' shall be deemed to include editors of London surburban newspapers.

newspaper editor elected by editors of newspapers in membership of the Scottish Daily Newspaper Society and the Scottish Newspaper Proprietors Association. The procedure by which these elections shall be carried out shall be determined by the respective organisations.

(vii) On or before 1st June, 1953, names of nominees and elected members shall be sent by the constituent organisations to the secretary or acting secretary of the Council for the time being accompanied by the written consent of the persons nominated to serve. In the event of the same nomination being put forward by more than one organisation, the nomination first made shall have priority and the organisation or organisations submitting the subsequent nomination of the same person shall be asked to put forward another nomination.

5. *Chairman.*—At its first meeting the Council shall appoint from its members a Chairman and vice-Chairman, each of whom shall hold office until the first meeting of the Council in 1954 and be eligible for re-election. At the first meeting in 1954 and each subsequent year the Council shall elect a Chairman and vice-Chairman who shall hold office for the ensuing twelve months. Persons so appointed shall be eligible for re-election.

SOURCE: General Council of the Press. *The Press and the People,* first *Annual Report* (1954), 32–4

*The 1963 Constitution also changed the title of the Press Council to its present form, but still left much of the public complaining that the lay element in its composition was inadequate. Accordingly, ten years later, a third constitution was drawn up, its membership determined on the following basis:*

(i) A Chairman who shall be a person otherwise unconnected with the Press.
(ii) Twenty members nominated by the following bodies in the proportions indicated:

| | |
|---|---|
| The Newspaper Publishers Association Ltd. at least two of whom shall be editorial—as distinct from managerial—nominees | 5 |
| The Newspaper Society at least one of whom shall be an editorial nominee. | 3 |
| Periodical Publishers Association Ltd., including one editorial nominee | 2 |
| The Scottish Daily Newspaper Society | 1 |
| Scottish Newspaper Proprietors' Association | 1 |
| The Guild of British Newspaper Editors | 2 |
| The National Union of Journalists | 4 |
| The Institute of Journalists | 2 |

(iii) Representatives of the Public who shall not exceed one-third of the Council's total membership entitled to vote   10
(iv) Additionally each constituent body may nominate one of its officials to attend meetings of the Council in a consultative capacity. Such nominees may speak but not vote. Constituent bodies may change these nominees by giving seven days' notice to the secretary of the Council.

SOURCE: Article 3 of the Press Council Constitution, as amended (1973)

## 60 Press Council
## A STATEMENT ON FOUR-LETTER WORDS

*Publicity remained the only sanction of the Press Council and its first lay chairman, Lord Devlin, thought that the system worked well; many observers thought it was beginning to help eliminate from the Press in Britain certain of the abuses for which Fleet Street had earned fruitless criticism in the past. Although the Press Council, in one form or the other, has now accumulated 20 years of judgements and precedents, no complete code of rules governing the conduct of journalists has developed. None the less there has emerged a general feeling that a set of guidelines exists in the profession of journalism, although the judgements of the*

*Council may be rejected by newspapers and journalists, who are not legally or even professionally bound to respect them. The Press Council's decision on four-letter words following the Lady Chatterley obscenity trial in 1961 would not, for instance, necessarily act as a guide to the conduct of newspapers a decade later. Indeed the Press Council has, as in a complaint against the* Evening Standard *in 1969, upheld the right of the editor to print a four-letter word 'on a rare occasion as part of a factual description and not unduly emphasised in the narrative'.*

After its meeting on February 14, the Council issued the following statement to the Press:

The Press Council has considered the action of The Spectator, The Guardian and The Observer in publishing certain 'four-letter' words mentioned in the Lady Chatterley's Lover trial. In the opinion of the Council this was both objectionable and unnecessary. The Press, in general, demonstrated how a Court case of this kind can be adequately and broadmindedly covered without debasing standards of decency. The Council received a complaint from Mr. R. Inglis, editor, and Mr. B. Levin, deputy-editor of The Spectator, about its procedure. They said that The Spectator had not been given any opportunity to submit evidence and defend itself. This representation was considered and after its meeting on April 25, the Council issued a further statement that the issue was discussed as a matter that affected Press standards and that no specific complaint had been lodged. No issue of fact had arisen since there was no dispute that the words were published. In these circumstances, in the Council's opinion, there was no necessity to call evidence.

SOURCE: Press Council. *The Press and the People*, eighth *Annual Report* (1961), 32–3

## 61 Press Council
## UNSAVOURY MEMOIRS DEPLORED

*After the reconstitution of the Council the number of complaints received rose sharply; it gained a much greater credibility among the public. After the Profumo affair of 1963 there was a great deal of public criticism about the role of the Press in persuading some of the individuals involved to publish their personal stories of a highly scandalous nature. The Press Council in publishing its censures on this practice took the opportunity of quoting at length the concluding paragraphs of Lord Denning's report on the scandal.*

The Press Council makes the following adjudication on the issues raised.

1. The extensive reporting of court proceedings in the Ward case was justified as news of exceptional interest and public concern. Nevertheless, some intimate detail should have been omitted.

2. In their presentation, headlines and photographs, a number of newspapers gave excessive prominence to and thus glamorised the people concerned in the prostitution and vice revealed in this case. This is strongly condemned.

3. The Council deplores, as it has done on previous occasions, the publication of personal stories and feature articles of an unsavoury nature where the public interest does not require it and it urges editors and managements of newspapers to discuss what arrangements can be made to avoid publication of material of this sort.

4. The action of the News of the World in paying £23,000 for the confessions of Keeler and publishing in these articles details of her sordid life story was particularly damaging to the morals of young people. By thus exploiting vice and sex for commercial reward the News of the World has done a disservice both to public welfare and to the Press.

It is interesting to observe Lord Denning's concluding paragraphs in his Report.

After urging that newspapers should not seek to put names to those whom he had deliberately left anonymous, he said:

341. This brings me to the end. It might be thought—indeed it has been thought—by some that these rumours are a symptom of a decline in the integrity of public life in this country. I do not believe this to be true. There has been no lowering of standards. But there is this difference to-day. Public men are more vulnerable than they were: and it behoves them, even more than ever, to give no cause for scandal. For if they do, they have to reckon with a growing hazard which has been disclosed in the evidence I have heard.

Scandalous information about well-known people has become a marketable commodity. True or false, actual or invented, it can be sold. The greater the scandal the higher the price it commands. If supported by photographs or letters, real or imaginary, all the better. Often enough the sellers profess to have been themselves participants in the discreditable conduct which they seek to exploit. Intermediaries move in, ready to assist the sale and ensure the highest prices. The story improves with the telling. It is offered to those newspapers—there are only a few of them—who deal in this commodity. They vie with one another to buy it. Each is afraid the other will get it first. So they buy it on chance that it will turn out profitable. Sometimes it is no use to them. It is palpably false. At other times it is credible. But even so, they dare not publish the whole of the information. The law of libel and the rules of contempt of court exert an effective restraint. They publish what they can, but there remains a substantial part which is not fit for publication. This unpublished part goes around by word of mouth. It does not stop in Fleet Street. It goes to Westminster. It crosses the Channel, even the Atlantic and back again, swelling all the time. Yet without the original purchase, it might never have got started on its way.

342. When such deplorable consequences are seen to ensue, the one thing that is clear is that something should be done to stop the trafficking in scandal for reward. The machinery is ready to hand. There is a new Press Council already in being.

343. Although I have felt it necessary to draw attention to this matter, I would like to say that I have had the greatest co-operation and assistance from the newspapers and all

concerned with them; and not least from those whose practices I hold to be open to criticism.

SOURCE: Press Council. *The Press and the People*, eleventh *Annual Report* (1964), 19-20

## 62 Press Council
## CHEQUE-BOOK JOURNALISM

*There are certain areas of journalistic practice where it is extremely difficult to decide precisely where proper practice differs from improper. It is one thing to create a code of conduct as to personal behaviour; it is another to create a code in areas where values are constantly shifting and definitions are hard to come by. One of these areas is that of 'cheque-book journalism', on which the Press Council has attempted to improve newspaper practice without being able to state any very firm laws.*

*The problem is that 'cheque-book journalism' defies accurate definition; while newspapers can indeed misuse their wealth by bribing witnesses or attempting to buy exclusivity of information which should be generally available, there is no moral reason why information should never be purchased from willing sellers. The practice of buying information can range from entertaining a contact for lunch to paying tens of thousands of pounds to convicted criminals. The Press Council has tried to provide guidance on newspaper practice in the following document.*

What then are the objectionable elements of the practice? In the wider aspect of acquisition of exclusive news they centre on exercise of the power of the purse to deny competitors legitimate access to news or facts that the public ought to know. This limitation of circulation of news is a grave matter. It is at the heart of the anti-social side of cheque-book journalism. If the public good requires that news shall be generally known it is completely unethical for any newspaper, by exercise of the power of the purse, to block dissemination for private gain.

The yardstick of measurement of public interest is not always national. A news event that may be trivial considered nationally may be of great importance to the public of a given provincial area. The Press Council, for instance, has knowledge of cases in which national newspapers have bought exclusive rights to news and pictures of local events not only to the exclusion of national competitors but to the deprivation of the local Press. Because local people rely primarily upon their town or county newspapers for their local news such instances of artificial restriction of news must, on the face of things, be against public interest.

The difficulty of enunciating a standard of conduct applicable to all cases of purchase of exclusive rights to news is obvious. Circumstances can be almost infinitely variable and the Press Council cannot do otherwise than judge each case on its merits.

The second objectionable element of cheque-book journalism is its tendency to induce unseemly conduct in the quest of special-purchase stories. In one instance which the Press Council considered there was a street fracas between journalists of rival newspapers when some of them tried to interview a man leaving a Court on a 'Not Guilty' finding in a charge of murder. Others claimed that their newspapers had 'bought his story' and the conflict between the groups was unedifying. Such conduct serves only to bring the Press into discredit. There is no redeeming feature about behaviour of this kind. The best antidote to it is removal of the cause.

The third element is 'body-snatching', a term devised to describe extreme steps sometimes taken to ensure that a bought source of information shall not be in a position to divulge anything of what he knows to persons other than his paymasters. It is one thing to rely on a seller's promise of silence and another to take almost forcible steps to make certain that it is kept. The Council finds this practice most objectionable.

The glamorisation of vice and the rewarding of criminals are the aspects of cheque-book journalism that make the biggest impact on the public. The Press Council has not hesitated to condemn this practice and it is heartened to note that since its outspoken comments on the Christine Keeler memoirs in 1963 there has been marked improvement in the standards of newspaper approach to the publication of unsavoury matters which are not dealt with in the way of public duty.

This point of public duty, although of primary importance, is sometimes overlooked by critics of the newspapers. The Press has a responsibility to the community to record what is going on. It would err ethically if it ignored unpleasant matters of public consequence simply because they were unpleasant. Vice and sex should not be swept under the carpet. They should be adequately reported and commented upon in an adult manner, and this generally can be achieved without going into excessive detail.

When the Press exceeds its duty to inform in these events it panders to the baser element in man's nature and descends to the level of trafficking in scandal. The claim that a large section of the population demands this sort of journalism is no excuse for providing it. One does not give a sick man poison because he fancies it!

The Council unhesitatingly condemns as immoral the practice of financially rewarding criminals for disclosure of their nefarious practices by way of public entertainment. Crime is anti-social and it cannot be other than wrong that an evil-doer should benefit—oftentimes substantially—by his offences against the community. These payments for revelations by the notorious might also be held to constitute encouragement to others. To some people the prospect of wide publicity and a monetary reward being obtainable for details of their illegal exploits could be a vivid and compelling inducement to criminal activity.

Some degree of reservation was expressed within the Council about publication of revelations by convicted spies because the spy, in the minds of many, is a criminal only to the side he injures. When he spies for his country he could even be something of a hero to his compatriots. It was also advanced in discussion that publication of a foreign spy's work in Britain served the positive good of exposing weaknesses in the nation's defensive mechanism. In the final analysis, however, the Council felt that it is contrary to public welfare to reward criminals whether they be vicious or treasonable.

The Press Council regrets that it cannot provide an all-embracing definition of cheque-book journalism. The facets of the subject are so many and varied that each case must be considered in light of its facts and circumstances. The Council will, however, keep the matter under review and will issue, from time to time, its views on individual cases which come to its notice.

SOURCE: H. Philip Levy. *The Press Council*, Appendix IV (1967), 484–6

## 63 Press Council
## STATISTICS ON ADJUDICATIONS

*The Press Council has published the following figures on the number of complaints it has handled in one typical year, 1971.*

### COUNCIL ADJUDICATIONS

|  | Upheld | Rejected | Total |
|---|---|---|---|
| National Mornings | 6 | 9 | 15 |
| Sundays | 2 | 1 | 3 |
| London Evenings | 1 | 1 | 2 |
| London Weeklies | 3 | 2 | 5 |
| Provincial Dailies | 3 | 8 | 11 |
| Provincial Weeklies | 2 | 3 | 5 |
| Scottish | – | 2 | 2 |
| Irish | – | – | – |
| Periodicals | 2 | 1 | 3 |
| Agencies | – | – | – |
| General | – | – | – |
| Giveaways | 1 | – | 1 |
|  | 20 | 27 | 47 |

SOURCE: Press Council. *The Press and the People*, nineteenth *Annual Report* (1972), 6

PART FOUR

# Newspapers and Workers' Participation

In a celebrated piece of invective Prime Minister Baldwin attacked the *'power without responsibility'* of the owners of the Daily Mail *and the* Daily Express *which were goading him with constant attacks:* 'The newspapers conducted by Lord Rothermere and Lord Beaverbrook are not newspapers in the ordinary acceptance of the term. They are engines of propaganda for the constantly changing policies, personal wishes, personal likes and dislikes of two men.' *Perhaps the greatest of the dilemmas of the present time in regard to the nature of Press freedom is that, with newspapers secure from interference by government, it is now not clear in whose hands the freedom of the Press is placed—on that of corporate owners, editors or journalists. The question has not been a particularly vexatious one until the present decade, when the general spread of participatory ideas has involved Fleet Street in an incipient and important crisis of authority. The Press is a source of concentrated power in a society dominated by many such concentrated power centres; the cause of 'freedom' in other spheres is intimately involved with the task of opening up those centres or making them publicly accountable in some way. Inevitably, the Press has become subject to the same kind of attention, from within as much as from without.*

*On the continent of Europe a number of prominent newspapers,* Le Monde *among them, have created for themselves internal constitutions which give a far greater say in the editorial process to members of the journalistic staff than has been the traditional practice.* In Britain several newspapers have concluded house agreements with the National Union of Journalists which provide for a greatly increased amount of internal consultation on questions of staffing and policy. In the case of one weekly, the New Statesman, the staff has won from the Board the right to have the editor of its choice. It is not yet clear whether this movement towards journalistic democracy is going to spread into a general movement throughout the profession or whether it will remain the special preserve of a small group of journalists working in the 'quality' Press. If it develops as a general movement among all those who work on newspapers (of whom journalists comprise about one-tenth), then it could have far-reaching effects on the nature of the daily Press in Britain.

The industrial climate in Fleet Street since the late 1960s has been at times very strained. There have been continuing fears for the survival of certain papers and production costs have escalated enormously. Inevitably, the unions, concerned for the future of their members, have taken an interest in material published in the Press which deals with the newspaper industry itself. A number of disputes have broken out—the first of them on the Observer—over the way industrial news affecting newspapers should be presented to the public. That tension has spread to other subject matter, and production unions as well as journalists have become involved in disputes over what their newspapers should publish.

The purpose of Part Four is to illustrate certain aspects of this developing issue.

## 64 Jeremy Tunstall
## THE CAREER OF THE JOURNALIST

*In one of the very few thorough professional investigations of the social environment and outlook of journalists in Britain Jeremy Tunstall gives the following description of the career pattern of the British journalists whose working lives he studied. It provides a valuable starting-point to a consideration of the new tensions at work in the journalistic community, and indicates how the young journalist might tend to see the life ahead of him as a jungle, in which a small élite begins with unfair privileges and retains them throughout life in Fleet Street.*

Most recruits to British newspaper journalism during the 1960's began on *weekly* provincial newspapers. 'Juniors' made up about two-fifths of the journalists on these small papers in each of the years 1964–7.\* During the late 1960's the majority of recruits had academic qualifications below the usual university entrance requirements.† Most came from middle- and lower-middle-class families, and were indentured for three years on a newspaper near their parents' home. Most journalists started in the sort of places where the weeklies were strongest—namely in towns and suburbs too small to have a daily newspaper. Editors of small newspapers in such centres were thus front-line recruiters for all British newspapers.

Over half of the young journalist recruits in his study told Oliver Boyd-Barrett that they were writing, or intended to write, a novel. Perhaps most relevant to the young journalist recruit was a desire to escape from set routines. In addition to early rejection of routine, another career-long journalism theme was the importance of personal contacts. Personal contacts, alliances and recommendations play a part in most occupational careers. But in journalism they assume a special significance, because not only examinations, but any other impersonal criteria are widely regarded as poor guides to ability in journalism. Moreover, from the local Editor's point of view it might be quite rational to select recruits from candidates who approach him through personal contacts. Some journalists claimed that to be successful a journalist required ambition and determination to overcome obstacles, and consequently a little difficulty in getting into the occupation was no bad thing. But job opportunities were unevenly spread geographically; moreover, many young people still entered journalism without difficulty and without any special 'ambition' or noticeable attributes relevant to journalism.

\* In 1967 Newspaper Society figures showed 1,404 juniors out of a total 3,450 journalists on weeklies.
† In 1967–8 of recruits to provincial newspaper journalism, 12·1 per cent were graduates, 11·5 per cent had three or more GCE 'A' levels, 17·6 per cent had two 'A' levels and 8·3 per cent one 'A' level.

In his first months and years a journalist learnt the role of the local journalist and the discipline of writing to order; he internalized news values. The technique most emphasized by small provincial papers in Britain was shorthand, which stresses accuracy, the spoken word, the formal statement, and personalization. The young journalist learnt the 'house-style' and the art of the 'intro'—the riveting first sentence. He was socialized to unusually intense work in the hours before the main deadline. He was exposed to a wide variety of social areas including accidents, death and the social arrangements for dealing with them. He might interview famous entertainers on their appearance at the local theatre. Such small pieces of power and 'inside dope' were quoted to support the romantic-derisory judgement 'it's better than working'. In addition to his enthusiasm for the occupation of journalism in general, a young journalist was often aggressively disillusioned, for instance by the lack of criticism in the local paper—whether of local politicians or the films at the local cinema.

Within only a year or two of entry to the occupation, some journalists found themselves already earning substantial amounts of money beyond their ordinary pay by working for other news organizations. Much of this activity was 'linage'— local news supplied on order to agencies or national news organisations. Often linage was 'owned' by one of the senior journalists such as the news editor, for whom the young recruit might find himself working in both his regular and irregular capacities. The young journalist learnt the practice of getting a foot into the doorway of another news organization in the interest of security; he also learnt the rules and available roles in another news organization for which he would like to work, by first working for it on an occasional freelance basis.

Almost all recruits to newspaper journalism started as general reporters. Photographers were the one type of journalist who specialized strongly from the start. The first chance for a young reporter to specialize was in sports reporting. On a typical provincial daily 5 per cent of the staff were sports reporters in the head office and a fair proportion of work done by the 28 per cent of total staff located in district offices was sport. Other specialist newsgathering was weakly developed on most provincial papers—apart from the odd rather senior industrial correspondent or other specialist responsible for a major local interest (e.g. agriculture). But the young reporter anxious for promotion must look elsewhere, in particular to sub-editing.

On a provincial daily of 60 staff there were about a dozen or so seniorish jobs. Any journalist who stayed on the paper, by the age of 40 could regard himself as having a fair chance of getting one of these jobs. Remembering the opportunities for extra earnings and the jobs available in regional television and public relations, there was no need to be too cynical about statements by some provincial journalists that they did not wish to go to London.

Preliminary interviews for the present study suggested that only a minority of all journalists on London papers had started their careers in the North of England or Scotland. This was consistent with the social processes by which journalists joined London national news organizations. National jobs were usually obtained through some kind of *personal* contact; news organizations with jobs to fill alerted relevant staff members to suggest suitable people. Secondly, another important aspect was *observation* of a journalist's work. This combination of printed (or broadcast) output plus personal contact reinforced the dominance of the South of England. Because most national journalists' beginnings were in the south, social contact networks were stronger in the south; news executives in London when studying the competition also studied mainly *London* (not Manchester or Glasgow) editions. Similarly, young journalists on local papers in the south sent stories to the London offices of national papers, whereas those working in the north sent them to the Manchester offices.

The 'traditional' emphasis given to provincial 'experience' was something of a myth if any kind of clearly pursued policy was indicated, although most journalists had worked outside (central) London previously. National news organizations avoided the short-term costs of a vigorous national recruitment policy and exploited provincial papers which in turn often exploited young journalists. Weak emphasis also was given to experience on one of the larger provincial news organizations; 'experience' primarily meant previous work on any news organization of almost any size or character—and thus experience mainly in avoiding elementary mistakes.

There were two polar extreme career paths to London: Firstly the *élite career* path straight into national journalism without previous 'experience'. Secondly the *provincial career* path—based on 'experience' on a weekly provincial newspaper, then a provincial daily, then some provincial/national job (such as in the London office of a provincial daily, or in the Manchester office of a national paper) and finally a post on a national news organization in London. But so lacking in an orderly career structure was journalism that only a minority of careers followed even this *provincial career* path at all closely. Moreover, the *élite career*, although followed only by very small numbers, was especially important in three high prestige specialist newsgathering fields—foreign, financial and political—fields from which national Editors were disproportionately drawn.

The lack of a career structure and the lack even of accurate information about the prevalent disorderly career processes reinforced the emphasis upon personal contacts, the forging of career alliances, the pursuit of promotion tactics and the prevailing sense of insecurity and anxiety on the issue of careers.

'On your 35th birthday they push you down the rubbish chute.' This statement was made by a journalist in a national newspaper newsroom where the majority of journalists looked past age 35. Indeed over 60 per cent of national journalists were past this age. Nor was there any evidence for the often-repeated assertion that journalists die young. Alcoholism, mental illness, coronaries and suicide were claimed to be common; but a sociologist interested in occupations may come to believe that most occupations make such claims.

Apart from the closure of publications there was also little evidence to support assertions that many journalists were sacked. During 1965–8 only two examples could be discovered of sacking involving more than the occasional individual—both multiple cases followed from the sacking of Editors of popular daily newspapers. But at least as common as sackings were examples of older men being kept on in a state of semi-retirement. Perhaps the latter type of case contributed more to the prevalent sense of unease.

In line with their rather dated personnel policies national newspapers combined a flamboyant organizational concern (e.g. free cruises) for seriously ill journalists with a reluctance to concede that pensions should be transferable. The 1947–9 Royal Commission on the Press (Report, p. 171) expressed concern on this topic, but twenty years later the situation was improving only slowly. The lack of transferable pensions schemes was one factor in the sharp contrast between rapid job mobility in the early part of most national careers followed by rigid immobility in the later years. It was probably one factor also in the sharp divorce between most provincial and national careers in the later years, and the segmented nature of the whole occupation. It contributed to the paradoxical position in which to an outsider older journalists on national news organizations *looked* fairly secure, but still felt insecure. One new executive said: 'Older journalists get steadily more paranoid.'

Older men knew that journalists of some seniority were seldom fired outright; but 'encouragement' was more common, such as promoting men's juniors over their heads, making new appointments in border areas, and also giving some people roving commissions—seen by others as a licence to trespass. Many small events from day to day connected with the coverage of this story, the arrangements for that man's day off, the preferences of a newly promoted executive—each of these could

K

be read by an insecure journalist as evidence of intrigue. Hence the prevalence of gallows humour, talk of rubbish chutes, and the *Daily Mirror*'s local pub familiarly known as 'the-stab-in-the-back'.

SOURCE: Jeremy Tunstall. *Journalists at Work* (1971), 60–64

## 65 Free Communications Group
## NEWSROOM DEMOCRACY

*The most prominent group to spearhead a change of professional consciousness among journalists was the Free Communications Group, which published, for the brief period of its existence, a journal entitled* The Open Secret. *In 1971 the FCG published what was to have been the first of a series of special pamphlets,* In Place of Management, *which provided a guide to the journalist wanting to work in a new system of control; it set out the kind of changes he should press for and how he should go about influencing the National Union of Journalists to develop its thinking along these lines. As later documents in this section will show, the movement was responsible for a number of significant achievements in the period when the FCG was most active.*

1. *NEWSROOM DEMOCRACY.* There are ways of starting at the bottom, small changes in practical, everyday working which give people experience in sharing decisions and break up the old fashioned hierarchies.

(a) *News Teams.* In most papers copy filters up through horizontal layers, from reporter to news editor to sub, to make-up, to copy-taster . . . Each little trade keeps itself to itself, and processes the story according to its tastes.

There is a better way of doing things. This is the news team system, already used in parts of several papers. Sections of the paper are turned over to groups of journalists who work as a unit with its own reporters, subs, lay-out and production men. The news editor's responsibility is decentralized and journalists work together in single compact operations: the days of the 'Reporters' room versus the subs' room' are over.

Many sports departments already function like this. The 'Insight' team on the Sunday Times is another example. The FCG, in a blueprint for a new 'Sun' drawn up last year with the NUJ chapel members there, proposed a complete news team system, believing that this was the way to guarantee good morale and good journalism. In a framework like this bright ideas get listened to.

(b) *Consultation.* This, simply, is the setting-up of a framework in which journalists meet the editor and heads of departments at regular intervals, to talk about the way the paper is being run and its contents, to criticize and to make suggestions.

The most recent model of this is the Times, a good example of the rapid way the turbid frustrations and anxieties in Fleet Street are suddenly taking solid form in a quite new type of militancy. Exasperated by uncertainty about the paper's future and goaded by rumours of change ranging from the sellout of the Times to mass sackings, a group of chapel members won management consent to an editorial consultative committee.

This body meets monthly. No holds are barred—except, significantly, policy as expressed in leaders. The committee, divided into precise components, 6 permanent journalists, 6 journalists who change each month etc, and convened by a management representative, has worked well as a forum in which journalists have argued, demanded information and won considerable concessions to their 'right to know'. A confidential—and very outspoken—bulletin is produced and circulated after each meeting. Another scheme of this kind is being introduced on the Mirror. There will be a series of teach-ins or seminars at department level to discuss local problems, and at a higher level to discuss, criticize and suggest improvements in the newspaper's problems or its handling of various issues. Circulation, advertising, profitability and labour relations will also be the subject of special teach-ins. A chapel member will be in the chair to ensure that the meetings do not turn into a public relations exercise for the management.

Something of the same kind has emerged with the Observer house agreement. This is a verbal agreement providing for quarterly or more frequent meetings with the editor and management representatives at which the whole editorial, political and financial strategy of the paper may be discussed.

Some version of a 'consultation' framework is being considered on the Sunday Times, where the next house agreement is being planned.

2. *SHARING CONTROL.* This is the next step upward in the process of winning democratic control. A 'consultative committee', after all, is just that: it doesn't give you more than the right to be heard. What you will need, in the long run, is actual power, expressed through some body or agreement which editor and management have been obliged to accept. And in the first stage this is going to be mainly 'blocking' power—a veto over policies or appointments or other developments of which you don't approve.

For us in Britain this is likely to be the main battlefield as the press crisis worsens and journalists struggle for a handhold over their own destinies.

Sharing control has three elements. Experiments made so far, here and abroad, don't include all three. But they are interdependent in practice. They are:

(a) access to information.
(b) share in control of editorial and managerial sides.
(c) share in ownership.

(a) *Access to information.* This is often the motive which sets off a general demand for a share in control. It is the demand to know, as of right, what new appointments at the editorial, managerial and head of department level are being planned, what is the true financial state of the paper, what the strategic plans of editor and management are (changes in content, readership, political line), what reorganisations in terms of staff are contemplated.

In times of crisis, this demand may crystallize round the need to know to whom, or to which group, the paper might be sold, and who are the candidates for the editorship.

(b) *Share in editorial and managerial control.* Experiments on the continent suggest that the best way to achieve a share in editorial control is through the setting-up of an editorial council. All members of the staff, preferably including regular contributors, combine to elect a council of, say, eight members. This council, which can be re-elected annually, has certain watch-dog and veto functions which can include:

—Defining the broad political stance of the publication and ensuring that it is maintained,
—Seeing that no staff member is required to write material which conflicts with his conscience, and that he or she is not penalized for refusing to do so,
—Operating control over appointments. A new editor, for instance, could require a two-thirds approving majority in the council before management endorses his appointment. Other staff appointments, like those of heads of departments, and major changes in responsibility or dismissals, could be made subject to the same council approval.

Once this system is working, the aim should be to extend it. Management, for example, affects everybody who works on a paper. The definition of 'staff' can be extended to include all employees, printers, clerical workers, cleaners etc. meeting as a general assembly to elect councils which will exercise control functions over managerial appointments. The final development might be

(a) a single council representing all employees and controlling all appointments, as well as general policy;

(b) a move forward from the idea of 'blocking power' through vetoes to direct selection and appointment by those who work on the publication.

3. *SHARING OWNERSHIP.* This is the ultimate step. Those who make the paper own it. It seems a long way off. The existing structure of newspaper ownership has got to collapse first. But in fact it is destroying itself amazingly efficiently, from year to year. Sometime in the next ten years a state of breakdown will be reached at which only two or so men can afford to keep a national paper going, and when—as a result—public and political opinion will force through a total recasting of the way British newspapers and magazines are financed.

SOURCE: Free Communications Group. *In Place of Management*, No 1, 'Free the Press—the Case for Democratic Control', 6–15)

## 66 Jak
### CARTOON ON THE ELECTRICAL WORKERS— HOMO-ELECTRICAL-SAPIENS-BRITANNICUS

*On 9 December 1970, production of the London* Evening Standard *was halted when union members objected to a cartoon by Jak depicting 'Homo-electrical-sapiens Britannicus, circa 1970'. It was a mordant attack on the electrical workers who were striking throughout the country at that time in the course of a bitterly fought industrial dispute. After two hours, production restarted, when the house chapel was allowed to publish a letter stating its objection fairly prominently on the page close to the cartoon. The paper's branch of the National Union of Journalists issued a statement in which it declared that 'It was agreed that this chapel will not countenance any censorship of the contents of the* Evening Standard *by any union. It is and must be the decision of the editor what the editorial columns contain.' The stoppage at the* Standard *was attacked by prominent politicians of both parties and by the editor of the paper in a leader the following day.*

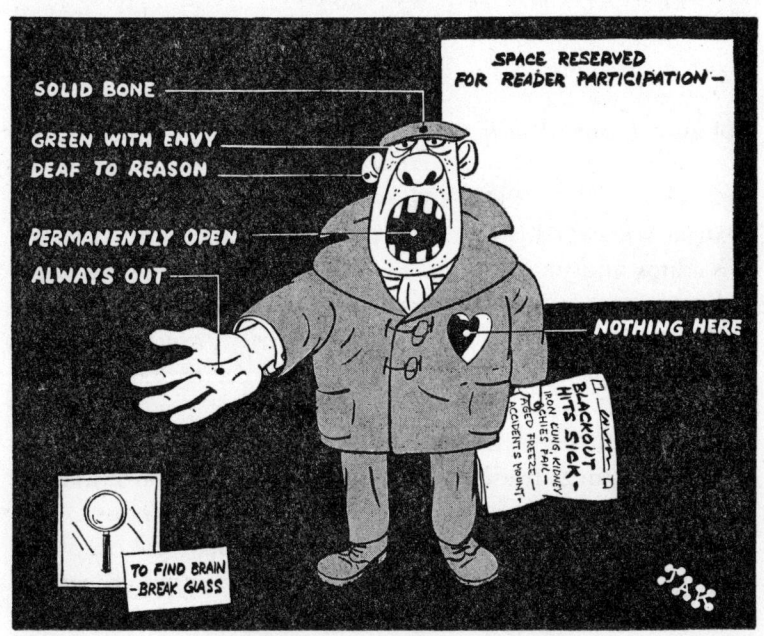

Homo-electrical-sapiens Britannicus, circa 1970

## 'WHY WE OBJECT TO JAK'

The cartoon by Jak which appears on Page 14 expresses his own opinion. We wish to make it clear that the opinion is not shared by members of the Evening Standard Federated House Chapel, which represents the trade unions within this newspaper.

The Federated House Chapel most strongly deprecates the cartoon and feels that it goes above and beyond the bounds of humour and fair comment. However, to show that we are not boneheaded as portrayed and because we firmly believe in the freedom of the Press we have not refused to print once given this opportunity to express our opinion.

Evening Standard<br>Federated House Chapel

SOURCE: *Evening Standard* (9 December 1970)

## THE JAK CARTOON

A strike was called yesterday in this office in an attempt to force the editor and management of the Evening Standard to withdraw a cartoon by Jak. This cartoon portrayed in aggressive and vigorous terms Jak's view of the electricity worker, 'Homo-electricus-sapiens, 1970.' It was not a joke cartoon—it was not intended to raise a laugh—it was a direct attack on the strikers by the cartoonist.

It is a proud tradition of the Evening Standard that its cartoonists have always had complete political freedom. Low and Vicky could and did attack this newspaper's policies when they felt like it. Jak carries on the same tradition. Everyone who works for the Evening Standard knows that the cartoon expresses the cartoonist's point of view, and not necessarily that of the newspaper.

SOURCE: *Evening Standard* (10 December 1970)

### 67 Scottish Daily Express
## THE IRA AND FATHER O'BREZHNEV

*On 28 September 1971 the* Scottish Daily Express *(the semi-autonomous Scottish version of the* Daily Express) *lost 350,000 copies of its edition in the course of a dispute arising from a Cummings cartoon (see p 297). Denny McGee, the father of the NUJ chapel on the paper, objected to a cartoon which implied that the IRA was communist-inspired or operated to the advantage of the communist world and drew it to the attention of the compositors. The dispute, which lasted for some hours, was a confused affair in which the father of the compositors'* chapel, the journalists working on the paper, the editor and the managing director of Beaverbrook Newspapers in London attempted to work out a formula whereby an objection to the cartoon would be published somewhere close to it or on the following day. The day before the dispute there had occurred the first major outbreak of sectarian violence in Glasgow since the new wave of fighting had begun in Ireland, and some workers believed that the cartoon would attract violence to the newspaper.

The distinguishing character of this particular dispute was that the ultimate stoppage of work was supported by sixty journalists who voted against the cartoon at a hurriedly called chapel meeting; it was the first case of journalists supporting such a stoppage, although the National Executive of the NUJ condemned their action severely. The incident, although exceptional, indicated how far the traditional demarcations between editorial functions and workers' functions had become blurred in the context of modern industrial psychology.

"Oh dear! If we make a fuss about this, Mr. Wilson will accuse us of gimmickry and spy mania..."

SOURCE: *Scottish Daily Express* (28 September 1971)

## 68 Press Council
## THE COUNCIL'S WARNING ON PRESS CENSORSHIP FROM WITHIN

*Following a series of incidents in which production unions brought about brief stoppages after disputes over editorial content the Press Council decided to issue a statement of principle which attacked the growing practice as an interference with the freedom of the Press.*

Press controversy followed the withdrawal of a letter from the *Observer* on May 31 1970 in response to demands made by members of SOGAT who objected to its publication. On December 9 1970 the production of the *Evening Standard* was interrupted because newspaper workers objected to the publication of a cartoon. These events led to the Press Council issuing the following statement:

> The Press Council has not entered the area of industrial disputes and its policy is to avoid that area. But it has a paramount duty to protect the freedom of the Press. It feels bound to emphasise the importance to the public of that freedom and of the right of a newspaper to publish what it lawfully may.
>
> The Council has noted that the printing of the *Evening Standard* was interrupted in circumstances which seem to indicate that it is desirable to re-iterate firmly the importance of Press freedom. The Council believes that those involved in the interruption will appreciate the desirability of ensuring the protection of that principle.

On January 12 1971 there was a stoppage at the *Evening Post*, Bristol, when some of the men in the print room objected to the newspaper's account of a meeting of print workers. Arising from this incident the Council issued another statement which said:

> Objections to the contents of newspapers have recently led to industrial action by employees of the newspapers, causing interference with their publication. To stop publication or to threaten to do so in order to suppress news or comment, however unpalatable to some the item concerned may be, is censorship.

NEWSPAPERS AND WORKERS' PARTICIPATION                     299

The functions of the Press Council are to resist censorship and to provide to all a means of registering complaints about misconduct by newspapers. It offers remedies which have shown themselves over the past seventeen years to have a large measure of effectiveness. The Council believes that it is entirely unacceptable in a free society that protests should be allowed to take the form of a direct attack upon the freedom of the Press and denial of the right of a newspaper to publish what it lawfully may. The destruction of Press freedom in this country would be disastrous to the public as a whole and to both sides of the industry. It is the Press Council's first duty under its Constitution to preserve the established freedom of the Press. Therefore the Council urges both management and employees' organisations speedily to seek agreement within the industry to preserve the essential freedoms of free speech, a free Press and the right to protest.

On March 17 1971 a stoppage of the *Evening Echo*, Southend occurred after trade union members in the office had objected to some proposed contents. The Council considered the circumstances but no action was taken on this occasion.

SOURCE: Press Council. *The Press and the People*, eighteenth *Annual Report* (1971), 67–8

### 69 Editor of the Observer's Memorandum
### THE PROBLEM OF THE 'UNQUALIFIED' JOURNALIST

*During the 1960s the National Union of Journalists had gradually advanced its area of negotiation into that of journalist recruitment; in the 1950s it was possible for an editor still to hire and fire almost any journalists he wished, whether or not their careers had advanced along the traditional path of training through the provincial Press. Many very prominent journalists were simply appointed from the ranks of undergraduate journalists of a given year.*

*In a memorandum drawn up by the Newspaper Proprietors' Association and the National Union of Journalists in February 1970, it was noted that in most cases journalists would be expected to train out of*

*Fleet Street for three years; graduates could be taken on to Fleet Street papers after two and a half years. Where an editor wanted to recruit a special correspondent (with a knowledge of a specific subject), he could do so after consultation with the Union. The Union, however, did not recognise that the ability to write well in itself constituted the specialist knowledge necessary to vary the rule. The Editor of the* Observer, *in signing his own house agreement with the NUJ, felt it necessary to add a special memorandum of warning. In the* Observer *agreement the relevant clause states that while the employment of unqualified journalists will be guided by the 1970 industry agreement, the* Observer *Chapel will adopt a 'reasonable attitude' towards the interpretation of that agreement—both parties took note of David Astor's special memorandum attached and dated 13 February 1970.*

We should like to record our reservations about the proposed memorandum. We fear that unless this is interpreted in a very liberal way—as we have interpreted the memorandum of June 1965—it must have serious consequence for the Press as a whole and certainly for newspapers such as 'The Observer'. We have decided to spell out our reasons for taking this view at some length, because we believe this agreement raises fundamental issues that will call for further consideration.

First, as a matter of general principle, we believe that journalism is not simply an industrial process in which the manpower needs can be met by a form of technical apprenticeship, but that it is a creative or semi-artistic occupation, with important political aspects. We believe that it depends for its quality on a free supply of talent; enforcement of any formula limiting recruitment would have, among other disadvantages, the objection that it would be likely to deter gifted people from entering journalism.

Our own experience since the last agreement on 'unqualified' journalists in 1965 has failed to convince us that three years in the provinces are either a necessary or a sufficient training for the kind of journalists we need. To put it quite simply, most of our best people didn't have this training.

Incidentally, the memorandum, as it stands, imposes an unwitting penalty on small firms with only a London-based publication (such as 'The Observer') in that they are effectively debarred from training their own staff, whereas a larger group is not. But a main objection to the new agreement (like its predecessor) is that it overlooks one quality of special value to journalism—a talent for writing. This talent can appear without any form of training or advanced education, and should, in our view, count as a 'specialist' quality of immediate value to Fleet Street newspapers. Indeed, individuals with this special talent are among those most likely to be deterred from entering journalism if a specified period in the provinces is made a rigid condition of entry. A similar case can be put for the capacity to express a powerful political argument; to deny direct entry to a person with an exceptional talent of this kind is to limit a newspaper's freedom to say what it wants.

Furthermore, we believe it is fundamental to the health of journalism that an editor should be free to judge what are the talents that his newspaper needs. It is a main part of his creative function to attract and make use of talent, and for this reason we feel that in any dispute his judgement should be given special weight. That is to say, the burden of proof in a disputed case should rest on those who make the objection, not those who make the appointment. Accordingly, in the sentence of the agreement which reads, 'Where the appointment of any unqualified journalist is proposed, it is agreed that the management will consult the NUJ in advance of the appointment', we would feel it right to 'inform' rather than to 'consult'.

We fully recognise that the NUJ has a legitimate and reasonable right to protect the interests of its members, and that it believes this can best be done through an agreement of this sort. We also fully recognise the value of some training in provinces for many journalists. And we have no objection to the financial clauses in the agreement.

Our immediate point, as stated earlier, is to register concern that our interests as a newspaper could be damaged by a rigid interpretation of this memorandum. We regard the points we have made above as being of such cardinal importance to us that we have felt it imperative to make our viewpoint clear to you.

SOURCE: *Observer* House Agreement (1970)

## 70 Guardian House Agreement
## JOURNALISTS ON THE BOARD

*The movement towards various forms of participation by workers (at least those on the editorial side) in the management of newspapers has been spreading.* The Times *has an Editorial Consultative Committee which meets monthly, bringing together twelve members of the NUJ chapel with the Editor and some of his senior executive colleagues. The* Daily Mirror *house agreement now contains provision for a monthly meeting between management and chapel. It is in the London chapel of the* Guardian, *however, that the movement has, in discussion at least, moved furthest.* The Open Secret *published an account of the discussions between the chapel and the* Guardian *management on a series of three demands: for representation on the Board, for a kind of bi-annual staff parliament, and for consultation on senior appointments.*

At the final meeting in the recent house agreement talks the London chapel put in these proposals. It was agreed that discussion of them should not delay the signing of the house agreement and that they should take appendix status.

1. Editorial staff shall be represented on the parent board of the *Guardian* by two elected staff members accountable to those who elect them.
2. Twice yearly, preferably at time close to the publication of half-yearly circulation figures, a full dress meeting between editorial staff and editorial management shall be arranged. Its purpose will be to review progress and future possibilities and to resolve difficulties in the editorial sector.
3. Appointments to senior positions on the *Guardian* will form

a subject for consultation with editorial staff. Management will seek the views of staff before making such appointments. Staff reserve the right to veto appointments.

On the management side the proposals were received with two comments. Firstly, that in negotiations for a house agreement with the *Guardian* chapel some participation scheme would have been surprising only by its absence. Secondly, management asked for documents giving an outline of chapel thinking on the subject. What follows is a response to that request.

Two main ideas inform the proposals. The first is that the *Guardian* continues to survive by fighting hard for success in an environment that does not grow less hostile. There is need for lessening tendencies for hostility within parts of the organisation, and for recruiting all the talent available to the paper and harnessing it to positive ends. Secondly, the trend in the 1970's, a trend recommended and endorsed by the government, is towards a greater degree of staff participation in the running of their companies. This looks to be the main hope for coping with wage hysteria.

*Board Membership*
In the last decade the *Guardian* has altered from being a well established provincial paper with an international reputation into a national paper. One important effect has been to enlarge the editorial staff and to force competition for that staff to be more directly, and more broadly, against other national papers. This has lessened the numbers of people willing to work for the paper at less than competitive rates just to be on the *Guardian*. The monastic overtones of the *Guardian* tradition has not survived well in London.

Its end was hastened by the crisis in 1966 which is regarded by those who remember it as being a challenge not properly met. Attitudes since then have been more embattled and polarised. There has been a growing impatience with the repeated claim that the *Guardian* cannot afford whatever is being asked for, and that the editorial staff ought to display a sense of co-operative responsibility.

During the house agreement talks these pleas made within what remained of the old convention finally broke down. The editorial staff selected a target which it achieved at the price of anxious moments about the paper itself. For whatever complex historical or other reasons figures presented to negotiators and arguments made from them make little impact on a staff determined to remain firmly in the Fleet Street pay brackets.

This offers a most pressing argument for editorial staff directors. There seems little likelihood that any future sets of figures will carry any greater conviction with the staff increasingly aware—but hardly less baffled—by the proliferation of Guardian-based companies and projects. Financial figures presented to the staff through union representatives are suspected on grounds of incompleteness, and also because in the increasingly complex situation from which they arise, the viewpoint of the presenter matters more. The staff has an interest and a point of view about the division of the 'cake' and should be represented and have facts and proposals at first hand.

Three alternatives emerge for the future:

1. There will be a continuing slide towards an armed camp mentality as between staff and management. This would erode the valued informality and flexibility in the firm. It would also set up stresses, or increase those already present, between journalist and non-journalist parts of the management.

2. Deliberate effort—made for the sake of the working atmosphere—could minimise the growth siege mentality. There will remain a tendency to sceptical disregard for estimates, pledges, promises, warnings, and forecasts.

3. Staff members can be appointed to the board who will restore credibility to information and by adding a dimension make future management/union discussion more fruitful.

Because of the *Guardian*'s money difficulties its range of options in management terms is restricted and there is a growing danger of the irresistible force of staff demands for money meeting the immovable object of no cash with which to pay. The potentially disastrous sting can be drawn from this situation only by allowing the editorial staff a place in management.

There seems only one way—on the more general front—to take the hysteria out of the inflationary spiral and that is to give workers more say in the running of affairs at their plant. Only by this means can what are 'real truths' for management be made into convincing arguments for staff. The *Guardian* recommends increased employee involvement to others. It could confidently add example to precept as far as journalists go since hardly any other body of workers are as well qualified by outlook and practice for making a constructive contribution to the running of their own firms.

Editorial staff board members would be selected from London and Manchester. They would be elected by their fellow workers and would not be NUJ chapel officers. Their reports might, for convenience, be delivered at chapel meetings. Staff directors would be accountable to those who appoint them; to strengthen this accountability it is proposed that there should be an issue of shares —49 per cent—to the staff. Such an issue of shares would increase individual senses of involvement with the firm, underpinning the usefulness of the staff directors. Should profits ever be made, staff shareholding would be more important.

Benefits flowing from acceptance of this proposal are:

1. A growth of unified purpose and willingness to work to that purpose in a company that has expanded quickly and which now operates in equal parts in two centres.

2. A vital renewal of links between management and staff supplementing contact points now dangerously corroded.

3. Economy of time and effort in discovering for certain what the likely effect of plans and proposals made by the board will be on those affected. This will be particularly important with any work-study or other streamlining techniques.

4. A lift in staff morale from operating in a self-evidently progressive company.

*Elective component*
Implementing this proposal would give the editor a new and wider range of insight and opinion on the appointment of a candidate. The collection of this opinion could be on an individual and voluntary basis, or be anonymous, general and obligatory. Outside candidates for posts involving a supervisory role might be invited to talk to those over whom they are asking to be placed.

In addition to making useful contribution to the selection process, the fact that staff have been involved in the selection should make for a more cohesive working team when the appointment is made. There is no sufficient reason why the democratic principle should not have a place in the work context.

*The twice yearly staff meeting*
Journalists, like employees of other enterprises, are principally interested in pay and conditions. They are also concerned with their newspaper's success, or otherwise, as a business, partly because this bears on pay questions. But they are also interested, naturally, in the quality of the newspaper they help to produce. High pay cannot compensate for the sense of unease and dissatisfaction felt by journalists working for a paper whose standards are slipping or have measurably fallen from a previous high standard. Even if a journalist is satisfied with his own performance he will resent working for a paper which misses some stories, mishandles others, takes up foolish or reactionary policy positions, or prints other below standard material.

It is not suggested that the *Guardian* is in this position. But these things are a matter of degree, and the maintenance of the high general morale which produces high performance is not an easy thing. It can slip, temporarily or permanently, for a host of reasons: the co-incidental loss of two or three valued writers in a short space of time, an accumulation of mistakes of judgement in news gathering decisions, the hammering, in a series of leaders, of a policy position repugnant to the majority of the staff.

We need to draw the entire staff into a continuing effort to maintain and improve the standards of the paper. Senior staff have day to day opportunities to comment on the work of their colleagues and to explain and defend their own decisions, although pressure of work and considerations of politness may in fact prevent fruitful discussion. At least senior staff have that opportunity: more junior staff do not.

In an attempt to meet this need—and as a beginning and an experiment—we propose a twice yearly staff meeting at which the paper's performance in the previous half year could be debated in a constructive way.

The pattern we suggest is that there should be two fixed debates, one on leader policy and one on domestic news coverage, with a third debate on a particular department, these to be dealt with in rotation over a period of years. A fourth debate would consider resolutions concerning any department of the paper proposed by members of staff in advance, and consolidated in the normal way.

The debate on leader policy, we feel, should take the form of a paper read by the Editor, or, possibly, by the Deputy Editor, followed by questions from the floor. The debates on domestic news coverage and on particular departments (foreign coverage, arts coverage, sports coverage, etc.) should take the form of a paper read by the appropriate head of department followed by a paper read by a 'shadow' department head appointed at least a month or two early by the junior staff. General discussion would follow. The 'shadow' department head would be expected to produce a critical paper but could if he wished, after a brief general critique, move on to a narrower area e.g. crime coverage, regional reporters v. occasional regional forays, use of correspondents, etc. (in domestic news coverage). The idea of the two papers is principally to provide a framework, a certain amount of material, and a starting point for the rest of the discussion.

The meeting would not have the right to pass resolutions in the debate on leader policy. It would have the right to pass resolutions in the three other debates. These would not be binding on the head of a department, but would be, according to the size of the majority, an indication to him of the general feeling. For the fourth debate, the one considering various general resolutions, a consolidated list of resolutions would be produced in the weeks before the meeting. If few resolutions were forthcoming, the debate could be dropped.

Clearly, there are numerous ways in which the scheme outlined above might fail. Lack of interest could cripple it, attacks on personalities could turn it into a slanging match, shyness and deference could blunt its purpose. But we think it is worth trying.

All staff should attend, which means that the meeting would have to be held on a Saturday, that a hotel or similar establishment would have to be taken. We suggest that the debates should take place during the day and that they should be followed by a grand dinner and drinking evening. The firm would meet general costs, and staff would pay for meals and their own fares. The meeting would be held alternatively in the North and the South. We feel that attendance should be regarded as virtually compulsory, with only the most compelling personal reasons acceptable for absence.

The possibility of bringing in outsiders is not ruled out. There seems no reason why we should not ask, for example, a newspaper critic, a Baistow or a Grundy; or a particular academic, whose work is relevant to a topic up for discussion, or an admired journalist from another paper or a foreign paper to take part in one or more of the debates. Or even an MP.

SOURCE: *The Open Secret*, No 7, 63–5

# Suggestions for Further Reading

There have been newspapers in Britain of one kind or another since the early 1620s, yet in three and a half centuries, despite the enormous historical and biographical literature which has developed around the Press, there has been very little written on the development of many of the issues which principally interest us today.

There is, for instance, no general history of the newspaper in Britain, apart from the official *History of The Times* (1935–52), and Stanley Morison's *British Newspapers* (1931), which deals mainly with the evolution of the production of papers. There is a large assortment of personal historical essays of a sketchy kind, which are mainly based on large out-of-print Victorian volumes; among those which are more easy to obtain one might suggest Harold Herd's *The March of Journalism* (1947) and also his *Seven Editors* (1955); and Francis Williams' *Dangerous Estate* (1957). However, there exists no history of the profession of journalism in Britain.

On the biographical side the picture is far more promising. There are some recent major biographies of great newspapermen and great newspaper-owners, of which the best is A. J. P. Taylor's *Beaverbrook* (1972), though Tom Driberg's shorter biography of *Beaverbrook* (1956) should not be ignored. Russell

Braddon's *Roy Thomson of Fleet Street* (1965) contains much useful material for the reader who has the patience to read the lives of men whose biographers believe their subjects have done no wrong. Donald McLachlan's *In the Chair—Barrington-Ward of The Times* (1971) is similarly interesting though undercritical in tone. A. P. Ryan's *Lord Northcliffe* (1953) is readable, as is the vast official biography of *Northcliffe* by Reginald Pound and Geoffrey Harmsworth (1959). So many newspaper biographies are written by old colleagues, former suppliants and close relations that in order to reach the factual material the reader must become used to the sometimes sycophantic presentation. One biography which requires no apology, however, is Sir Edward Cook's *Delane of The Times* (1915), which gives a vivid portrait of that great editor and his struggles and triumphs. A. M. Gollin's *The Observer and J. L. Garvin 1908–1914—a study in a great editorship* (1960) contains an enormous reservoir of information on the role of newspapers in Britain before World War I. James Aronson's *The Press and the Cold War* (1970) is a study of how the Press, mainly the American, was induced into a long period of self-censorship after World War II, and is salutary reading after wading through the more hagiographical material I have referred to.

There is a group of histories of specific newspapers which are most rewarding for anyone who wants to see what papers were like from the inside at different periods. David Ayerst's *The Guardian—Biography of a Newspaper* (1971) is probably the best of these, but *The Pearl of Days—an intimate memoir of The Sunday Times 1822–1972* (1972) is written by its team of writers in part at least with the detachment that is required. The five-volume *History of The Times* is of course the heaviest and most detailed of all individual newspaper histories and cannot be avoided by any serious student of Press history, and Robertson Scott's *History of the Pall Mall Gazette* (1950) contains a great deal of anecdotage on one of Britain's most distinguished (deceased) newspapers. Clement J. Bundock's history of The *National Union of Journalists 1907–1957* (1957) is one of the few books which deal with the other side of newspaper history from that of the owners and editors. Lord Burnham's *Peterborough Court—the Story of the Daily Telegraph* (1955) is decidedly written from above the salt.

Among histories of the popular Press, there are Hugh Cudlipp's *Publish and be Damned* (1953), an account of the *Daily Mirror*, and that paper also enjoys a history of itself written by Maurice Edelman, *The Mirror—a Political History* (1966).

Among general personal and anecdotal accounts of the world of British newspapers there are a few which, almost at random, one might select from different periods out of several shelves available. Lord Beaverbrook's *Politicians and the Press* (1924) is good vigorous special pleading. Beaverbrook's later book *Men and Power 1917–18* (1956) is full of valuable historical material. Kennedy Jones' *Fleet Street and Downing Street* (1919) is an invaluable account of the growth of the mass Press in Britain at the beginning of the twentieth century as seen from inside; it shows how the world of newspapers changed under the impact of mass circulation and the discovery that vast fortunes could be made from the new classes of reader available. My own favourite book of reminiscence is Hamilton Fyfe's *Sixty Years in Fleet Street* (1949), which contains much fascinating gossip on the principal characters of the Street in the first half of this century. H. Simonis' *The Street of Ink—an Intimate History of Journalism* (1917) looks at the rise of the modern newspaper empires of Britain at a period just before pessimism set in and the sense of endless financial and journalistic adventure began to wane.

One of the most difficult things for the reader interested in newspaper history to do is to find somewhere to read newspapers which are more than a month old. The appalling quantity available has apparently defeated the task of selection and boiling down. However, one existing American collection entitled *A Treasury of Great Reporting*, edited by Louis L. Snyder and Richard B. Morris (1962), contains some very useful pieces of journalistic writing from the seventeenth century until modern times. David Ayerst is publishing a collection of pieces from the *Guardian,* and there are several collections of journalistic pieces from the major weeklies.

In the field of newspaper design and journalistic practice there is now a five-volume work by Harold Evans, Editor of the *Sunday Times,* which brings up to date the work of Stanley Morison. The volumes deal with *Newsman's English, Handling Newspaper Text, News Headlines, Picture Editing* and *Newspaper Design.* The final volume was published in 1973. For up-to-date information on the financial and corporate state of Fleet Street there is no substitute for reading the regular articles of Sheila Black.

The greatest gaps in the literature of the Press exist in the area of general policy. *Pressures on the Press—an editor looks at Fleet Street* by Charles Wintour of the *Evening Standard* (1972) is essential reading for anyone who wishes to develop further his knowledge of the issues dealt with in Part Three of this book; Charles Wintour gives many accounts of specific classic cases of recent times when journalists and editors have fallen foul of the law or have narrowly avoided doing so. Ben Bagdikian's *The Information Machines—their impact on Men and the Media* (1971) examines the news system of America, in broadcasting as well as the printed Press, and shows the directions in which it is evolving both financially and technically. Francis Williams' *The Right to Know—the rise of the World Press* (1969) is an attempt to examine the areas dealt with by Wintour and Bagdikian on a world scale, but it does not really work. More useful on the theoretical and philosophic side is Bernard C. Cohen's *The Press and Foreign Policy* (1965), which looks in some critical detail at the interrelations of newspapermen and government officials. Another invaluable short American work is *Four Theories of the Press—the authoritarian, libertarian, social responsibility and Soviet Communist concepts of what the press should be and do* (1956, paperback in 1971) by Fred Siebert, Theodore Peterson and Wilbur Schramm; this cannot be too highly recommended. *The Times'* special supplement on

'The World's Press' (23 July 1973), contains a great deal of information and international comparisons on all the questions of general Press policy.

The best compendium of material on the British Press from an academic standpoint is Colin Seymour-Ure's *Press, Politics and the Public* (1968). Three very useful essays on the sociology of the Press (selected from a very large shelf) are *Communications* by Raymond Williams (revised 1966); Graham Martin's *The Press*, in a collection edited by Denys Thompson entitled *Discrimination and Popular Culture* (1964); and James W. Carey's *The Communications Revolution and the Professional Communicator*, which is to be found in the Sociological Review Monograph of Keele University, No 13 (1969).

On the legal issues which have been outlined in very simple terms in this book the reader is referred to Thomas Dawson's *The Law of the Press* (1947), which, though old, has not been overtaken. On libel the most illuminating book of all is surely Randolph Churchill's *What I Said About the Press* (1957), which contains much of the transcript of a dazzling libel action in which Churchill successfully (£5,000 damages) fought a newspaper which had called him a paid hack. On the official secrets problem Peter Hedley and Cyril Ainsley's *The D-Notice Affair* (1967) supplements Jonathan Aitken's book very well, and on obscenity the best documentary account of a relevant trial is undoubtedly Tony Palmer's *The Trials of Oz* (1971); the best general résumé of the issues is to be found in the Arts Council Working Party's report *The Obscenity Laws* (1969). For further information on the issue of privacy, I can safely refer the reader to Mervyn Jones's collection of documents in the same series as this book (1974).

The best compendia of information on the British Press are the two *Royal Commission Reports*, extracts from which appear in Part One of this book. Together with the volumes of evidence that go with them, they remain, despite the passage of time, the best single source of material. Readers interested in American comparisons are referred to the various publications of the

*Hutchins Commission*, which met in America in 1947 to consider the problems of the American Press. Their main publication, *A Free and Responsible Press—a general report on Mass Communication*, is obligatory reading for anyone interested in the shape of journalism in the last 25 years. That work has been, in one sense, brought up to date by a report by the Twentieth Century Fund Task Force, entitled *A Free and Responsive Press* (1973); the document recommends the creation of an American version of the British Press Council and is a background paper by the former Editor of the *Columbia Journalism Review*, Alfred Balk. Perhaps this is the point to mention an excellent history of the profession of journalism in America, which is Bernard Weizberger's *The American Newspaperman* (1961). Another work in the area of general disquisition on the Press in the American context is V. O. Key Jr's *Public Opinion and American Democracy* (1961).

The function of this book, it is hoped, has been to indicate the issues around which general readers and students interested in newspapers should build their reading. The papers, books and documents from which the extracts have been drawn (which I have not referred to again in this reading list) form one important part of any Press bibliography and should be the subject of further, more extended reading. Extracts are useful only to a very small extent; there is no substitute, especially on the legal topics, for reading the whole thing.

# Acknowledgements

I am indebted to the trustees of the Leverhulme Trust Fund for their continuing support and encouragement. A stiff and formal acknowledgement of this kind considerably underestimates the true extent of my indebtedness to them. I am similarly obliged to the Warden and Fellows of St Antony's College, Oxford, for the warmness of their continued hospitality to me, which has made this and previous work possible.

I should like to thank the following for their kind permission to reproduce extracts from the works listed: Penguin Books Ltd (Wickham Steed, *The Press*), Prof Jeremy Tunstall (*Journalists at Work*), James Curran ('The Impact of TV on the Audience for National Newspapers'), Anthony Lewis and Chapman Pincher (for the texts of their speeches at the Institute of Journalists), Cecil H. King (*Granada Lecture, 1966* and his essay in *Wicked, Wicked Libels*), John Whale (*Journalism and Government*) and Jonathan Aitken (*Officially Secret*).

I am indebted also to G. G. Eastwood, General Secretary of the Printing and Kindred Trades Federation, for permission to quote from the Survey conducted by his union, to the Economist Intelligence Unit for permission to use extracts from the EIU report on the National Newspaper Industry, and to Noël S. Paul, Secretary of the Press Council, for early access to the Press Council's new constitution and for permission to quote a number of important adjudications. Tom Sargent, Secretary of

Justice, the British Section of the International Commission of Jurists, kindly allowed me to quote from the various reports issued by his organisation.

I am obliged to the Rt Hon Harold Wilson, MP, for permission to quote in full his letter to *The Times* following the thalidomide affair. I have had a great deal of help from several newspapers: in particular I should like to thank *The Times* for permission to quote from one leading article and several Law Reports, the *Evening Standard* for permission to use the Jak cartoon of 9 December 1970 and other extracts, the *Scotsman* for permission to quote an important article on Press privilege at some length, the *Sunday Telegraph* for permission to quote from its first issue, the *Sunday Times* for permission to use extracts from some of its most important contributions on the problem of Press restraints, the *Sun*, the *Sunday Express* and the *Daily Express* for their assistance and permission to make various quotations.

Extracts from Command Papers, *Hansard*, Bills, Acts, Royal Commission Reports, Select Committee and Tribunal Reports, White Papers and reports of the National Board for Prices and Incomes and the Monopolies Commission appear by kind permission of the Controller of HM Stationery Office. I am indebted to Martin Barnsley of the Bodleian Law Library for his assistance, and to Neal Ascherson and Nicholas Garnham for helping me to obtain various documents. I must also acknowledge, as on several previous occasions, the miraculous efforts of Mrs Pat Kirkpatrick in producing an immaculate manuscript out of chaos. All errors and omissions are my own.

# Index

Aberfan disaster, 115, 155
Aberfan Tribunal, 120, 121; contempt of court issue, 115
Aitken, Jonathan, 179, 180
Aitken, Sir Max, 171
Allighan, Garry, 229, 230
Associated Newspapers Ltd, 30, 31, 32, 49
Astor, David, 300

Bank Rate Tribunal (1957), 122
BBC Programme Complaints Commission, 203, 204, 205
Bernstein, Alex, 193, 194
Biafran secrets trial, 179–80
Brown, George, 171
Budget Leak Tribunal (1936), 121

Cadbury family, 43, 49
Cairns, Colonel, 179, 180
Cameron, James, 44
Caulfield, Mr Justice, 179, 180
Christiansen, Arthur, 177
Clarke, Windsor, 194, 197
Committee of Privileges, 229, 230
Contempt of court, 110–61; Committee on Contempt in Tribunals, 126, 150; Govt views on Committee's report, 127
Cross, Lord, 157, 158
Cudlipp, Hugh, 101, 102, 103
Cummings cartoon on IRA, 296, 297
Curran, James, 105
Curtis, Michael, 43, 44, 45

*Daily Dispatch*, Manchester, 44

*Daily Express*, 59, 119, 170, 171, 173, 174, 177, 283
*Daily Graphic*, 25
*Daily Herald*, 16, 25, 31, 43, 45, 49, 50, 63
*Daily Leader*, 60
*Daily Mail*, 22, 32, 33, 49, 53, 119, 141, 210, 283
*Daily Mirror*, 19, 24, 25, 30, 31, 32, 50, 53, 58, 63, 100, 102, 210, 229, 230, 291, 302
*Daily Sketch*, 25, 32
*Daily Telegraph*, 16, 25, 30, 31, 42–3, 45, 46, 74
Davies, Lord Justice Edmund, 115, 116
Defamation Act (1952), 213, 214, 224
Denning, Lord, 132, 157, 277; thalidomide case ruling, 132–42
Devlin, Lord, 275
Distillers Company (Biochemicals) Ltd, 132–5 *passim*, 139–44 *passim*, 149–57 *passim*
D-Notice Committee, 162, 164, 166, 174, 194–7 *passim*; Granada TV and, 192
D-Notices, 166, 167, 176–9 *passim*, 187, 195, 196

Economist Intelligence Unit, 65, 69, 93
Editorial Liaison Committee, 190
*Empire News*, 30
Evans, Harold, 133, 134, 144; on privacy and Lambton-Jellicoe affair, 205
*Evening Echo*, Southend, 299
*Evening News*, 230

*Evening Post*, Bristol, 298
*Evening Standard*, 24, 110, 230, 276, 294, 296, 298; Federated House Chapel, 295, 296

Farnhill, Admiral, 193
*Financial Times*, 25, 74
Forman, Denis, 193, 194
Francis-Williams, Lord, 19
Franks Committee, 183–9 *passim*, 191, 193; opposition to report by ELC, 190
Franks, Lord, 20, 183
Fraser, Hugh, MP, 179
Free Communications Group, 290

Goodman, Lord, 215
Granada Television, 192, 193
*Guardian*, 16, 25, 26, 30, 31, 71, 74, 79, 80, 92, 210, 276; House Agreement, 302

Haley, Sir William, 74
Heath, Edward, 182, 205
Herbert, Sir Alan, 230; definition of obscenity, 239
Hill, Lord, 115
Hobson, Sir J., MP, 116, 117
Hooson, Emlyn, MP, 118
Howard, Lee, 177
Hutchins Commission, 35

Industrial Relations Act and Court, 159, 160
Inglis, R., 276
Institute of Journalists, 119, 177; memorandum to Franks Committee, 183
International Publishing Corporation Ltd, 31, 100–4 *passim*
ITA Complaints Review Board, 203, 205

Jak cartoon on electrical workers, 294, 295, 296
Jones, Sir Elwyn, QC, 115–19 *passim*, 126
Journalists: career pattern, 284; classes of, 92; earnings, 90, 92; on the board, 302; protection of sources, 252; sources, 162, 247
'Justice' reports: on contempt of court, 112, 135; on libel, 222; on official secrets, 185; on privacy, 199, 200

Kaldor, Nicholas, 55, 56
Kemsley Newspapers Ltd, 30
Kemsley, Viscount, 269
King, Cecil, 103; on libel, 216; on Press behaviour, 245

Lambton-Jellicoe affair, 205, 208
Lambton, Lord, 209
*Le Monde*, 23, 283
Levin, Bernard, 276
Levy, Colin and Norma, 207, 209
Lewis, Anthony, 267
Libel, 213–28
Littman, Mark, QC, 199
Lobby system, 248, 260, 262; criticism of, 267
Lohan, Colonel 'Sammy', 170, 171, 173, 177
Lynskey Tribunal (1948), 122
Lyon, Alexander W., MP, 117, 200

Macmillan, Harold, 109, 235
Manchester Guardian & Evening News Ltd, 31, 32
Monopolies Commission, 25, 41; on independence of Thomson editors, 85; on merger of *The Times* and *Sunday Times*, 74
*Morning Star*, 16
Murdoch, Rupert, 24, 31

National Union of Journalists, 32, 91, 119, 284, 294, 297, 299, 301; code of conduct, 249
Neild, Robert, 55, 56
*New Statesman*, 23, 215, 284
*News Chronicle*, 25, 53, 54, 65; character, 41; demise, 25, 30, 41–2, 49
*News of the World*, 24, 30, 31, 205, 206, 207, 209, 277
Newspaper Proprietors' Association, 91, 299
Newspaper Society, 119

Obscene Publications Act (1959), 238–9
Obscenity, 238–43
*Observer*, 30, 45, 74, 79, 210, 276, 284, 292, 298, 300, 301; memorandum on the 'unqualified' journalist, 299

INDEX 319

Odhams Press Ltd, 30, 50, 53, 63, 100
Official secrets, 162–97
Official Secrets Acts (1911, 1920), 20, 162, 163, 164, 166, 168, 176, 177, 180, 190, 195, 196, 212; attacks on, 180–6; Section 2, 162, 163, 164, 180–94 *passim*
*Open Secret, The*, 290, 302
*Oz* obscenity case, 239

*Pall Mall Gazette*, 206
Palmerston, Lord, 15
Pannell, C., 118
Parke, Baron, 214
Parliamentary privilege, 228–38; historical origins, 234
Pearson, Lord, 155, 156
*People, The*, see *Sunday People*
Peterson, Theodore, 21
Phillimore, Lord Justice, 127, 159
Pincher, Chapman, 170, 171, 173, 177
Porter Committee on libel, 214, 217, 224
Press: chain of distribution, 100; changing technology, 93–6; circulation, 24, 25, 97; commercial TV and radio holdings, 26, 45, 50–1; contempt of court and, 110–61; EIU survey, 65, 69, 70; exposure of corruption by, 210; finance, 18, 19, 24–5; freedom, 108–10; Govt restraints on, 20; impact of TV on, 105; 'levy' scheme, 55; libel and, 213–28; manpower and productivity, 93; newsroom autonomy, 23; obscenity and, 238–43; official secrets and, 162–97; ownership, 22, 98–9; Parliamentary privilege and, 228–38; popular, 16, 25; privacy and, 197–213; quality, 16, 25; 'social-responsibility' theory of, 21; workers' participation, 283
Press Amalgamations Court, 52, 53–4
Press Council, 21, 35, 51, 52–3, 119, 204, 208, 209, 213, 244, 245, 269, 270, 271; constitution, 271; on censorship from within, 298; on chequebook journalism, 279; on contempt of court, 120, 121; on four-letter words, 275; on 'intrusion', 198; on unsavoury memoirs, 277; statistics on adjudications, 282

Prices and Incomes Board, 25, 97, 98, 100; on changing technology, 93; on journalists' earnings, 90
Printing and Kindred Trades Federation, 30
Prior, James, 159
Privacy, 197–213; Right of Privacy Bill (1967), 200

Radcliffe Committee (1962), on D-Notice system, 166
Radcliffe Committee (1967), on cable-vetting affair, 170; report rejected by Govt, 173
Radcliffe, Lord, 167, 171; on Govt and a free Press, 175
*Railway Gazette*, 109
Rawlinson, Sir Peter, 142
Reed International Ltd, 31, 100–4 *passim*
Reid, Lord, 142, 157, 158; thalidomide case ruling, 142–53
Reynolds, G. W. McM., 83, 84
*Reynolds News*, 31, 82
Robens, Lord, 115
Royal Commission on Tribunals of Inquiry (1966), 121, 122; Govt's views on report, 127
Royal Commissions on Press, 21, 25, 31; 1947–9 Commission, 32, 33, 35, 50, 59–60, 269, 289; 1961–2 Commission, 49, 50, 51, 52, 55, 65, 81, 88, 92, 271
Ruck, Peter Carter, 199

Salmon, Lord Justice, 122, 126, 127, 150
*Scotsman*, 50, 77; on Press privilege, 238
Scott, Colonel, 179
*Scottish Daily Express*, 296
Scottish Television Ltd, 50, 51, 77
Select Committee on Obscenity Bill (1958), 239, 242
Shawcross, Lord, 50, 112, 135, 222
*Spectator*, 276
*Star*, 30, 43, 49
Stead, W. T., 206, 207, 209
Steed, Wickham, 26, 27
Stewart, Michael, 179
*Sun*, 16, 24, 25, 31, 93, 119, 291; inception of, 63
*Sunday Citizen*, 31, 82

*Sunday Dispatch*, 30, 48, 49, 53
*Sunday Express*, 30, 48, 49, 53
*Sunday Graphic*, 30
*Sunday Mirror*, 31
*Sunday People*, 32, 50, 205, 207, 209, 212
*Sunday Pictorial*, 31
*Sunday Telegraph*, 31, 119, 179, 183, 184, 249; inception of, 45
*Sunday Times*, 31, 45, 74, 76, 161, 205, 210, 225, 292; thalidomide affair and, 131–59

Tangley, Lord, 225
Thalidomide affair, 131–59
Thomas, Denis, 41
Thomson, Admiral, 166, 170, 177
Thomson, Lord, 31, 53, 74, 78, 79, 85, 86, 87; on libel, 225
Thomson Organisation Ltd, 30, 31, 49, 50, 76–82 *passim*, 85–90 *passim*
*Times, The*, 15, 16, 24, 25, 31, 60, 104, 119, 131, 208, 212, 227, 231, 291, 302; change of format, 69; merged with *Sunday Times*, 74
Trades Union Congress, 30, 31, 63

Tribunals of Inquiry (Evidence) Act (1921), 121, 122, 130, 131; inquiries under, 122, 252
Tunstall, Jeremy, 262, 284

Vassall, Christopher, 109, 252
Vassall Tribunal (1962), 109, 122, 252, 253

Waller, Ian, 249
Webb, Maurice, 32
Whale, John, 260
Widgery, Lord Chief Justice, 154
Williams, Prof David, 182
Wilson, Harold, 102, 115, 170, 171, 173; on need for Press information, 159
Wintour, Charles, 110
*Workers' Press*, 60
*World in Action*, 193, 194
*World's Press News*, 229

Younger Report on privacy, 201, 203, 208, 212
Younger, Sir Kenneth, 201

DATE DUE